Kids & Computers:
A Parent's Handbook

Kids & Computers: A Parent's Handbook

Judy Salpeter

with

Dan Derrick

Carol S. Holzberg

Michael Milone

Cindra Tison

Mary Jo Woodside

SAMS

A Division of Prentice Hall Computer Publishing

11711 North College, Carmel, Indiana 46032 USA

International Standard Book Number: 0-672-30144-x
Library of Congress Catalog Card Number: 91-67085

94 93 92 91   8 7 6 5 4 3 2 1

Interpretation of the printing code: the rightmost number of the first series of numbers is the year of the book's printing; the rightmost number of the second series of numbers is the number of the book's printing. For example, a printing code of 91-1 shows that the first printing of the book occurred in 1991.

Printed in the United States of America

Publisher
Richard K. Swadley

Associate Publisher
Marie Butler-Knight

Managing Editor
Marjorie Hopper

Acquisitions/Development Editor
Mary-Terese Cozzola Cagnina

Manuscript Editor
Linda Hawkins

Editorial Assistant
Hilary Adams

Cover Designer
Tim Amrhein

Cover Illustrator
Ned Shaw

Designer
Scott Cook

Indexer
Joelynn Gifford

Production Team
*Audra Hershman, Betty Kish, Phil Kitchel,
Bob LaRoche, Joe Ramon, Linda Seifert*

Table of Contents

Introduction

During the past few years, there has been a surge of interest in home computing. IBM, Apple, Tandy, and a host of other computer manufacturers have introduced machines geared specifically at the home market. Software developers with strong roots in the business world have suddenly begun producing titles designed to entertain and educate adults and children in a home setting. And publishers of educational software for school use are now designing many of their newest titles with families in mind.

What is it that these hardware and software producers are responding to? Why the increased interest on the part of home users—so many of them parents? In a sense, what you are seeing is the maturing of an industry. The personal computer is no longer a newcomer, and interest in it no longer relates to its value as a novelty item. Instead, microcomputers have become a regular part of everyone's daily lives. Adults rely on them at work, children are exposed to them at school, and we all see them in use every day in the world around us. It's only natural that parents would wonder about the best ways to use these tools at home with their kids.

Equally important, the technology has matured to the point that software incorporating vivid images, high-quality sound, varied information, and true interactivity is commonplace. This is not to say that the technology has reached a standstill; hardware and software will continue to improve, and the programs that amaze people with their capabilities today will seem no more than satisfactory in the years to come. But now the refrain we heard so often in the 1980s—"There is no good educational software"—is far from true.

What we *have* found lacking in recent years as we perused the shelves in book shops and software stores is information for parents about everything from locating the best software to deciding how, when, and whether to use computers at home with their kids. This book grew out of our conviction that such information is sorely needed.

Whether you're an experienced computer user thinking of turning your own personal computer into the family computer, or a total newcomer curious about what the technology has to offer your child, this book is for you. One of our goals is to respond to the questions and concerns we hear most frequently from parents. Is the computer harmful to my child's health? How can I help my kid if I don't know about computers myself? What will happen to my children if they don't learn about computers at a young age? Part 1 addresses these and many other questions you might have, and takes a close look at some of the different groups—including girls, boys, kids with special needs, and very young children—that can benefit from home computing.

The rest of the book is focused on another broad question asked so frequently by parents: "What should we buy?" In Part 2, we address the topic of hardware, providing an overview of the issues and options to consider when purchasing a computer system to use at home with your kids. We assume no computer expertise on the reader's part and try to explain potentially confusing terminology as we go along. In addition, much of the information included in this section of the book should also be relevant to more experienced computer users looking for advice on upgrading a home computer system or adding to it.

In Parts 3 and 4, we focus on building a software library for your family. While you're likely to be called upon to make hardware decisions only once every few years, software decisions are ongoing. Perhaps you're looking for a program to help in a subject area your child is having trouble with at school. Or a program that builds on your kid's existing interests. Or maybe you're in search of a fun package to give a young person as a gift. Before getting into specific recommendations, we provide (in Part 3) some general guidelines for selecting and shopping for software. By discussing the criteria we used to arrive at our decisions and recommendations, we hope to provide you with a good basis for evaluating future software titles.

In Part 3, we also include information about how and where to shop for commercially produced titles such as those reviewed in this book. And we discuss "public domain" software—what it is and where you can find it.

Part 4 is where you'll read about our favorite programs. Some of these are titles that have been around for several years; we've watched many kids use them, talked to many teachers and parents about them, and concluded that they were worthy of your consideration. Some are brand-new programs that, although they have not yet withstood the test of time, received favorable first reviews from kids and adults with enough experience to know how these new titles compare with what's available.

Our focus is on programs with "educational value," although we are not defining "education" in a narrow or entirely traditional sense. As you will see in the pages that follow, we believe strongly that educational software for the home must be fun to use. Furthermore, we have not limited our reviews to titles related to specific academic areas but have also included tools and general-purpose games that we think are worth considering for your kids. In recommending software, however, we do place a high priority on programs that require kids to think, that encourage curiosity and

creativity, and that help excite young people about learning.

Our primary focus is on children between the ages of 2 and 13. Although many of the issues addressed and a number of the programs reviewed are relevant to older teenagers as well, parents of a typical 15- or 16-year-old are not likely to have much say in that youngster's software-purchasing decisions. Furthermore, many of the programs most useful to a high school student at home are likely to be business-oriented tools—word processors, graphics packages, graphing programs, and other adult software that would take up far too much space for us to review in the pages of this book. We hope, however, that if you do have a teenage son or daughter, you will find some of the references in Chapter 2, "Getting Up to Speed Yourself," helpful for your teenager as well.

Acknowledgments

This book was a collaborative effort. Dan Derrick contributed chapters on cooperative learning, getting up to speed, and on-line services; he also helped with the reviews of games and graphics programs and had primary responsibility for the reviews of social studies/science and language arts software. Dr. Carol Holzberg wrote most of the hardware chapters and reviewed CD-ROM titles and games. Dr. Michael Milone wrote about special education, computer-related health issues, public domain software, and computer maintenance. Cindra Tison and Mary Jo Woodside reviewed preschool software, publishing programs, and math software. I filled in the rest and added my two cents' worth to everybody else's chapters.

In addition, there are many other people who contributed in important ways to this book. Mike Albanese of Davidson & Associates, Mary Cron of Rymel, Ben Shemuel of Diaquest, Bill Volk of MEDIAGENIC, and Jay Whitney from the Campus Store, University of Massachusetts, Amherst, all helped tremendously with the hardware chapters. We also want to thank Pam Barnett, formerly of *Technology & Learning* magazine and Broderbund Software; Connie Connors of Connors Communications; and Mary Beth Coyne of Broderbund for getting us up to speed on the ins and outs of the software market.

For their help with the chapters on early childhood, gender issues, and special education, we want to thank Dr. Douglas Clements of the State University of New York at Buffalo; Janet Coburn of *Early Childhood News*; Sharon Edwards (personal friend and author of an upcoming book from Viking Press about writing with your child); Susan Elting and Barbara Sorenson from the Council for Exceptional Children; Kay Gilliland of EQUALS; Charles Hohmann of High/Scope; Sally Narodick, Tina Ruppelt, and MaryAnn Trower of Edmark; Dr. Suzanne Thouvenelle of MOBIUS Corporation; and special education consultant Richard Wanderman.

We appreciate the contributions made by Professor Giora Shaviv of the Technion, Haifa, Israel; and Dr. Len Weiss, optometrist, to the chapters on computer-related health issues; and also want to thank Professors Miriam and Edwin Salpeter of Cornell University for tracking down additional research on these and many other relevant issues.

Leslie Eiser, educator, parent, and free-lance writer, deserves a special mention for her help with everything from technical reviews to advice on software worthy of consideration for the book. Thanks also to everybody at Peter Li, Inc.—to Publisher Peter Li, Editor-in-chief Holly Brady, and corporate Editor-in-chief Carl Fischer—for being so supportive of this venture; to Dave Hoffman, Associate Editor, for lots of good software leads; and to everybody in the San Rafael office for all the phone messages they took and software packages they tripped over during the months this book was being written.

Many thanks also go to our editors, Mary-Terese Cozzola Cagnina and Linda Hawkins, for their faith in this book and their patience with us. And, of course, to our spouses for behind-the-scenes support. (Mine, for one, has proven himself to be a marvelous single father for the past several months—thanks, Ian.)

Finally, this book wouldn't have been possible without the kids— ranging from 2 to 14 years of age— who tested the software for us. An extra special thanks goes to T.J. and Rachel Derrick; Adrienne, Alexander, and Robert Eiser; Jacob and Shoshona Holzberg-Pill; Jamie Salpeter Irvine; Katy Rusnak; Beau Tison; and Michael Woodside.

Judy Salpeter
October 1991

Biographies

About the Author

Judy Salpeter is managing editor of *Technology & Learning*, a national magazine for technology-using teachers and school administrators. An educator with 10 years of teaching experience at the elementary and junior high school levels, Salpeter earned an M.Ed. from the University of Massachusetts, Amherst, and an M.S. in Interactive Educational Technology from Stanford University. She lives in Berkeley, California, with her husband, Ian, and their son, Jamie.

About the Contributing Authors

■ Dan Derrick is an author and consultant who specializes in computer topics. His credits include *Master SimCity/SimEarth* and *Learning DOS*, both published by Sams. Dan resides in Brownsburg, Indiana, with his wife, Cathy, and their children, T.J. and Rachael.

■ Carol S. Holzberg, Ph.D., is an anthropologist, a mother, and a computer journalist. She writes for numerous publications, works as a computer consultant, and serves as the computer resource person at the Shutesbury Elementary School in Shutesbury, Massachusetts.

■ Michael Milone, Ph.D., is an adjunct assistant professor at Ohio State University, a free-lance software developer, and the author of five computer-related books. He holds graduate degrees in counseling with deaf people and in education and psychology research.

■ Cindra Tison and Mary Jo Woodside are consultants who specialize in helping teachers, parents, and children learn to use the computer. Tison has experience in retail sales and marketing of software. She lives with her husband, Hack, and son, Beau, in Carmel, Indiana. Woodside is a former teacher who resides in Indianapolis with her husband, Jack, and son, Michael.

I

Your Questions Answered

The 5th Wave   By Rich Tennant

"OH SURE, $1.8 MILLION DOLLARS SEEMS LIKE ALOT RIGHT NOW, BUT WHAT ABOUT RANDY? WHAT ABOUT HIS FUTURE? THINK WHAT A COMPUTER LIKE THIS WILL DO FOR HIS S.A.T. SCORE SOMEDAY."

CHAPTER ONE

Computers in Today's World: What Your Child Needs to Know

■ *How important is it for my kid to be computer literate?*

■ *What does my child need to know about computers in order to get along in this world?*

■ *Why should I consider buying a computer for my family?*

Some parents today are fearful that their children will "fall behind" or have serious problems if they are not "computer literate" by a certain age. Given the speed at which computers have changed almost every aspect of modern society, these parents worry that children who don't know how to program a computer, name its components, and use the most popular business software by the time they leave high school will be unprepared for the world that lies ahead of them.

To a limited extent, we agree. The information age we live in *does* require new skills on the part of our children—skills such as the ability to access, evaluate, and interpret large quantities of data. On the other hand, we don't believe that your child needs a computer in order to become an educated citizen or that you should be concerned if courses on computer literacy and programming are not given high priority by his school.

Let's look at the source of so many of these information-age fears. In the early days of microcomputing

(10 to 15 short years ago), computers were relatively difficult to use and good software was scarce. If you wanted to take advantage of what the computer had to offer, you needed to learn to program. Many people found the whole world of computers and programming intimidating. Perhaps you plunged in and learned anyhow; or perhaps you put it off indefinitely. In either case, you might have come away from the experience with a sense that these strange, new machines were challenging and a little bit scary.

Today, much has changed. Computers are far easier to use, featuring "user friendly" software with simple menus, easy-to-follow instructions, and information presented clearly with the help of realistic graphics and sound. Programming is no longer necessary in order to get the computer to do what you want it to do, and the new technology is visible everywhere in the world around us. The average young child today has no more fear of a computer than of a stereo system, a VCR, or any of the other modern tools she sees every day.

While computer programming is interesting and fun for some of us (and a good way of developing problem-solving skills), knowing how to program or how to open the computer and make repairs is no more necessary to the average user than expertise in auto mechanics is to the average driver. And a complete course devoted to learning how to use a computer (how to turn it on and off, to identify its parts, etc.) makes only slightly more sense than a course in using the telephone or VCR.

Yes, there are some computer "basics" that kids should know when they do find themselves using the computer. They need to be taught to save files, care for disks, and so on, just as they need to learn how to use the brakes on their bikes or pump up the tires when they get flat. But young people pick up these basics quite willingly and easily in the course of working with software. In the same way, it is safe to assume that if we raise our kids to be confident, flexible problem solvers, they will have little difficulty learning to use whatever spreadsheet, database program, word processor, or other tools they encounter in their life beyond high school. In fact, teaching them to use specific applications for the purpose of "preparing them for the real world" is pointless because technology is changing so rapidly that there's no way to predict what tools will be popular a few years from now.

Why This Book?

Why, then, have we bothered to write a book about computers and kids? And why are all the authors of this book committed to using computers with our children at home and with the kids we work with in a variety of other settings? Because we believe that technology can change our children's lives.

We own automobiles or live near public transportation not because we want our kids to learn about cars, buses, and trains, but because these vehicles make it possible for us to go places—to visit family and friends, participate in sports events, explore new, interesting spots, and much more. In the same way, we are interested in computer technology because of the places it can take us and our children.

A good software program, like a good book, can transport a child into an exciting new world, bringing a variety of experiences to life. It can be a patient tutor, an encouraging assistant, or an entertaining playmate. With the help of computer technology, children who used to have difficulty writing can now compose and revise with relative ease—and with attractive, satisfying results. Children who once found mathematics boring can now practice math skills with the help of highly entertaining games. And children who never before were interested in geography can now travel to far-off places with the help of interactive globes and appealing simulations.

Is a computer necessary to bring such meaning and excitement to learning? Probably not. In fact, it's possible to own a computer and equip it with uninspiring software that does nothing but bore your child and turn him off to learning. It's equally possible for a child growing up with inspiring teachers, creative and caring parents, a stimulating environment, and *no computer* to be well educated, happy, and creative.

Computers provide no magical cures. They are not objects to be studied with awe (or fear), nor are they perfect teachers that can do no wrong. With the right software, however, a computer can have an extremely positive impact on your child's attitudes towards learning and his ability to comprehend and affect the world around him. It's for this reason—because of the computer's potential to help and to delight your child—that it's worth thinking about investing in a computer system and good software to run on it.

Learning About Computers

Although we don't believe that it's essential for every child to know a great deal about computers and how they work, we certainly don't mean to discourage you from exploring this topic with your kids. Computers—like dinosaurs, cars, animals, and a variety of other topics that have fascinated children over the years—can be lots of fun to learn about. If and when your child shows an interest in the computer itself, expressing a desire to learn how it works, what's inside it, how to program it, and so on, we hope that you and your child's teachers will encourage such an interest. It certainly presents a wonderful opportunity for you to learn together with your kids.

Once you begin looking for examples of computers and computer technology in the everyday world, you and your children will find them everywhere. You'll notice travel agents using the computer to access data on every commercial airplane due to fly anywhere in the world; grocery store bar code readers sending computerized information to cash registers that instantly display the brand and type of food about to be purchased; special effects on television created with the help of computer animation; waiters entering information into hand-held computers that then relay orders back to the kitchen; and kiosks with interactive computer programs that help orient you to museums, amusement parks, and shopping malls.

But whether your kid sees computers primarily as tools to help her explore other areas of interest to her or also as interesting objects to study in their own right, we think that if you invest in a computer, you'll come to view it as a welcome and educationally valuable addition to your household.

The 5th Wave   By Rich Tennant

"WELL, RIGHT OFF, THE RESPONSE TIME SEEMS A BIT SLOW."

CHAPTER TWO

Getting Up to Speed Yourself

- *How do I deal with the fact that my kid knows more about the computer than I do?*
- *Do I have to be a computer whiz to help my child at the computer?*
- *Where do I go for help to learn to use a computer?*

As we pointed out in Chapter 1, computers are much easier to use than the average novice expects. If you're new to computers, you might be surprised at how simple it is to become "computer literate." With each passing year, computer software is becoming more "user friendly" and less difficult to learn. This is particularly true of good software for children. In fact, if it takes you and your child more than 20 minutes to get up and running on an educational program, a game, or a tool designed for kids, you should probably send the program back and request a refund.

We do acknowledge, however, that knowing some basics will help first-time users feel more comfortable at the computer. For example, you will want to spend some time learning about your computer's operating system—the commands that you'll need in order to *format* new disks, *install* programs on a hard disk, *name* and *rename* files, *copy* files from one place to another, *create* directories (or *folders* as they're known in the Macintosh world), and so on.

In addition to these computer basics, once you've invested in a computer system, you may be motivated to plunge deeper into the world of computing and learn how to use business-oriented tools, such as advanced word processors, desktop publishing programs, and so on. This is certainly not necessary in order to help your child at the computer, but you might enjoy acquiring the knowledge and using the computer to meet your own needs, as well as those of your child.

In setting out to learn more about computers and computer programs, you will have many resources to choose from. Depending on the age of your child, you might also have the opportunity to learn with (or, in some cases, from) your child. Let's take a closer look at some of the options.

Tutorials—In Print or on Disk

Several years ago, it was hard to find a computer manual written in plain English. The documentation that accompanied hardware and software—when it existed—was often cryptic and filled with technical jargon. Fortunately, many computers and software packages today are sold with easy-to-follow manuals, which walk you through the steps necessary to become comfortable with the product. Some are even accompanied by computer-based tutorials, which allow you to try things out on the computer and provide feedback and guidance as you work.

In addition to whatever help is provided with the product itself, you can generally find at local stores computerized tutorials, videotapes,

and books that will teach you everything you want to know about your computer, its operating system, and the most popular business-oriented products on the market. Software-based tutorials (also referred to as *computer-assisted instruction* or *CAI*) sometimes work *with* the program you are trying to learn, making it necessary for you to own the product before you begin the lessons. Other CAI programs run on their own. The best way of finding a program that will really help you learn what you want to learn is to ask around; a recommendation from someone who has had success with a particular CAI package is extremely helpful.

Videotaped instruction is another approach that is gaining popularity because users can relax in front of the television while "learning" how to use the computer. This form of training can be quite helpful in providing an overview of a program or in showing what the software can accomplish. However, watching TV is not necessarily the best way to acquire detailed information about a program, because—for step-by-step training—being at the computer and trying out what you are learning is generally more helpful.

Despite all the high-tech options, many people still find books the most convenient way to learn about computers. Even if you're pleased with the documentation that accompanied your latest purchase, good books on the topic are likely to provide you with additional, valuable information. Experienced computer users typically own at least one book on each of the major business software packages they use regularly. Fortunately, if you're looking for information on MS-DOS, *Windows*, *HyperCard*, most programming languages, or virtually any popular business application (whether it's a word processor, spreadsheet, database, graphics package, desktop publisher, or presentation tool), you're likely to have several titles to choose from. Look for a book that is targeted at your experience level, is easy (even enjoyable) to read, and is organized in a way that makes sense to you. (Look at the table of contents, the chapter subheads, and the index to see how easy it is to find what you want to know.)

Workshops and Classes

All of the methods discussed in the preceding section are ideal for people who like to learn on their own and are motivated to keep working until they've mastered a subject. For those who prefer a more personal approach or work better in a more structured setting, a workshop or class may be the best choice. Local computer dealers and software stores sometimes offer evening classes or weekend workshops on topics of interest to many of their customers. They are also likely to have information on local and regional computer fairs and conferences tailored to the average computer user. In addition to being ideal places to gather information about new products, such fairs also offer workshops (ranging in length from one hour to one day) on everything from using computers with your kids to creating presentations with a particular tool.

In addition, many high schools and most colleges and adult-education centers offer classes focusing on various uses of computers. Before enrolling in a class, think carefully about what sort of help you need. If you're simply interested in becoming comfortable with a particular tool, you may decide that a one-time workshop that presents an overview of the product is sufficient. If, on the other hand, you definitely want the in-depth knowledge offered by an ongoing class, it's important to find a course that is tailored to your needs. If at all possible, find someone who has taken the class you are considering. In addition, try to talk with the instructor before signing up to determine if you like his or her approach. Finally, make sure that you can get at least a partial refund if, after attending the first class, you decide it's not for you.

User Groups

At sites all over the country, computer users meet on a regular or semiregular basis to discuss hardware and software and share what they know with one another. Such gatherings are known as *user groups*. Some groups are organized around a specific computer (a Macintosh user group or an Amiga user group, for example), while others focus on specific interest areas (computer-using educators, desktop publishing groups, and so on). Six people may meet casually every week in a restaurant, or the group may be large enough to have paid officers. Whatever the structure, user groups can be a valuable resource for people at all levels of experience.

Computer stores in your area will probably know about local user groups and can give you information or a copy of a group's newsletter. If you attend a meeting, don't be afraid to ask questions. Although the group's members may be very experienced with computers (some may even seem like fanatics), most groups welcome new members. If the user group is large enough, it is likely to have special interest groups (SIGs) that focus on specific software or topics of interest. Various SIGs may meet separately from the main meeting to discuss such subjects as accounting software or the basics of telecommunications. You might even start a special interest group about family computing.

Other Resources

Magazines can be another source of valuable information for new computer users. Although many of the computer magazines on the newsstand or available by subscription are too technical or focused on too specific an area for the average casual computer user, there are a few publications that *do* focus on beginners. In particular, there's *PC Novice* (published by Peed Corporation, Lincoln, Nebraska), a magazine packed with tips, product information, explanations, and introductory articles for newcomers to the world of computing; and its partner publication, *PC Today,* designed for the slightly more experienced user.

Try purchasing several different magazines and reading them carefully before deciding which one or two are worth subscribing to. You are much more likely to read a magazine when it arrives every month.

Still another way of learning about computers is to connect with a friend who can help you. Remember that many people who know how to use computers may have difficulty (or be uninterested in) explaining what they do. On the other hand, you may have a friend or neighbor who enjoys both using computers and teaching about them. If so, make sure you offer an exchange of services. For example, you might wash your friend's car in exchange for a half-hour session.

Finally, if your child is old enough and knowledgeable enough about computers, he may be able to assist you. This can be a wonderful opportunity for both of you to learn valuable skills. Your child will solidify his knowledge of the topic he is

teaching and, even more important, learn to explain things clearly and patiently; and you will acquire the computer knowledge you desire.

It's possible that your child's school offers some sort of classes for parents and other interested adults. Even elementary school students can play the role of teachers in such a setting. If your child's school has an exciting computer program, you might want to suggest that the school establish such classes for the community, led at least in part by the kids. If each participant is charged a small fee, such events can even serve as fund-raisers to help the school purchase additional computer equipment.

The 5th Wave By Rich Tennant

"KEVIN HERE HEADS OUR MACINTOSH SOFTWARE DEVELOPMENT TEAM. RIGHT NOW HE'S WORKING ON A SPREADSHEET PROGRAM THAT'S SORT OF A COMBINATION 1-2-3 LOTUS,-DONKEY KONG."

Fun, Games, and Learning

■ *My child seems to be having fun, but is she learning anything?*

■ *What sorts of things can a computer teach my child?*

■ *Is there any value in pure "entertainment" software or in tools that allow my child to print or paint?*

Years ago, when micro-computers first began making their way into homes and schools in significant numbers, many publishers rushed to create "educational" software for kids and adults. Given the limitations of the technology at the time and the narrow definition of education many of these developers brought to the task, a large number of the titles they produced were deadly.

Some of the programs, billing themselves as *tutorials*, presented page after page of text interspersed with multiple-choice questions. Others took a *drill-and-practice* approach, asking students to answer questions and then providing feedback in the form of a brief message ("No, try again" or "That's right!"). After the student responded correctly to several problems, the drill programs generally offered a special reward (music, the screen's lighting up, an animated effect, and so on).

Software has come a long way since then, but a number of developers and potential purchasers still have a rather old-fashioned view of what is and is not educational. Many of us fall into the trap of thinking that unless a program feels like "serious" hard work, our children won't learn from it. We sometimes look at programs that focus on factual information and drilling kids on a specific body of knowledge and say, "Now, *that's* educational!"

There are at least two problems with viewing software this way. First, it's easy to lose sight of other aspects of learning when we focus exclusively on right or wrong answers and facts to be memorized. Although there is a definite place for such factual information in any child's education, an even more important role of education is to help our children learn to *think* and to *create*—neither of which can be taught through straight drill. In fact, some of the most educationally valuable programs on the market are tools with no obvious instructional content. For example, the writing tools described in Part 4 of this book are likely to motivate your child to create stories, letters, and cards for friends, relatives, and teachers—and to refine those writing, spelling, and visual skills necessary to create satisfying results.

A second problem with old-fashioned drills and tutorials is that they usually aren't much fun. In the past, children may have put up with deadly-dull programs because the computer was new and exciting to them. Today, the novelty has worn off and young people have come to expect much more. Not all software has to be "fun" in the sense that a good game or an entertaining movie is fun; publishing programs that allow kids to produce outstanding results or reference tools that make their schoolwork much easier have their appeal as well. But if your child sees a program as "boring," he will never stick with it.

Games and More

A number of the programs that hold children's interest for hours at the computer are educationally oriented games. Some of these are *simulation games* that place kids in a historically, geographically, or scientifically accurate environment and challenge them to explore, make choices, and overcome obstacles. Many others are today's much-improved versions of drill-and-practice; the drill is now in an entertaining context involving game-playing elements (arcade action, mazes, etc.) plus appealing graphics and sound.

In trying to determine what your child is learning from a particular game, you should first consider whether the enjoyment is *intrinsic* (internal, closely related to the content being covered) or *extrinsic* (external, unrelated to the content).

To explain, let's start with a noncomputer analogy. Suppose that you want your child to practice spelling and vocabulary skills. Many popular activities focus on those skills, including crossword puzzles; games such as Scrabble and Boggle; and television quiz shows, such as "Wheel of Fortune." All of these activities rely primarily on intrinsic motivation. In each case, the content (letters and words) is central to the game; although there are some external rewards in the form of points or money earned, the enjoyment that players experience is derived mostly from successfully manipulating letters to form words or sentences.

An alternate approach, one that focuses more on extrinsic motivation, is often taken in schools. Imagine that, instead of suggesting one of the games listed above, you encouraged your child to take part in a board game or baseball game involving a set of words she needed to memorize. Each time she correctly spelled and defined one of her words, she would be able to progress to another spot on the board or take another base in the ball game. In this case, the game-playing elements (moving around the board or baseball field) are far removed from the content being studied.

Which approach is more educational? In part, that depends on your exact goal. If the point is to master a specific list of words for a test the teacher will give at the end of the week, the extrinsic approach is more efficient. After all, with games such as Scrabble or Boggle, it's impossible to predict which letters players will get and which words they will practice as a result. On the other hand, if your goal is to develop in your child a fascination with letters and words, the first set of games is much more helpful. If your child enjoys playing any one of them, she is likely to walk away with a more positive feeling about word play and language. When walking away from the baseball game, however, she's much more likely to think, "Baseball is fun. I'm glad I got those words right so I could run the bases."

In the software world we have the same sorts of choices to make. Like the noncomputerized games that encourage word play, some software programs manage to create environments in which the fun, the challenges, and the game-playing aspects are all closely related to the learning that is taking place. Some of the best examples are geography and history programs, such as the *Carmen Sandiego* series (see Chapter 23, "Learning About the World," for a description of this series and several other geography/history programs that use a similar approach). These programs send players on imaginary trips around the world, using maps to help them navigate and geographic or historical clues to steer them in the right direction. It's hard to separate the game from the content in this case, which increases the likelihood that kids will acquire a renewed interest in maps and in learning about the world.

Many more of the popular educational computer games are on the other end of the spectrum, relying heavily on extrinsic rewards: answer this math problem correctly and you can progress through a maze, spell this word right and you'll shoot down a missile, and so on. In these examples, there are two sets of activities taking place (the maze navigation or arcade action on the one hand and the math or spelling on the other), and there's little logical connection between the two. While we are clearly more enthusiastic about the intrinsic approach, we are not ruling out extrinsic motivation. In fact, many of the educational games we recommend in Part 4 of this book rely more heavily on extrinsic than intrinsic rewards. (It's definitely a spectrum, by the way, and most programs do a little bit of both.) In part, that's because there are so few intrinsically rewarding programs to choose from. But it's also because there are many occasions when the extrinsic reward does work.

As with the baseball example, such an approach can be more efficient at conveying a set body of knowledge. Furthermore, some topics lend themselves better to exploration than others: if the subject is mathematical estimation, it's easy to imagine a game in which children navigate through a magical math land, estimating how far they need to go at each turn; if the goal is to memorize multiplication facts, it's much harder to think of a game with intrinsic rewards.

A final, and very important, reason for considering games with extrinsic rewards is that some kids respond best to them. The active child who needs to move and run might reject even the most entertaining word game but be willing to play the baseball game and learn a bit of spelling and vocabulary on the side. In the same way, kids who find games like *Where in the World Is Carmen Sandiego?* too slow-paced, might stick with a geography arcade game, learning to identify countries on a blank map of the world in order to have the opportunity to steer a speeding race car along a track. The social studies content that they are learning may not be as rich, but if the game succeeds in exposing them to a topic they previously ignored, then it certainly has educational value for that child.

Looking at What Else They Are Learning

Whenever you do consider a program that relies heavily on extrinsic rewards, it's helpful to look at those external game-playing elements to see how valuable you think they are for your child. In a sense, there are two types of learning going on, the *primary* learning related to the content area this educational game says it's teaching and the *secondary* learning related to the game elements that provide the rewards.

In the case of an arcade-style game, the secondary learning generally involves developing fast reflexes, good aim, and so on. You may decide that these skills are valuable for your child—perhaps he has some difficulty with fine motor coordination but enjoys arcade action and improves his fine motor skills as a result, or perhaps you feel that by "burning off some steam" in this way, your very active kid will be able to concentrate better on other tasks. Or you may choose to steer your child away from the arcade-type games if you feel that they are too violent, if you're convinced that they simply reinforce skills that he already practices for hours each day, or if he is on the other end of the spectrum and hates arcade action.

Other types of secondary learning are also common in educational games. When you take into account how much time is often taken by these external tasks, you may feel that some of these games are not worth the time and energy your child spends on them. On the other hand, other skills introduced may be ones that can really help your child. Perhaps a game your child loves involves strategy, problem solving, and deduction— thinking skills that will help her in many aspects of her life. Or perhaps it includes a maze or jigsaw puzzle that encourages her to focus on spatial relations without the time pressure associated with an arcade game. Even if none of these secondary skills are closely related to the program's primary goals, they can often be valuable in their own right.

In fact, it's worth considering some games that focus entirely on secondary skills. So far, the games we've discussed in this chapter are the ones that bill themselves as "educational," offering practice in content or skills that fit neatly into specific areas of the school curriculum. But there are a number of other valuable programs that make no such claims even though the skills that they reinforce—problem solving, logical reasoning, spatial relations, and so on—do indirectly relate to a child's performance at school and in life. That is why we've chosen to include a chapter in Part 4 that focuses entirely on "entertainment" software, and why we want to reassure parents whose kids already spend considerable time with such programs that your child might, just might, be learning more than you realize.

In the end, there are many types of learning and many approaches that are educationally valid. If your kid is having a good time using a particular program, if that program focuses on content and skills you feel are important, and if it does so in a way that encourages thinking and creativity, you can feel confident that valuable learning is taking place.

The 5th Wave — By Rich Tennant

"NO, YOU'RE IN THE CASTLE COMPUTER ROOM. THAT'S THE 'WIZARD OF NERD'. YOU WANT 'OZ'— TWO DOORS DOWN ON YOUR RIGHT."

CHAPTER FOUR

Working Together at the Computer

■ *Are computers bad for a child's social development?*

■ *If my child spends lots of time at the computer, isn't there a danger that he will become an isolated "nerd"?*

■ *How can I encourage group work and cooperation at the family computer?*

■ *How much time at the computer is too much?*

Many people think of working and playing at the computer as a solitary activity. After all, the computer has one screen and one keyboard, so it's easy to assume that only one person can use it at a time. We imagine a lone computer "nerd" sitting hunched over the keyboard, staring intently at the screen. The glow of the screen is the only light in an otherwise darkened room as this solitary soul shuts out the rest of the world and computes.

This image alone is enough to convince some parents not to buy computers for their children. But, although a number of tasks require solo time at the computer, many other computer activities promote group involvement. In fact, educators frequently report that children in their classes work particularly well together when engaged in group activities at the computer. Working together toward a common goal, the children get to know one another better and discover the usefulness of teamwork.

How can you cultivate "cooperative learning" of this sort in your home? The first step in turning your child's computer time into a social activity is to look for programs that lend themselves well to group use.

Software to Use Cooperatively

Many computer games allow more than one user to play at one time. In most cases, the players take turns trying to win the most points. The computer signals each player when it is time to take his turn. A few of the programs allow two players at the keyboard or two joysticks in use at once. The players may oppose each other or, in rare cases, cooperate and compete against the computer.

Competitive games are frequently very appealing to kids. While not the ideal way to encourage cooperative attitudes, such games do allow two or more children in your family (or your child and some friends) to socialize at the computer. By making the rules harder for the player who indicates that he is older or more advanced, some programs, such as Broderbund's *Treehouse*, even allow children at different skill levels (an older and a younger sibling, for example) to compete equitably.

If you're concerned about the effects of too much competition on your children, you can try helping them "turn around" the goals of a competitive game. Rather than competing to get the highest individual score, everyone can work together as a single team to see how high a score the entire group can get. Or, if you have at least four people interested in playing, you can combine both competition and cooperation by encouraging your kids to form competing teams of two or more players.

In addition to the software created specifically for multiple players, many programs designed for individual users can also be used cooperatively. Almost any software that provides a story line or multiple choices lends itself to a group effort. Adventure games, simulations, interactive storybooks, and programs that allow users to explore freely an imaginary environment are all great ways of getting a group to work together, stopping to discuss possible next moves at each decision point and proceeding once a consensus has been reached.

Even tools such as word processors and paint programs can be used cooperatively. A cooperative effort with this sort of software focuses on the end result and not the process. For example, several members of your family might try writing a group letter to somebody you all care about. The "team" might first create a basic outline of points to cover in the letter. Then each point could be filled in to form a paragraph. Each person might be responsible for a different paragraph, or everybody might contribute to each one. Since all participants can see what is being written and corrections can be made easily, the letter evolves as the group works together.

Team effort can go a long way toward making a challenging program easier and more fun to use. As long as one team member is familiar with the software, the others can learn the ropes relatively painlessly. With a task to focus on and a little bit of coaching, each member of the team is in an ideal position to learn to use the program independently.

Rules and Roles

When children work together at the computer, you will often find them taking turns voluntarily or dividing up the roles based on individual skills and interests. In other words, they may not need your help learning to cooperate if they're motivated by the software and glad to be working together. There are times, however, when adult guidance is needed to help children (especially siblings) learn how to cooperate at the computer.

One approach that works particularly well with children who are at similar skill levels is to agree on a specific role for each participant and then rotate roles periodically so that everyone has the chance to "play" them all. If only two players are involved in a game, for example, one might be the *pilot* in charge of typing at the keyboard or using the mouse or joystick; while the other could be the *navigator,* providing verbal instructions, reading aloud whatever appears on the screen, and having the final say whenever the two disagree on a move. With additional players, roles such as *tactician* (in charge of finding hints, rules, and shortcuts in the documentation), *historian* (the note taker who keeps track of what actions the group has taken), and *site manager* (responsible for reminding people of their roles and determining when jobs rotate) can be added.

Of course, you'll want to be flexible about these roles because the kids will probably want to modify them or create new ones. If players are at very different skill levels, you might need to establish nonrotating roles that take advantage of each kid's abilities. For example, a nonreader might never have to take a turn reading at the monitor but could always be in charge of deciding where the group should go next. This can be a great way of allowing younger children to participate in games that might otherwise be too hard for them.

However, as the adult, you may find it necessary to monitor play to make sure nobody is ignored or made to feel bad.

If your children respond well to formal rules, you might want to work with them to come up with a list of guidelines to be posted near the computer. In addition to basic computer rules such as "No food near the computer" and "Keep disks in their jackets," the list would include rules related to cooperative play. For example: 1) No one touches the keyboard/mouse/joystick except the pilot; 2) No making fun of other players; 3) Rotate jobs every 20 minutes; and so on.

Working with Your Child at the Computer

So far in this chapter, the role we've described for you is that of a monitor or supervisor, helping your children and their friends learn how to cooperate at the computer. But you may want to be even more actively involved. In fact, if your child does not have a sibling or friend with whom he plays well and is suitably matched, his social time at the computer might be well spent with *you*. This can be an excellent time for you and your child to relax together.

A larger group of children might welcome your participation as well. For example, kids who are easily frustrated by typing at the keyboard might prefer to have you serve as pilot much of the time while they give the orders. Or you might take the role of *special advisor,* loading the program and explaining the rules. In either case, your biggest challenge will be to step back and let the kids take the lead. If you're the typist, be sure to type exactly what you are told, even if you know the instructions won't work. If you're an advisor, try to speak up only when your advice is requested. In general, if you spend too much time telling your kids how to use the computer, they will resent the intrusion and come to view computing as just another area in which parents get to tell kids what to do.

If you're lucky (or plan it right), your kids will know more about the program than you do—allowing them the unique opportunity to explain something to you that you don't understand. If you admit that you do not know much about a program but are interested in learning more, your child is likely to delight in teaching you all he knows.

Sometimes the most helpful role you can play is as an interested observer. Acknowledge your child's discoveries and ask her broad questions about the program, the characters, her favorite and least favorite parts, and so on. Simply watching what she chooses to do and letting her know that you are interested can be an excellent way of strengthening your relationship and her self-confidence.

Ownership

If you want your children to view the computer as a tool to be shared, it's important to think carefully about who has access to it and when. Who really owns the computer in your family? If family members view the computer as jointly owned, if they all have some say in the decision to purchase it or in what type of computer to buy, they are apt to feel freer to use it. If the computer was purchased in part for a parent to work on at home, it's important to set aside time when the kids know the computer is *theirs*—and then to step back and let them use it.

If you want your children to work effectively together at the computer, it's also important to find software that appeals to everyone. This may require research and a consensus on which program to purchase. Some families find it helpful for everyone to make a financial contribution. The

parents might pay 50 percent of the cost of a program, big sister might pay 35 percent, little brother 15 percent, and so on. With everybody agreeing on the purchase and providing their fair share—or at least some share—of the cost, the software will definitely be viewed as an item to be shared.

Location

The location of the computer is also important. With sibling rivalry being as intense as it is, placing the computer in one child's room is not likely to encourage sharing, much less group participation. Ideally, the family computer should be located in a room where everyone can use it and in a position suited to group viewing.

Some families find it useful to place the computer near the television, since most TV rooms are set up to accommodate a large group of viewers. However, this can cause conflicts between those who want to use the computer and those who want to watch TV. It's virtually impossible to accomplish anything at the computer with a television set blaring a few feet away. If you do decide to put both pieces of equipment in the same room, it's important to designate certain times for using the computer and others for watching TV.

A preferable solution is to find a relatively quiet common room—for example, a study, a den with no television, or even the corner of a dining room—where individuals can work alone without being disturbed and where it's also easy to pull up several chairs for a cooperative activity. For those times when a large group will be working together, it's helpful to find a way of placing the screen at a slightly higher level than usual so that everybody can see. A deep computer table helps here as well. By moving the keyboard back away from the screen, more people can view the image on the screen. Keep in mind that even with the best vision, most people cannot read small type on the screen from more than three feet away.

In addition, check to make sure the screen does not have a glare caused by large windows or bright lights: Look at the screen with the computer off. If you can see bright reflections, it may be difficult for several people to view the screen from a slight distance. Close the curtains or leave the light off when using the system.

Watching the Clock

All of us want our children to be able to work and think independently. Equally important is the fact that we want them to develop social skills, learning to work cooperatively with other people. The computer can help with both.

Some parents fear that their children will become "addicted" to computers. For them, the concern is not simply that the child will work alone, but that he will become obsessed, unable to think about anything but computing. The truth is that *certain children*, during *certain periods* of their life, will indeed become "hooked" on particular computer activities, working on them at every free moment of the day. But, then, kids quite commonly get hooked on all sorts of activities—from reading mystery books to playing baseball.

There's no such thing as "the right amount of time" at the computer, but as with almost any activity your kid loves, you may find it necessary to encourage (or even require) moderation. (See Chapter 5, "Computers and Your Child's Health," for information about the eye strain, muscle aches, and other health problems that can be caused by *excessive* computer use.) Just as the serious "bookworm" should be encouraged to put down her book occasionally and go outside to play, the serious computer "hacker" should be encouraged to turn off the computer frequently, as well as to welcome others into the experience. Whether your child is a fanatic or a reluctant computer user, you can also help by being supportive, making suggestions that will help her broaden her tastes and outlook—and remembering that whatever game or activity she's obsessed with today will undoubtedly give way to something else in a few months, a few weeks, or even days.

The 5th Wave — By Rich Tennant

"WHOA, HOLD THE PHONE! IT SAYS, 'THE ELECTRICITY COMING OUT OF A SURGE PROTECTOR IS GENERALLY CLEANER AND SAFER THAN THAT GOING INTO ONE, UNLESS-UN-LESSS-YOU ARE STANDING IN A BUCKET OF WATER.'"

Computers and Your Child's Health

- *Is it dangerous for my child to spend too much time at the computer?*

- *What does all the talk about VDT health hazards mean? Should I be concerned?*

- *Is there any way I can protect my child from harmful effects caused by the computer?*

For the most part, a computer is as safe as any other household appliance. But just as with other household appliances, there are some potential health hazards associated with computer use. (Many of them, by the way, are just as applicable to video games as they are to computers.)

Concern about the health effects of computers focuses on several general categories of risk. These include:

- Problems related to electromagnetic emissions

- Visual problems

- Muscle and joint problems

In every case, these risks appear to be directly related to the amount of time spent working on or being near the computer.

Let's begin with the most controversial topic: the possible harmful effects of the electromagnetic field produced by your computer monitor.

Electromagnetic Emissions

Every device that transmits or runs on electricity gives off *electromagnetic radiation*. This radiation surrounds the object and creates an *electromagnetic field (EMF)*. Some devices, like your toaster or refrigerator, emit very low levels of electromagnetic radiation. Other devices, like high-voltage wires, a kitchen microwave oven, a television, or a computer monitor, give off significantly higher levels. You can't see, hear, smell, taste, or touch electromagnetic radiation, but in today's world, it is everywhere.

No one is certain how normal levels of electromagnetic radiation affect the health of children or adults, but many people are concerned. Occasionally, the fears are based on a misunderstanding of the term *radiation*. Used to refer to a full range of electromagnetic emissions, "radiation" to many of us connotes X rays (also known as ionizing radiation), a high-frequency form of radiation that has been proven to increase the likelihood of cancer in animals and human beings. Actually, everybody who has studied the technology behind computer monitors (also referred to as *video display terminals* or *VDTs*) agrees that X-ray radiation is not the issue; the tiny amount of ionizing radiation emitted by the *Cathode Ray Tube (CRT)* within the monitor is effectively screened out by the surrounding glass.

What scientists and consumer advocates do not agree on, however, is the effect on humans of lower frequency electromagnetic radiation—

the *VLF* (for *Very Low Frequency*) and *ELF* (for *Extra Low Frequency*) radiation given off by computers and a variety of other appliances. A number of studies on the subject in recent years have raised concerns—and many unanswered questions.

Most of the studies that have been conducted into the health effects of electromagnetic fields fall into one of three categories: 1) studies on the miscarriage rate for pregnant women working many hours a day at computer terminals; 2) experiments with animal embryos to examine the relationship between prolonged exposure to EMFs and birth defects or miscarriages; 3) statistical analyses of cancer rates in children and adults to determine whether proximity to high-power lines (or other wiring configurations causing high levels of electromagnetic radiation) increases cancer risks. The results of the research thus far have been confusing and inconclusive. In each of the three categories, there have been several studies indicating a relationship between EMFs and health problems, and an even larger number of studies refuting such a connection.

Even the studies that do find connections frequently raise more questions than they answer. For example, a 1988 study (conducted by Kaiser Permanente Hospital in

Oakland, California) that helped draw attention to the potential risks of computer usage by pregnant women, found that only one group of women studied (those with clerical jobs) experienced a higher miscarriage rate the more time they spent at the computer, while other groups (including women in sales or management positions) did not. (These findings suggest that other factors, such as stress, may have been responsible for the increases that were found.)

Research in the other two areas has been equally confusing. For example, some of the studies of embryos exposed to EMFs showed an increase in miscarriage but not in birth defects, others showed an increase in birth defects but not miscarriage, and still others had results that were not reproducible from one trial to the next. And one of the most recent studies (conducted by the University of Southern California) on the effects of power lines pointed to a link between wiring configurations (related to number, capacity, and proximity of power lines) and leukemia risk but found little evidence that the locations considered riskiest actually had a higher measured level of electromagnetic radiation. Perhaps location with regard to power lines

has more to do with other factors, such as traffic patterns, use of defoliant sprays, or socioeconomic status, which in turn might be connected to increased leukemia risk.

Playing It Safe

What, then, can you conclude about the risk that computing poses to your child's health and yours? There is no conclusive evidence that the electromagnetic field created by your computer's monitor can be harmful, but clearly there is a lot of information yet to come in this confusing area. (If scientists do some day conclude that EMFs present a health risk, we'll clearly have to think about protecting our children from much more than computers and TVs; electric lights, hair dryers, and other appliances will be implicated as well.)

In the meantime, it can never hurt to take a cautious approach. Here are some suggestions, gathered from a variety of sources, for playing it safe when it comes to computers and EMFs:

■ Because electromagnetic radiation is emitted from all parts of the monitor (in fact, many measurements indicate higher emissions from the sides and back than from the front), it's safest to place a computer in a corner of a room or somewhere else where nonusers are least likely to find themselves near the sides or back of the machine.

■ Don't leave the computer or monitor turned on for long periods of time. If the computer is not in use, turn it off. This can be a nuisance (and might have a *slight* effect on the life expectancy of your computer), but it is a small price to pay if EMFs do prove to be hazardous.

■ Encourage your children to sit as far as they comfortably can from the computer (or television) screen. According to tests conducted by *Macworld* magazine (reported in the July 1990 issue), users sitting at least 28 inches from the screen were exposed to only a minimal amount of electromagnetic radiation. *Macworld* recommended placing the monitor at arm's length (that's an adult arm, with fingers extended) when working at the computer.

■ Children and pregnant women should not spend an excessive amount of time (more than a few hours a day) at the computer.

You may also be wondering whether there is any way of reducing the electromagnetic radiation given off by your monitor. Actually, two approaches are being taken by manufacturers challenged with this question. Some companies now offer special screens that you can place over your monitor to decrease the glare associated with eye strain (see the next section) and, supposedly, to decrease electromagnetic emissions. However, according to tests reported in the *Macworld* article, the grounding wires used by the protective screens they tested succeeded only in decreasing the *electrical* field, not the *magnetic* field—which is considered to be the risky portion of the EMF.

On the other hand, according to a follow-up article in *Macworld's* October 1991 issue, some of the producers of computer monitors have succeeded in building models that do emit lower magnetic fields. You might want to check out such a monitor for your family. If you do, look for proof that the model does indeed decrease VLF and (more importantly) ELF *magnetic* fields, not just electrical fields.

If You'd Like to Read More About Computers and Health

Some useful overviews:

Macworld magazine's July 1990 and October 1991 issues each include articles addressing health hazards and the computer. The Special Report in the July 1990 issue provides a comprehensive but one-sided summary of all the studies that have concluded that electromagnetic fields can be harmful, while other articles in that issue summarize test results and offer suggestions for playing it safe. The October 1991 issue provides an update, written in a much more balanced tone, about new studies in the field, plus test results on a number of monitors designed to decrease EMFs.

For back issues, look in your local library or send $6 for each issue you want to: Back Issues, Macworld, 144 Townsend St., San Francisco, CA 94107.

The Labor Occupational Health Program (LOHP) of the University of California, Berkeley, publishes a quarterly publication, *Monitor*, which includes in each issue a special section about the hazards of VDTs and computers. (A one-year subscription costs $15.) LOHP will also send you a free packet of information or (for $10) a more extensive collection of research on the subject.

For information or to order, contact LOHP, 2515 Channing Way, Berkeley, CA 94720.

Science magazine's September 7 and September 21, 1990, issues provide an excellent (and balanced) overview of much of the research related to the effects of EMFs on humans.

For back issues, look in your local library or send $6 per issue to: Science, AAAS, 1333 H St., NW, Washington, D.C. 20005.

Some studies to watch for:

Mt Sinai Hospital, with support from a variety of different organizations, is currently conducting a four-year study of 10,000 female office workers and the effects of computer usage on their health. The study is due to be completed in 1993.

The Food and Drug Administration (FDA) is conducting a number of studies, including one that attempts to reproduce earlier findings on the harmful effects of electromagnetic fields on chick embryos.

Visual Problems

While there's much controversy over the danger of electromagnetic fields, there's little disagreement about the fact that prolonged computer use can lead to eye strain. Whenever children or adults spend a great deal of time on a visual task, they suffer eye fatigue. You are probably familiar with this problem from driving long distances or from reading for extended periods of time. The muscles that control your eyes and focus them simply become fatigued from overuse. The potential for eye fatigue exists for all visual tasks, but it is greatest for those involving close work. Many feel that it's also more of a problem when the close work involves a high-glare device, such as a computer monitor.

Children are especially prone to eye fatigue because their eyes and the muscles that control them have not matured. Extensive reading, close-up television watching, and computing all put great demands on young eyes. The most common result of visual fatigue is that children will become tired and cranky. As every parent can attest, these responses are not unique to computing. When children overdo any activity, they frequently become irritable—and irritating. If your child is acting more temperamental than usual, and there is no other obvious cause, long periods of time spent in front of the computer may be the culprit.

Excessive computing may also aggravate existing visual problems. Many children suffer from minor visual impairments that fall into the "nuisance" category. Eventually, these problems require correction, but the remedy may not be necessary until adolescence or adulthood. When children are so taken with computing that they spend much of their free time at the keyboard, however, the "nuisance" visual problem may develop into something that requires correction at an early age.

While there is no evidence that computers can actually *cause* visual problems, some ophthalmologists worry that overuse at a young age might have a harmful effect on the muscles that control the eyes, making it more difficult for a child to focus his eyes, especially for close-up tasks such as reading. If this occurs, it might be necessary to correct the problem with glasses.

Fortunately, most of these computer-related visual problems can be prevented quite easily. Here are a few suggestions:

■ The most obvious solution is to limit the amount of time your kids spend computing without a break. For children, a brief break every 15 to 30 minutes is recommended. Although it may be difficult to enforce such a rigid time limit on an enthusiastic child, at the very least you should follow the guidelines set for many working adults these days and require a break once every hour. A nonvisual, physical activity—taking a walk, throwing a ball outside, or even accompanying an adult on a trip to the store—is the ideal "spacer" to separate computing sessions.

- Some professionals suggest the use of eye exercises to help children avoid the problems that might result from computer use. These exercises can be as simple as tracking objects that are moving across the field of vision or focusing on distant objects. One of the ancillary benefits of alternating computer use with other activities is that the alternative activity will often involve visual movements that actually exercise the eyes.

- It is also a good idea to vary the activities that children undertake on the computer. For example, time at a word processor might be alternated with an action-packed adventure full of moving objects. Alternating activities in this way will make varied demands on young eyes and prevent the fatigue caused by focusing on the same target for too long.

- Choosing a good monitor is another way of decreasing the risk of eye strain. Higher resolution monitors are easier on the eyes than low resolution monitors. If you and your child will be spending considerable time at the computer, it's absolutely essential to have a clear, crisp display.

- Finally, it may be important to take steps to decrease the glare from the monitor. Bright and uneven lighting in a room can cause disturbing reflections on the screen. Possible solutions to this problem involve turning off overhead lights, pulling the shades on windows that let in extremely bright light, and turning the monitor so it is neither directly in front of nor exactly opposite the brightest light source. Anti-glare screens to be placed over your monitor are available from a number of manufacturers and are definitely worth considering if your child appears to be bothered by reflections or the general glare of the monitor itself.

If, in spite of these precautions, your child complains about headaches and sore or itchy eyes or suddenly begins having problems with reading or other schoolwork, you should make an appointment with an optometrist or ophthalmologist. Be sure to mention that you have a computer at home and describe the amount of time your child uses it. The doctor may prescribe specific eye exercises, or might fit your child for glasses that are especially suited to the medium-range work involved in computing.

Muscle and Joint Problems

Among people who use computers to earn their living, the greatest number of health complaints is due to muscle and joint problems. For the most part, these problems are of the nuisance variety: a stiff neck, sore shoulders, lower back pain, or tingling in the legs.

There are a few more serious complaints, however. The most common is *carpal tunnel syndrome*, in which the nerves in the hand are damaged by long and repeated stints at the computer. In its most severe form, carpal tunnel syndrome is a painful condition that can permanently disable an individual.

Children rarely experience muscle and joint problems as a result of computing; they simply don't spend enough time at the computer for such problems to develop. However, it's wise to discourage your children from sitting for long periods of time in an uncomfortable position in front of the computer. One thing you can do is make sure that the chair your child uses is neither too high nor too low. (Special office chairs that can be raised or lowered easily might be helpful if several family members, all of different sizes, will be using the computer at different times.) In addition, encourage your child to sit with correct posture when she is computing. If you can get your child into the habit of sitting up straight and facing the computer directly, it is likely that muscle and joint problems will not develop in the future.

We don't want to exaggerate the risks of extended time spent at the computer, nor do we want to minimize them. By following the guidelines suggested in this chapter, and by encouraging your children to be moderate rather than excessive in their use of computers, we believe you will succeed in creating a safe and happy computing environment for your family.

CHAPTER SIX

How Young Is Too Young? Preschoolers on the Computer

- *Is my three-year-old ready for a computer? Will he be able to handle a mouse or find things on the keyboard?*
- *What can computer programs offer to very young kids?*
- *Is there any danger in exposing kids to computers at too young an age?*

The topic of computers and young children is a controversial one. Many early childhood educators are reluctant to bring computers into the preschool classroom, and those in the position of advising parents are sometimes adamantly opposed to the idea of computers in the hands of preschoolers. Why?

Most early childhood experts today believe in the importance of a "developmental" approach to educating young children. Such an approach, based in large part on the research of Swiss psychologist Jean Piaget, assumes that children learn by "constructing their own knowledge," by being placed in a rich environment with plenty of opportunities to explore, to manipulate objects, and to solve problems. In the developmental approach, teachers view counting, reading, and writing in much the same way they view walking and talking; they are confident that children will acquire the new concepts and skills *when they are ready to do so*—as long as they are given the chance to practice and experiment in a supportive, non-pressured environment.

Some early childhood experts look at software packages designed to drill young children on letters, numbers, and shapes, and worry that computers in preschools will be used to push children faster than they are ready to go and will encourage them to learn skills in isolation. These educators fear that children who spend lots of time at the computer will become passive or antisocial users. In addition, they are concerned that computers are too *abstract* for the very young child. They suggest that experience with *real* paints, blocks, dress-up clothes, and musical instruments is far more beneficial than computerized versions of such experiences. As Ellen Galinsky and Judy David put it in their book, *The Preschool Years* (New York: Ballantine Books, 1991), "In our opinion, the computer offers no learning experience nor fosters any skill for preschool children that cannot be experienced more meaningfully and less expensively in play at home and in good early childhood programs. The value of computers for learning comes later on, when children are older."

But there are a number of other early childhood experts—also strongly committed to a developmental approach—who disagree. While they acknowledge that the market is flooded with software that is *not* developmentally appropriate for preschoolers, they believe that the *right kind of software*, used as *just one of many* learning tools, can make a tremendous difference to young children.

In the Preschool Classroom

In her book *Children and Computers Together in the Early Childhood Classroom* (Albany, N.Y.: Delmar Publishers, 1989), Jane Davidson summarizes much of the research in the field and reports on her own observations of children using computers in preschools. She concludes that computers tend to encourage rather than discourage social interaction and observes that "the children who use computers at the University of Delaware Preschool do not seem passive. Children are jumping up to observe each other's work, . . . moving their bodies with the actions of the characters on the screen, and in some cases even dancing to the music on the program."

Charles Hohmann, coordinator of curriculum for the High/Scope Educational Research Foundation (an organization that focuses on the education of young children), agrees. In his book *Young Children & Computers* (Ypsilanti, Mich.:

High/Scope Press, 1990), he explains that, for preschoolers in the High/Scope demonstration classroom, "the addition of computers and appropriate software to their environment has [had] positive social consequences," including an increase in cooperative activity (for example, children playing together and helping one another at the computer). And,

What Is Developmentally Appropriate Software?

Based on the books mentioned in this chapter and on interviews we conducted with a number of early childhood experts, we have arrived at a list of criteria for you to use when determining whether a software package is appropriate for your preschooler.

Developmentally appropriate software is:

- **Open-ended and exploratory**. It doesn't focus on right and wrong answers but allows children to investigate and discover for themselves.

- **Easy for a young child to use independently**. It does not require reading, has easy-to-understand directions, and only expects children to find a limited number of keys on the keyboard. Furthermore, it is flexible about input devices, allowing a child to use a mouse, the keyboard, or an alternate device—whichever is easiest for that child.

- **Focused on a broad range of skills and concepts**. It works on more than just the numbers, letters, colors, and shapes so often identified as preschool skills. In addition (or instead), it encourages children to classify, to experiment using trial and error, to create and, in general, to think.

- **Technically sophisticated.** It appeals to a child's multisensory learning style, offering attractive graphics, appealing animations, and outstanding sound. It loads quickly and does not have long delays between screens (during which time a young child can become bored).

- **Age-appropriate**. It doesn't push the child to master skills for which she's not yet ready. The images and examples it uses are from real life or are at least understandable to the young child (within her realm of experience).

- **Playful and fun**. It encourages children to imagine, might involve fantasy play, and is definitely enjoyable. Furthermore, the fun is derived from the activity itself, not from some extrinsic reward given if the child succeeds at a given task.

- **Encouraging.** Children experience success when using this software; it helps build their self-esteem.

although he agrees that "the computer provides a symbolic rather than a direct learning experience," he points out that "young children interact meaningfully with symbolic material they encounter in books read or shown to them by parents and other adults." Certainly, a good, interactive computer program is no more symbolic or abstract than a book—especially when you consider the new generation of software that allows a child to "turn pages," move objects on the screen, "click" on any word and hear it read aloud, watch and listen as selected characters "come alive," and make choices that determine the outcome of the story.

Finally, when comparing the value of computers to that of concrete objects that children can manipulate, many early childhood educators believe that the ideal is to expose children to *all* of these options. Computerized graphics programs, for example, should never replace painting, collage, or other "messy" materials in the preschool classroom, but that does not negate the value of the graphics package as a tool in its own right. As Davidson points out, computer art programs "allow the children to create with straight lines and segments of line, something not within their skill level when using crayons, paint, or markers." Her conclusions on this topic: "One would not ban crayons from the room because paint is available. . . . The computer is merely another possible medium with . . . its own limitations and possibilities."

In addition to refuting many of the common fears about computers and young children, the researchers point to a number of other benefits of developmentally appropriate software in the early childhood classroom. For example, educators involved in a Head Start/IBM Partnership project that studied the effects of computers placed at selected Head Start classrooms around the country, concluded that developmentally appropriate computer activities increased young children's ability to attend to task, take turns, and follow directions; had a strong positive impact on self-esteem and self-confidence; and enhanced student creativity. (These results were summarized in an article by Tsantis, Wright, and Thouvenelle in the Jan./Feb. 1989 issue of *Children Today* and in a booklet entitled *Computers in Head Start Classrooms*, published by MOBIUS Corporation of Alexandria, Virginia.)

In the Home

So far the studies of computers and young children have focused on the school setting. But what does this mean for you as a parent considering a computer for your three- or four-year-old to use at home? Many of the issues are the same; a few are different.

A number of critics of computers for preschoolers have focused on the question of expense. Cost is an issue in a preschool setting because one has to weigh the benefits of a single computer (and accompanying software) against the value of art supplies, puzzles, rubber balls, and so on—all of which can be purchased for less money and used by more children at once. In your home, the issue takes on a slightly different twist. Instead of worrying about how many children you can schedule for this expensive piece of equipment in a single day, you need to worry about how much use your home computer will actually get.

If your only goal in purchasing a computer is to provide your preschooler with access, we suggest that you reconsider. Most preschool researchers find that young children rarely choose to spend more than 15 minutes at the computer before moving on to other activities. If you take the advice of early childhood educators and present the computer as an optional activity in your household, you may find that your youngster spends nearly an hour at the machine one day, 10 minutes the next, and then loses interest totally for a week. Unless there are adults or older children in the family interested in using the computer as well, you may find that you've spent a lot of money on equipment that gets used too rarely to warrant the investment.

On the other hand, if you already own a computer or are considering purchasing one for other purposes as well, we strongly encourage you to invest in a few developmentally appropriate programs for your preschooler to use. He will not be deprived if you *don't* expose him to the computer (for more on this topic, see Chapter 1, "Computers in Today's World"), but you may be pleasantly surprised at how quickly and positively he responds to the opportunity to play with this giant electronic toy.

In addition to the benefits found in the preschool studies mentioned in this chapter, there's another reason to consider using a computer with your little one: it's a tremendous opportunity for you to work closely together, to improve your child's communication skills, and to gain some insight into her thoughts and interests. Children as young as two years old can become involved in programs such as Tom Snyder's *Reading Magic* series, which encourages a parent to boot up the computer, place a child on his lap, and read the story that appears aloud, pausing at decision points within the program to ask the child to choose what should happen next. Other programs that are not necessarily designed as "lapware" can serve that purpose as well. For example, the *McGee* series from Lawrence/Broderbund, especially designed so a nonreader can make choices independently, can also be used with a child too young to use a mouse or other input device effectively; the child can point to a menu choice on the screen and say "go there" or "see chickens" and you can enter the selection she asks for.

Hardware Issues

While we do not suggest buying an entire computer system especially for your young child, there are a few types of add-ons you might want to consider. In particular, for owners of MS-DOS computers, there's the sound card (described in more detail in Chapter 12, "Peripherals and Other Options"). An increasing number of programs these days incorporate realistic-sounding speech and sound effects. While they might promise to "play through your PC speaker," they generally sound much better with the help of a special card. (On the Macintosh, such a card is not necessary because the hardware needed to play back high-quality sound is already built into the computer.)

Why should you care about sound quality for your young child? Because programs that "talk" to your preschooler can be extremely beneficial. With improvements in sound technology, software designers are finding themselves able to give directions to nonreaders by speaking those directions aloud. (While there are benefits to time spent with your child at the computer, it's also helpful to find programs that your child is comfortable using independently.) Speech can also provide vital feedback to your child. For example, a talking word processor that names each letter a child presses at the keyboard and reads back entire words (entered by the child or dictated to an adult typist) can be a tremendous tool for the child motivated to learn her letters or begin reading words. Other computerized sounds—conversations between characters on the screen, special effects, background music, and so on—can also add tremendously to the appeal of a program.

The other hardware issue that's worth thinking about is the question of input devices. Many people wonder whether young children can handle the complex task of using a mouse or can locate letters and other symbols easily on the computer keyboard. There is no simple answer to those questions, although the teachers at High/Scope have found that most three- and four-year-olds can learn to use a mouse quite effectively with a few hours of practice. Surprisingly, the children observed in this setting do not seem to have problems with the *concept* of moving the mouse on one plane (the desk) while the cursor moves on another (the screen); they generally plunge ahead, learning by trial-and-error. However, most observers agree that using a mouse can be very difficult for those young children who have problems with fine motor skills—especially if the program being used offers very small menu choices or features other tasks requiring precise control.

Evaluation Sources for Preschool Teachers

While we don't know of any ongoing software evaluation resources for parents of very young children, two groups publish an annual evaluation of early childhood software, aimed at preschool educators. Because both groups are quite comprehensive in their scope, critiquing many of the programs available to preschools today (including quite a few Apple II programs that have been on the market for many years), you may have to dig deep to find the titles that are not only developmentally appropriate but also designed to take advantage of today's computer technology. Nevertheless, both books provide valuable perspective on evaluating software for the young child.

High/Scope Survey of Early Childhood Software, by Warren Buckleitner, is published once a year. It contains reviews of hundreds of programs available for the early childhood market, with each program receiving a rating for user friendliness, educational value, and instructional design. The survey is available from High/Scope Educational Research Foundation, 600 North River St., Ypsilanti, MI 48198; (313) 485-2000.

Developmental Evaluations of Software for Young Children, by Susan W. Haugland and Daniel D. Shade, focuses on fewer titles than the High/Scope survey but rates them on a longer list of criteria. The 10 criteria used to judge the suitability of each title are based on guidelines set by the National Association for the Education of Young Children (NAEYC) for developmentally appropriate practices with four- and five-year-olds. This book is published annually and can be ordered from Delmar Publishers, Inc., 2 Computer Dr. West, Box 15-015, Albany, NY 12212.

The keyboard is physically quite easy for the average preschooler to use, although locating letters, function keys, etc., all over the keyboard can be painfully slow for many children. Here again, the issue has a lot to do with software design; developers of effective preschool programs make sure that the keys required for a child to operate the program are minimal and relatively easy to locate.

In general, you are likely to find that the standard input devices (keyboard and mouse) accompanied by well-designed software will be perfectly appropriate for the preschooler over the age of three or three and a half. However, if your child has special needs or generally has difficulty with fine motor coordination, you might consider a touch-sensitive screen that allows him to make choices by pressing directly on the screen. (See Chapter 7, "Special Solutions for Children with Special Needs," for more information on touch screens and other alternate input devices.)

The 5th Wave

By Rich Tennant

"IT'S AMAZING HOW MUCH MORE SOME PEOPLE CAN GET OUT OF A PC THAN OTHERS."

Special Solutions for Children with Special Needs

■ *My child has a learning disability. Can the computer help?*

■ *What special hardware and software is available to help children with physical or communication disabilities?*

■ *Our child has not been diagnosed as having a specific learning disability, but he has a hard time in school. What sort of software can we use to help him increase his skills?*

■ *Where can we find experts who really understand our child's special needs and the ways in which technology can help?*

The terms "special needs" and "disabilities" are very broad; used to refer to a variety of conditions, they include learning disabilities, behavior disorders, developmental disabilities, communication disabilities such as deafness and blindness, and orthopedic handicaps such as cerebral palsy and trauma-induced paralysis. While it is very hard to give any general advice about such a diverse group, it is safe to say that computers and related technologies have the potential to make a tremendous difference in the lives of children with special needs.

Computers allow "nondisabled" children and adults to accomplish tasks more efficiently. For those with special needs, the computer can play an even more important role: in many cases, it enables them to do things that were impossible (or at least much harder) to do before. This is particularly true of young people with physical or communication disabilities for whom special *adaptive devices* attached to the computer make it easier to communicate with the outside world. Adaptive devices run the gamut from text readers for blind children to special keyboards and head-operated switches for children with orthopedic disabilities.

Children with learning disabilities can sometimes benefit from special hardware as well. For example, the use of a touch-sensitive screen (built into some monitors or available as a separate unit to place over an existing monitor) can help a child who might otherwise have trouble making the connection between choices on the screen and the mouse or keyboard movements necessary to select them.

While it is beyond the scope of this chapter to list and describe all the adaptive devices that are available to you, the resource directory at the end of this chapter should help you locate an appropriate device for your child if she needs one. In addition, it's helpful to know that certain computers have built-in adaptive features. For example, the Macintosh allows users to modify their systems in order to magnify the screen, make it possible to enter all keyboard entries (Control key

combinations, capital letters, etc.) with only one hand, and so on.

What About Special Software?

Children with special needs often have difficulty accomplishing tasks that nondisabled children handle easily. A hearing-impaired child, for example, may have a hard time learning new vocabulary words. A child with a learning disability such as dyslexia may have trouble comprehending printed words.

For some children, especially those with developmental disabilities or other severe learning problems, special software that breaks tasks down into many simple steps is helpful. Such software, available from several of the companies in the directory at the end of this chapter, can be very satisfying to a child who rarely has the opportunity to learn at a comfortable pace and experience real success.

However, it's important not to assume that the average child with disabilities requires special *remedial* software, designed to drill him on the areas he finds difficult. That is a trap that too many school-based remedial programs fall into. Unfortunately, although children with special needs are frequently of average or above average intelligence, they often spend their time at school being drilled on lower-level skills such as vocabulary or "sounding out" words.

One of the problems with this approach is that it emphasizes a child's weaknesses, forcing her to focus on what she can *not* do rather than allowing her to learn compensatory skills and to experience success in other domains. As Richard Wanderman, an educational technology consultant who has years of experience working with students with learning disabilities, explains: "The biggest problem faced by children and adults with literacy problems is that they feel stupid. They need help separating their ability from their intelligence, realizing they can be very intelligent and learning disabled at the same time. As long as a child feels 'dumb,' as long as he's convinced that he'll fail at a task as difficult as reading or writing, why should he even try?"

The sense of failure that a learning-disabled student experiences due to repeated drilling in areas that he is weak in is compounded by the fact that many of the "supplemental" or "enrichment" activities reserved for children who have mastered these basic skills are much more fun than drill. Furthermore, by emphasizing

lower-level skills over higher-order thinking and problem solving, we deprive learning-disabled children of practice in the basic life skills that they need to be happy, contributing members of society.

In general, our advice to parents who are selecting software for a child with special needs—or, for that matter, for a child who is simply having trouble in certain subject areas—is to look for programs that are fun, that will help your child experience success, and that will encourage thinking, problem solving, and communication skills. Because these are some of the key criteria we used in selecting our favorite software for *all* children, you are likely to find a number of programs in this book that will be helpful to your special child.

This is not to say that every package that works with nondisabled students will work equally well with children who have special needs. In addition to the general guidelines that we just mentioned, there are other factors to consider when evaluating software for use with a child with disabilities. In particular, it's important for the software to be flexible and easy to customize. For example, if your child will be using a special input device, you'll need to make sure that the software works well with that device. (Fortunately, many adaptive devices today are designed in such a way that they will work with a whole range of standard programs—not just those that were designed specifically for use with that hardware. However, some screen designs or approaches to menuing might make it hard to control certain programs with certain devices.)

For a child with learning disabilities, it's often important to be able to control the speed at which action occurs on the screen, to turn sound effects on or off, and to be able to set difficulty levels. In addition, you'll want to pay attention to a program's overall design to make sure that the screen is not too busy or confusing, the graphics are clear and understandable, the feedback is supportive and encouraging, and the choices are open-ended enough to allow divergent answers and true exploration. A multisensory approach that takes advantage of the sound and graphics capabilities of the computer and somehow encourages tactile exploration as well is particularly helpful to children with special needs.

Self-Confidence and Problem Solving

Making the computer available and accessible is important for all children, but it is even more critical for those with special needs. If at all possible, the computer should be set up in your home so that your child can work independently and comfortably. This practice will promote self-reliance and will encourage your child to use the computer as a general problem-solving tool.

Likewise, you should teach your child how to start the computer, activate software, and use such devices as the mouse and the printer. Even though this might require considerable time and effort on your part and on the part of your child, the investment will be well worth it. In addition to fostering independence, you will be teaching your child skills that will be useful in school and in the world at large.

Although the ability to function independently is important, it's also helpful for you to spend relaxed, playful time with your child at the computer. This shows your child that you are interested in what she is doing, allows her to interact with you in a personal and meaningful way, and gives her an opportunity to do something that children with special needs rarely have the chance to do: "show off." By sitting down with your child at the computer, you give her an opportunity to say, "See what I can do!" Very few activities can contribute more to building your child's self-esteem and solidifying your relationship.

Educational games, such as *The Playroom* and the *McGee* series for younger children, or the *Super Solvers* and *Carmen Sandiego* programs for older, more advanced kids, can be excellent tools to promote problem solving and build confidence. From the moment your child sits down to learn how the program operates, he is practicing important problem-solving skills. As he progresses through the game, being called upon to solve practical problems through logic or trial-and-error, he is engaging in the type of thinking required in the real world. If these programs are difficult for your child, you can help eliminate frustration by making play a group experience—with the child taking on the roles at which he is best. Discussing the game with you (or a sibling) as he goes along helps him verbalize what is happening, often solidifying the learning that is occurring.

Communicating and Creating

The greatest challenge faced by most children with special needs is communication. The challenge may be obvious, as in the case of a hearing-impaired or blind child, or subtle, as

with a child who has an orthopedic handicap that prevents her from speaking fluently or intelligibly. Problems with *receptive communication* (listening and reading) or *expressive communication* (speaking and writing) often frustrate children with special needs and create the impression that they are much less intelligent than they truly are.

Learning to use a computerized writing tool is perhaps the single most important factor in improving a young person's communication skills. For older students, the appropriate tool might be a full-fledged word processor complete with such writing aids as a spelling checker, grammar checker, and on-line thesaurus and such customizable options as macros (automatic commands that can be created to simplify complex functions to a few keystrokes). For younger children, a simple printing tool like *The Print Shop* or a large-text word processor to which graphics can be added might be best.

Such writing tools allow children with special needs to think and write far more fluently than might otherwise be possible. The child who lacks the fine motor skills necessary to form letters, who reverses letters and words, or who gets frustrated trying to set a complete sentence on paper, now has the opportunity to produce legible letters with single keystrokes—and to revise as many times as necessary without ruining the appearance of his finished product. Paint programs and other easy-to-use graphics tools also provide special-needs students with the chance to explore, create, and take pride in the attractive art that results.

In addition to providing your child with the tools that make it easier for her to write or paint, it's also important to help her find reasons to *want* to communicate. One way to promote communication is by subscribing to an on-line service such as Prodigy or CompuServe. (See Chapter 10, "Getting into On-Line Services," for more information about these and other on-line services.) Such a service can provide your child with access to games, reference materials, and—most valuable—forums where they can interact with electronic pen pals. Parents, too, may find an on-line service useful. Both CompuServe and Prodigy offer forums and other resources that deal with parenting, education, disabilities, and related topics.

A less expensive approach involves using your computer and printer to create a variety of printouts, each with a real purpose. Perhaps there's a person in your child's life with whom he'd like to correspond. If not, you might be able to put him in touch with a pen pal or a mentor to whom he'd enjoy writing. Encouraging children to do other writing with a purpose (for example, shopping lists or Christmas wish lists that will actually be used, fliers for family events such as parties or garage sales, and so on) can do a lot to build self-confidence and to motivate them to improve their communication skills.

Learning More

Parents of children with special needs have a variety of resources available to them. The organizations and information services listed in the following section don't all deal specifically with computers, but most of them will help you locate support services and other valuable materials (including hardware and software) for use with your child.

Another place to seek help is through your local school district. Your special-needs child should already be receiving services from trained special-education teachers appointed by the district. While there is no guarantee that your child's teachers will have had a lot of experience with her particular disabilities, they should have access to a variety of resources that will help them—and you—learn more. For example, most states have a number of regional centers set up to provide technology demonstrations and other assistance to special-education teachers and administrators. If you're interested in paying a visit to such a center or tapping into other resources that are available to special-education professionals, let your child's teacher know. There's a good chance that he or she will welcome your interest and support—and that you can work together as a team to locate the best materials for your child.

Some Valuable Resources for Children with Special Needs

Organizations with a Focus on Technology for People with Disabilities

ABLEDATA, *Newington Children's Hospital, 181 E. Cedar St., Newington, CT 06111; (800) 344-5405 (used for both voice and TDD) or (203) 667-5404*

This organization maintains a database of thousands of products for people with disabilities. If you are trying to locate computer hardware, software, or any other equipment (seating systems, furniture, and so on), ABLEDATA will take information about your child's disability and the type of device you might be looking for and then mail you a printout with relevant product descriptions and ordering information.

Alliance for Technology Access, *1307 Solano Ave., Albany, CA 94706; (415) 528-0747*

Originally founded by Apple Computer, ATA is now an independent organization with many corporate partners (including both Apple and IBM) and 45 resource centers in 34 states around the country. Each center has its own board of directors and areas of expertise, but all agree on a common goal: to provide people of all ages, with all sorts of disabilities and at all income levels, with access to technology. Most of the centers offer demonstrations of hardware, lending libraries, workshops, clubs, and more. Call ATA's main number to find out if there is a center near you.

CAST, Inc. (Center for Applied Special Technology), *39 Cross St., Peabody, MA 01960; (508) 531-8555*

This center offers training for teachers and evaluation of children with special needs both locally and nationally. In addition to presenting at numerous conferences, representatives of CAST will fly to various sites to help with evaluations and training, or will help connect you with local professionals who can assist you in similar ways.

Closing the Gap, *P.O. Box 68, Henderson, MN 56044; (612) 248-3294*

One of the better-known organizations for teachers, parents, and others interested in the use of technology with special-needs students, Closing the Gap sponsors a national conference each year and publishes a bimonthly newspaper with ongoing hardware and software reviews. One issue a year contains a resource guide to software and hardware. (This guide can also be purchased separately.)

IBM National Support Center for Persons with Disabilities, *P.O. Box 2150-H06RI, Atlanta, GA 30301; (800) 426-2133; TDD (800) 284-9482*

The National Support Center is a clearinghouse of information about computer-related devices offered by IBM and other vendors. It provides resource guides with listings of equipment for people with mobility, hearing, speech and language, learning, and vision impairments and offers IBM computers and adaptive equipment to qualified buyers at a discount.

RESNA: Association for the Advancement of Rehabilitation Technology, *1101 Connecticut Ave. NW, Suite 700, Washington, D.C. 20036; (202) 857-1199*

An organization for rehabilitation professionals, RESNA is devoted to furthering the uses of technology to help people with disabilities. The organization publishes a comprehensive guide, *The Assistive Technology Source Book,* which is useful for both parents and professionals in the field.

TAM (Technology and Media), *Council for Exceptional Children, 1920 Association Dr., Weston, VA 22091-1598; (703) 620-3660*

The Technology and Media division of the Council for Exceptional children is a valuable resource for information about hardware, software, and other technology for children with special needs. TAM publishes a bimonthly newsletter and a quarterly journal, both with a focus on technology in special education.

Trace Research and Development Center, *S-151 Waisman Center, 1500 Highland Ave., Madison, WI 53705; (608) 262-6966*

Trace is a research center and clearinghouse for information about adaptive devices. If you're having trouble locating the right hardware (and accompanying software) for your child with special needs, Trace is the place to turn; the organization maintains a comprehensive database of adaptive devices on the market today and publishes the *Trace ResourceBook* with descriptions, ordering information, and help to find the right product for your child.

Worldwide Disability Solutions Group, *Apple Computer, Mail Stop 36SE, 20525 Mariani Ave., Cupertino, CA 95014; (408) 974-7910, TDD (408) 974-7911*

Through its Disability Solutions Group, Apple offers information to end users about adaptive hardware and software from Apple and third-party developers. Two brochures are available from this group: *Connections*, an overview of how computers are being used in special education and rehabilitation, and *Toward Independence*, a look at access technology.

Other Organizations That Can Help

American Speech-Language-Hearing Association, *10801 Rockville Pike, Rockville, MD 20852; (301) 897-5700, TDD (301) 897-0157*

The largest association of speech and hearing professionals, ASHA makes a variety of materials available to parents of children who have hearing and speech disabilities. The association publishes booklets on augmentative communication and

may be able to recommend a local professional who can help you with software selection.

Association for Retarded Citizens, *500 E. Border St., Suite 300, Arlington, TX 76010; (817) 261-6003*

ARC, with more than 1,200 local chapters, is a strong advocate for developmentally disabled children and adults. Local chapters can provide information regarding services for developmentally disabled citizens and their rights. The Bioengineering program, located in the national office, can make software recommendations.

Council for Exceptional Children, *1920 Association Dr., Weston, VA 22091-1598; (703) 620-3660*

In addition to its TAM division described earlier, CEC offers other resources for professionals interested in helping both disabled and gifted children. Two interesting organizations, located in the same building and loosely affiliated with CEC, are the Center for Special Education Technology, a federally funded national exchange, and the Information Center, an extensive library and ERIC clearinghouse with information on a variety of topics, including technology. These resource centers and CEC's two publications (*Exceptional Children* and *Teaching Exceptional Children*) are all geared towards professional educators rather than parents, but you can tap into CEC information with help from your child's teacher.

Easter Seal Society, *70 East Lake St., Chicago, IL 60601; (312) 726-6200, TDD (312) 726-4258*

Local chapters of the Easter Seal Society can be found throughout the country. They provide a variety of services to children and adults with head and spinal cord injuries or speech and language disabilities. These services include technological assistance, as well as therapy, vocational evaluation and placement, and prosthetic recommendations. The Easter Seal Society also offers low-interest loans to help individuals with disabilities purchase computers and related assistive devices. For more information, contact the Technology Related Loan Fund (attn. Sully J.F. Alvarado) at the national office in Chicago.

Exceptional Parent, *P.O. Box 3000, Denville, NJ 07834; (800) 247-8080*

Exceptional Parent magazine is published eight times a year. It contains a wealth of information for parents of children with disabilities, and periodically includes articles and special issues devoted to technology.

Learning Disabilities Association, *4156 Library Rd., Pittsburgh, PA 15234; (412) 341-1515*

Founded by parents, people with learning disabilities, and practitioners, this national organization offers free brochures, sells a variety of other publications, and will help callers find a chapter near them. Local chapters offer support groups and personal resources (medical and legal advice, advocacy with a school system, and so on).

March of Dimes, *1275 Mamaroneck Ave., White Plains, NY 10605; (914) 428-7100*

Through its local chapters, the March of Dimes provides information, referral, and support services to parents of children with birth defects. Although they have no special program for information about computer hardware or software, local chapters can be helpful in steering parents in the right direction.

National Association of the Deaf, *814 Thayer Ave., Silver Spring, MD 20910-4500; (301) 587-1788, TDD (301) 587-1789*

NAD is an advocacy organization that serves as an information and referral center for parents of hearing-impaired and deaf children. They have no special technology program, but they can generally refer parents to sources of information about computers, software, and telecommunication devices.

National Center for Learning Disabilities, *99 Park Ave., New York, NY 10016; (212) 687-7211*

This advocacy group promotes awareness of learning disabilities and lobbies for the rights of learning-disabled children and adults. A general information packet is available from the foundation as is an annual publication, *Their World.* The 1990 edition of this magazine was devoted to technology and its applications to special education.

National Federation for the Blind, *1800 Johnson St., Baltimore, MD 21230; (301) 659-9314*

Through its state chapters, the National Federation offers information and referral services to parents of visually impaired children. The NFB has a publication, *Future Reflections*, and an extensive collection of reference materials. The National Braille and Technology Center for the Blind is located at NFB's national headquarters and can provide relevant information on computers and software.

National Information Center for Children and Youth with Disabilities (NICHCY), *P.O. Box 1492, Washington, D.C. 20013; (800) 999-5599; TDD (703) 893-8614*

Although it offers no direct services, NICHCY is a clearinghouse for information dealing with all disabilities. If you are unsure of what information you need or where to get it, this is an excellent resource to consult first. In addition to providing information over the phone, NICHCY publishes several news digests each year. One of the recent issues focused on assistive technology.

Orton Dyslexia Society, *Chester Bldg., Suite 382, 8600 LaSalle Rd., Baltimore, MD 21204-6020; (800) 222-3123*

A national organization with regional branches, Orton was originally formed as a research organization for professionals studying dyslexia. While many of its members today are medical researchers, a number of teachers and parents are also involved. The society offers a national conference that includes a number of sessions on technology.

United Cerebral Palsy, 7 Penn Plaza, Suite 804, New York, NY 10001; (800) 872-1827

Like many other national organizations, UCP provides a continuum of services through its local chapters. These services range from diagnosis through medical treatment and adaptive housing. UCP offers technological support and is currently engaged in a national demonstration program in which computers are used by young children with cerebral palsy to improve their communication skills.

Some Hardware and Software Vendors

DLM Teaching Resources, P.O. Box 4000, Allen, TX 75002; (800) 527-4747 or (800) 442-4711 (in Texas)

DLM publishes several titles to help children with learning disabilities improve their math and reading fluency, plus a number of more general drill/tutorial programs that can easily be customized to meet the needs of special-education students. The company also publishes two valuable special-needs resource books compiled by Apple Computer: *Apple Computer Resources in Special Education and Rehabilitation* (a comprehensive guide to Macintosh and Apple II products and resources related to special education) and *Independence Day* (with a focus on adaptive technology and ways in which it can help people with physical or communication disabilities live independently).

Edmark, P.O. Box 3218, Redmond, WA 98073-3218; (800) 426-0856; TDD (206) 861-7679

Edmark is best known for its Touch Window screen, which can be placed over an Apple II, MS-DOS, or Macintosh monitor to turn it into a touch-sensitive screen. The company also produces special education and early childhood software and distributes products from a number of other publishers in the field.

IBM (see IBM National Support Center for Persons with Disabilities above for ordering information)

IBM produces a number of products for disabled users, including a touch-sensitive monitor; *SpeechViewer* software for use by speech therapists; *Phone Communicator* to help the hearing- and speech-impaired talk on the telephone; and *Screen Reader*, a product that reads the computer screen for blind and visually impaired users.

Don Johnston, *1000 N. Rand Rd., Bldg 115, Wauconda, IL 60084; (800) 999-4660 or (708) 526-2682*

This company manufacturers the Adaptive Firmware card (for the Apple II) and Ke:nx card (for the Macintosh), which allow users to plug a variety of alternate keyboards, switches, and other input devices into the computer. Don Johnston also distributes software and hardware from a number of other special-education companies.

Laureate Learning, *110 East Spring St., Winooski, VT 05404; (800) 562-6801 or (802) 655-4755*

Laureate offers talking software (and a limited amount of hardware) for children and adults with developmental disabilities, language and hearing impairments, emotional disturbances, and acquired cognitive and language disabilities.

Prentke Romich, *1022 Heyl Rd., Wooster, OH 44691; (216) 262-1984*

Prentke Romich sells a number of devices, including printers for the blind and other hardware and software that help with communication.

The 5th Wave

By Rich Tennant

"GATHER AROUND, KIDS. YOUR MOTHER'S WINDOWING!"

Girls, Boys, and Individual Differences

- *Is it normal for our son to be more interested in computers than our daughter is?*

- *What do researchers say about gender differences and computers?*

- *How can I encourage my daughter to have a positive attitude about computers and technology?*

During the mid-1980s a number of research studies focused on the differences between the way boys and girls viewed and responded to computers. (See the sidebar for a list of some articles that summarize these studies.) In general, the researchers found that boys were much better represented in computer electives, computer camps, and after-school activities involving computer technology (the boy-to-girl ratio in such voluntary activities was frequently as great as 3 to 1) and that they expressed much more positive attitudes about computers than did their female classmates. Girls generally expressed doubts about their own capabilities with regard to the technology, indicated that they saw computers as more appropriate tools for boys, and deferred to the males in their classes when there were disagreements about who should use the computer for recreational purposes.

Such differences were also reflected in the home, where parents were more likely to purchase computers for their sons than for their daughters and to spend more money on hardware and software purchases when a boy was involved. When girls did have access to computers at home, they generally spent less time on them than did boys with similar access.

The gap between male and female attitudes and behavior was most pronounced in studies that dealt with junior high and high school students. In fact, several of the studies of children under nine or ten years of age found no difference at all between the amount of time boys and girls spent at the computer or how much they enjoyed computer-based activities.

The tendency for girls to lose interest and become less confident about their abilities as they approach adolescence, closely parallels what happens to girls' attitudes towards math and science at the same stage in their lives—and raises many of the same questions. Why do our daughters suddenly become less interested and capable in the areas of math, science, and technology? There is little agreement about whether there are any physiological differences that somehow give boys the edge over girls when they reach adolescence, but it does seem clear that the strongest factor at work is social and peer pressure.

A number of studies have shown that girls do as well (or nearly as well) as boys in settings that require both to take the same math and science courses, but that girls in secondary schools generally don't gravitate to such courses when they are optional. (This, of course, increases the gender gap as time goes on, decreasing the likelihood that girls will have the prerequisites to major in math or

Some Helpful Research Summaries

The results reported in this chapter are summarized in more detail in the following publications:

"The Computer Gender Gap in Elementary School" by Mary DeRemer and "Girls and Microcomputers" by Alfred Forsyth and David Lancy—published in the journal *Computers in the Schools* (Vol. 6, Nos. 3 and 4, 1989)

"Mismeasuring Women: A Critique of Research on Computer Ability and Avoidance" by Pamela Kramer and Sheila Lehman—published in *Signs:*

Journal of Women in Culture and Society (Vol. 16, No. 1, 1990)

Does Your Daughter Say "No, Thanks" to the Computer?—a booklet published by the Women's Action Alliance, New York (see "Some Valuable Resources" at the end of this chapter for information on the Alliance)

science in college, even if their interest does increase.) One study of 1,200 ninth graders (reported in "Mismeasuring Women: A Critique of Research on Computer Ability and Avoidance" in the journal *Signs*) showed that boys did better than girls only in those schools where males and females had different self-perceptions about their ability to learn math and science; at sites where the girls *believed* they could do as well as the boys, there were few differences between the two groups.

Possible Changes

There are a number of research questions still to be answered about boys, girls, and computers. The majority of gender studies reported today were conducted in 1984 and 1985, at a time when computers were just entering schools in significant numbers and were being used primarily for computer programming. It's hard to know from these studies whether positive early experiences with computers over several years can make a difference in how girls feel about the technology when they finally reach adolescence. It's also worth asking whether girls continue to see computers as "male" even when they are used not for programming but for writing, art, and other activities

less associated with math and science. (This is definitely the direction the technology has moved in recent years.)

Two of the most recent studies, reported in 1989 in the journal *Computers in the Schools* (see the sidebar), do show possible evidence of changes in attitudes. In one of the studies, which focused on third and sixth graders who had been working with computers for several years, girls and boys were equally confident about their ability to learn from the computer, and girls were even more enthusiastic about computers than the boys in their class. Because many of the previous studies had shown attitudinal differences starting as early as fifth or sixth grade, the researcher concluded that the positive attitudes in the group she studied *might* have been the result of early exposure to computers.

The second study in the same journal also found that upper-elementary school girls enjoyed computers as much as boys and learned approximately as much from computer software that emphasized map reading and early geography skills. In this case, however, the conclusions focused on the *type of software* used. Many writers have pointed out in recent years that much of the kids' software on the market takes a traditionally "male" approach, featuring arcade action, explosions, battles, and other images that, for whatever reason, generally appeal to boys more than girls. The program used for this study included none of these elements; instead it focused on a fantasy world (A. A. Milne's *Hundred Acre Wood*). Perhaps this was the reason for the girls' positive response.

Most of the other evidence we have so far is anecdotal. A number of teachers report that when computers are used for word processing and other activities that appeal to girls as well as boys, there are few differences between the two groups in terms of their enthusiasm level or involvement. While it is still a serious concern that girls continue to be less interested in math and science than boys, the connection between computers and math and science seems to be decreasing in many young people's minds.

What Parents Can Do

One question you might be asking yourself is, "Does it matter if my girl doesn't love computers?" In Chapter 1, "Computers in Today's World," we suggested that parents and teachers may be overly concerned with the importance of raising "computer literate" adults. It is certainly not crucial for your child to be fascinated with computers and computer programming in order to do well in college or in the work world. What is crucial, however, is for each of our children to have a sense of confidence and personal self-worth that will allow him or her to deal with all sorts of challenges—on and off the computer—as they arise. Unfortunately, many girls seem to lose some of this confidence as they reach adolescence—at least in the areas of math, science, and related technologies.

What can we do about this problem? Following are some steps you might take to help your daughter keep an open mind about her capabilities and to encourage everyone in your family to examine some of the issues related to males, females, and computers.

We realize that there is a real danger in focusing too much on trends and differences. If your 12-year-old daughter loves computing, you certainly don't want her to get the sense that you're watching and waiting for the day that she'll change her mind. If your 13-year-old son has no interest in video games or "shoot-'em-up" action, the last thing you want is for him to feel that there's something wrong with him.

On the other end of the spectrum, it's important to recognize our children's choices and preferences even when they do conform to stereotypes. You can't force your daughter to be interested in math or science or your son to be interested in writing or human development. You can, however, encourage your kids to question their assumptions, to acknowledge (maybe even laugh at) peer pressures, and in general to be themselves.

What follows is a list of suggestions for ways of encouraging your kids to have open minds about technology. Many of the guidelines are adapted from the publications *Does Your Daughter Say "No, Thanks" to the Computer?* (Women's Action Alliance) and *Notes for Parents* (AAAS Directorate for Education and Human Resources Programs, Spring 1990). (For more information about both organizations, see the directory "Some Valuable Resources," which closes the chapter.)

- Display positive expectations. Don't assume that your daughter will find math, science, or computer programming difficult or that your son will have trouble working peacefully and cooperatively.

- If the computer is in your son's room, move it to a more neutral spot. Make sure that your daughter has equal time at the computer—even if she seems willing to defer to a more enthusiastic brother.

- Take an interest in what your daughter is doing with computers at school and at home. Let her know that you think her computer interests and skills are important.

- Encourage your daughter to enroll in math, science, and computer electives at school and to take part in technology-related after-school programs and summer camps.

- If your daughter is reluctant to join programs that appear to be dominated by boys, look for a local Girls Club or Girl Scout troop that offers science-oriented projects. (See the list of valuable resources at the end of the chapter for more information about projects that these two organizations are involved in.)

- Give your children nontraditional tasks. For example, next time you take a trip, have your daughter serve as "navigator" and map reader.

- Plan trips to science museums, planetariums, and computer museums with your daughter. Ask her to invite her friends.

- Hold family discussions about equity issues, stereotypes, and career options.

- Critique computer ads with your children. Compare how often males and females are portrayed and in what roles. Identify the stereotypes and sexist assumptions you encounter.

- Be good role models. Girls should see their mothers using the computer, not just their fathers. If you're a mother, take some time to sit down with your kids at the computer—even if it's a new experience for you. Perhaps your daughter can teach you how to use her favorite software.

- Visit places where computers are being used in interesting ways. Help arrange for your daughter to talk with women who have rewarding jobs involving math, science, and technology.

- If your daughter says she hates computers, pursue the topic further. Help her identify the types of computer activities she *does* enjoy and locate software that matches her interests.

- If your daughter *or* your son hates arcade action or other imagery used by a particular computer program, look around for alternatives. There are many titles to choose from and not all of them are targeted at the child who loves video games and fast action.

- Ask your children about the peer pressure and social attitudes they encounter at school. Does your daughter feel as if her friends *expect* her to hate math, science, or computers? Does she feel intimidated by the boys in her class and their attitudes towards computers? Does your son expect girls at school to do as well as his male friends?

- Talk with your children's teachers. Make them aware of your concerns and the resources you've found useful.

Some Valuable Resources

The American Association for the Advancement of Science (AAAS) has a division devoted to improving science, mathematics, and technology education in America. This division, the Directorate for Education and Human Resources Programs, publishes and distributes materials for parents, professionals, and policy makers, including suggestions for encouraging girls in math and science. The AAAS also provides materials to help Girl Scout councils train their leaders to conduct science and math activities.

Contact AAAS Directorate for Education and Human Resources Programs, 1333 H St. NW, Washington, D.C. 20005-4792; (202) 326-6670.

EQUALS, located at the Lawrence Hall of Science at the University of California, Berkeley, publishes a variety of materials related to math, computers, and equity issues. One of their publications, *Family Math*, outlines entertaining ways for families to work together to improve children's attitudes about mathematics and the role it can play in their lives. A number of community organizations now offer Family Math workshops based on the ideas outlined in this book.

Contact EQUALS, Lawrence Hall of Science, University of California, Berkeley, CA 94720; (510) 642-1823; or to find out about a Family Math program near you, call (510) 528-0560.

Girls Clubs of America (GCA) offers a program known as Operation SMART, focusing on science, mathematics, and related technology. Activities include building kites and model airplanes and taking apart computers to see how they work. Check with your local Girls Club to see if they offer Operation SMART. Or contact the GCA national office for the Operation SMART activity book.

Contact GCA, 30 East 33rd St., New York, NY 10016; (212) 689-3700.

Math/Science Network is an organization that works to increase the participation of girls in math, science, and technology. You can obtain literature, videotapes, and information about career awareness conferences from their office.

Contact Math/Science Network, Preservation Park, 678 13th St., Suite 100, Oakland, CA 94612; (510) 893-6284.

Women's Action Alliance offers a free booklet for parents (*Does Your Daughter Say "No, Thanks" to the Computer?*) and one for teachers (*Do Your Female Students Say "No, Thanks" to the Computer?*). The Alliance also sells a book, *The Neuter Computer: Computers for Girls and Boys* (New York: Neal-Schuman Publishers, 1986), which describes findings, based on government-funded research, about girls and their attitudes towards computers.

Contact Women's Action Alliance, 370 Lexington Ave., New York, NY 10017; (212) 532-8330.

The 5th Wave
By Rich Tennant

©RICHTENNANT

PRINCIPAL

"IT'S NOT THAT IT DOESN'T WORK AS A COMPUTER,
IT JUST WORKS BETTER AS A PAPERWEIGHT."

CHAPTER NINE

The Home/School Connection

- *If my child is enthusiastic about a program at school, should I consider buying it to use at home?*

- *Why can't I find many of the school titles in the retail stores?*

- *Can my kid's teachers help me get up to speed on computers and technology? How can I help them?*

Although your child's school may be a valuable resource in locating information about good software that will run on your family computer, it's important to realize that many of the programs that work well in schools have little place in a home. For example, there are a number of educational software titles—social studies simulations, graphing tools, and so on—that are designed to be used by a single teacher working with a group of students. Other programs have too narrow a focus to be of lasting value at home although they fit well in the classroom, where they are used to reinforce an important concept or skill (for example, how to estimate distances or place events in a proper order) and then set aside for re-use with a new group of students.

In general, parents have to be more conscious than teachers about the entertainment value of software. An educational program might compare favorably in your child's mind to a workbook or lecture—possible alternatives in a school setting. However, the same program might lose its appeal at home when it has to compete against Nintendo, baseball, or phone conversations with friends.

On the other side, there are some excellent home-oriented titles that do not perform well in a school setting. For example, an entertaining program with general educational value for the home market might not make it in the schools if it devotes more time to game playing (navigating through mazes, shooting at targets, etc.) than to the "content" being covered. In addition, such features as the ability to turn off sound in a program and to save information about how well a number of different players performed are generally far more important to teachers than to parents.

Titles for Both Home and School

In spite of the differences between the two markets, quite a few titles *do* work well both at home and at school. In fact, the majority of the programs included in Part 4 of this book are ones that we would recommend highly for school as well as home use. The publishers of these programs frequently build extra control features into their titles so that they can be altered by teachers to suit a school environment. And they often produce two different versions of the package, containing the same software but different documentation.

The school version of a title generally costs more and includes a backup disk (to avoid any delays if the main program disk fails and needs

replacement) and a teacher's guide with suggestions for classroom activities related to the software. The packaging is also different (frequently the school version ships in a loose-leaf binder rather than a box), which explains why, when visiting your child's school, you may find familiar titles in unfamiliar packages.

In trying to decide whether a program that your kid likes at school is appropriate for home use, it often helps to take a lead from the publishers themselves. While some publishers, including Broderbund and The Learning Company, produce virtually all of their titles for the home market and then create school versions of those they think will sell in education, school-oriented companies, such as Scholastic and MECC, offer home versions of only some of their titles. Of course, even if there is a home and a school version of a program your child enjoys, it's important to consider whether it's the sort of program that can maintain your child's interest at home after he has spent hours with it in class.

There are definitely some occasions when a school product not marketed aggressively to families is nevertheless worth considering for your home. While we did not include such programs in Part 4, a directory at the end of this chapter describes some of the best school-oriented software companies and their products. If you're involved in home schooling your kids, working with your child over the summer to help him get caught up in certain areas, leading any sort of computer-related club for kids, or making technology-related recommendations to your child's school district, these companies and programs should be of interest to you.

It's also very helpful to pay attention to what your child is using at school if you're thinking of buying her a word processor or other computerized tool. If you select the same tool she is using at school, she will have to spend less time getting up to speed on the software, and it will be easier for her to complete assignments at home that can then be loaded into the application at school.

The same is true for authoring programs (from programming languages to hypermedia tools such as HyperCard). It's the rare parent or child who has the time and energy to learn to program for pleasure at home, but if your child is already excited about such activities at school, you might want to build on this interest by purchasing a version of the authoring tool for use at home.

Give and Take

In this country, the technical expertise of teachers and school administrators varies tremendously. If the public school system in your state and district (or the private school if your child attends one) has invested resources in buying computers and related technology and in educating teachers about using these tools effectively to enhance the curriculum, your child may be participating in an exciting computer program that will inspire you to learn more as well. Or your child may be lucky enough to be working with dynamic teachers who have taken it upon themselves to make computers and exciting software a part of the classroom. On the other hand, there are many school districts (as well as individual schools within a district) where teachers and administrators are afraid of the technology, where software is outdated or practically nonexistent, or where the computer experts on the staff have lost their jobs due to budget cuts.

If your child's school is staffed with experienced computer-using teachers or a knowledgeable computer resource teacher, chances are these educators will be happy to talk with you about products and ideas that will help your child's computer use at home complement what is happening at school. If, on the other hand, you turn out to be more computer-savvy than the school personnel, you may have the opportunity to help shape the ways in which technology is used in your child's school or district.

Many teachers and administrators will welcome help in this area if it really feels like help and not criticism. For example, if you play an active role in fund-raising for new technology purchases, you will be doing a lot to earn the right to help decide how the funds are spent. You might also volunteer to spend some time in your child's classroom demonstrating those computer uses your family finds most exciting. If you want to lobby for new technology expenditures in the district, you will also need to identify and seek out the key administrators, those who understand the potential of computers and exciting software to improve education.

When spending time in your child's school—either as an observer or as an adviser—it's helpful to be aware of some differences in the home and school technology markets that go beyond the issues of software design described earlier. If you're thinking only of computers and computer software when talking to your kid's teachers about technology, your focus

is too narrow. Schools often have access to additional forms of technology that are not found in the typical home. For example, laser videodiscs (an alternative to videotapes that never really took off in the home market because one cannot tape onto a videodisc) are playing an important role in schools today. The videodisc is appealing to educators because it allows them to jump to any segment of the footage, branch to relevant portions of the video, and step through freeze-frame images with the help of a remote-control device or a computer hooked up to the videodisc player.

Local area networks that link computers together to share data and peripherals are also becoming widespread in schools, opening up an entirely new world of software possibilities. In addition to the many existing software packages that can run on a network (eliminating the need for floppy disk storage and management), there are some new titles that go a step further, taking true advantage of the network's features. These programs involve children working together on different computers in cooperative learning experiences, such as large-group simulations or collaborative writing projects.

Some schools use networks to deliver complete curriculum packages known as *Integrated Learning Systems* (or ILS) to students. ILS are controversial because they tend to be quite expensive and take a fair amount of control out of the hands of the teacher (for that period of the day when kids are "plugged in" to the network). On the other hand, as the software delivered by the ILS becomes more sophisticated and open-ended (some ILS now offer tools on the network as well as straight instructional titles) and school districts see positive results from a number of the systems, more and more administrators and school boards are taking a serious look.

Finally, there are some technologies familiar to many home users that take on new uses in the classroom. For example, schools interested in telecommunications (see Chapter 10, "Getting into On-Line Services," for more on this technology) have access to a variety of school-oriented services that connect students in different cities, states, and countries so that they can share everything from information about their families to data on acid rain and pollution. Educational television is used in many schools to supplement other teaching materials, and in a number of districts, the medium is becoming increasingly interactive as

schools participate in "video teleconferences" with other sites or enroll in "distance learning" courses in which an instructor at a remote site teaches classes via TV. In addition, CD-ROM technology, already well established in school libraries, is of growing interest to educators as well as home users.

If you're interested in staying informed about these and other computer-related technologies in the schools, you may want to subscribe to one of the magazines listed in the next section. At the very least, they will provide you with insights about what is possible in education today with the help of powerful electronic tools.

Some School-Oriented Producers and Products

Software Publishers

In addition to the software companies in the appendix at the end of this book (most of whom sell both home and school products), here are a few other publishers worth watching if you want to know what's available to schools around the country:

Claris, *P.O. Box 526, Santa Clara, CA 95052; (800) 747-7483*

Claris, Apple's own software publishing branch, does not bill itself as a school publisher, but several of its products are bestsellers in K–12 schools. If you own an Apple II computer, you'll no doubt want to try *AppleWorks*, an integrated tool (word processor, spreadsheet, and database) that's used by most Apple II-using schools. The other Claris product that schools are excited about is *HyperCard*. Although a working version of *HyperCard* ships with every Mac, if you want to do some "scripting" (program design) with your kid at home, you'll have to contact Claris for the documentation and other tools to help you with the process.

IBM, *PC Software Dept., One Culver Rd., Dayton, NJ 08810; (800) IBM-2468*

IBM's education group publishes a number of educational software titles of its own. Many are designed for large groups, require a network to run, or have a strictly tutorial approach that would make them inappropriate for home use. On the other hand, some of IBM's tools for kids and adults, including *Primary Editor Plus* (a talking word processor for children), *Linkway* (a hypermedia tool designed especially for education), and various versions of *PC Storyboard* (a presentation tool used in both businesses and schools) might be of interest to you as well. In addition, if you own a CD-ROM drive, you might want to find out more about *Stories and More*, a collection of interactive storybooks on disc.

If you do want to order from IBM, be aware that, unlike other publishers that offer school versions (with additional components) at higher cost than home packages, IBM offers schools a sharp discount. As a parent, you'll have to pay about 35 percent more than the school price.

Logo Computer Systems, Inc. (LCSI), *P.O. Box 162, Highgate Springs, VT 05460; (800) 321-LOGO*

At those elementary and middle schools where computer programming is taught, the programming language they're most likely to teach is Logo and the version they're most likely to use is LCSI's *LogoWriter*. If your child enjoys the opportunity to create interactive programs at school, you may well want to get a version that will allow her to continue at home. LCSI offers a home version of *LogoWriter* for MS-DOS computers, the Macintosh, and the Apple II family.

MOBIUS, *405 N. Henry St., Alexandria, VA 22314; (800) 426-2710 or (703) 684-2911*

This early childhood publisher sells an integrated learning package with a variety of developmentally appropriate activities (involving art, shapes, nursery rhymes, etc.) for children in preschool and kindergarten. The package is meant to run off the hard disk of an IBM or compatible computer and works best in that context because of its flexible management system for teachers. However, certain of the program's components are also available in "stand alone" versions and might be of interest to parents of young children.

National Geographic, *Educational Services, Washington, D.C. 20036; (800) 368-2728*

Aside from the company's *encyclopedia of mammals* (reviewed in Chapter 26), very few of National Geographic's titles are appropriate for home use. However, this is a company worth following if you're interested in new technologies in the schools. National Geographic offers software accompanied by filmstrips, CD-ROM programs, and videodisc packages. In addition, National Geographic's *Kids Network* is a telecommunications project that allows students at different schools to work together via modem on scientific projects involving data collection and analysis.

Optical Data Corp., *30 Technology Dr., Warren, NJ 07060; (800) 524-2481*

This is another publisher of most interest to parents involved in advising or working with local schools. Optical Data is one of the largest distributors of videodisc programs, selling several of its own science series (some designed to be used with a computer, others without), history and current events titles from ABC News Interactive, and a number of other exciting multimedia products.

Roger Wagner Publishing, *1050 Pioneer Way, Suite P, El Cajon, CA 92020; (619) 442-0522*

HyperStudio, Roger Wagner's hypermedia tool for the Apple IIGS, is very popular in schools that use Apple II computers. If your family owns a IIGS and your kids are into creating their own interactive programs, this easy-to-use tool is worth knowing about.

Sunburst, 101 Castleton St., Pleasantville, NY 10570; (800) 628-8897
WINGS for Learning, 1600 Green Hills Rd., P.O. Box 660002, Scotts Valley, CA 95067; (800) 321-7511

Sunburst and its newer subsidiary, WINGS, have made names for themselves in the school market over the years as publishers of problem-solving software, tools for kids, and (more recently) multimedia titles. Neither company offers a home catalog nor home versions of its software, but both will send out school catalogs or take orders for school versions from parents. If you have a less powerful MS-DOS machine or an Apple II computer, Sunburst's older software in the early childhood and problem-solving areas is some of the best around.

Tom Snyder Productions, 90 Sherman St., Cambridge, MA 02142; (800) 342-0236

Aside from its two early childhood titles (reviewed in Chapter 20), Tom Snyder Productions specializes in software for the "one-computer classroom." Most of its titles are social studies, science, and math simulations designed to be used by a teacher with a large group of kids. A few of the titles, however, would work equally well with a smaller group of kids in a home setting. If you request a catalog, you might want to look closely at *National* (or *International*) *Inspirer* (two geography search games that require cooperation between team members) and *Inner Body Works* (a database game focusing on the human body).

William K. Bradford Publishing Company, P.O. Box 1355, Concord, MA 01742; (800) 421-2009

While marketed primarily to schools, the story-writing collection, developed by Learningways and sold by William K. Bradford, will appeal to many parents as well. The collection, which consists of several different series (Explore-a-Story, Explore-a-Classic, and so on), features interactive storybooks that allow kids to "step inside" each book, adding words, objects, and characters to the scenes, manipulating what they see on the screen, and printing out the results.

Publications

The Computing Teacher,
*1787 Agate St., Eugene, OR
97403-1923; (503) 346-4414*

This journal, which focuses on the instructional uses of computers, is published eight times a year by the International Society for Technology in Education (ISTE). An annual subscription to *The Computing Teacher* costs $46 and includes ISTE membership fees.

Electronic Learning, Scholastic, Inc., 730 Broadway, New York, NY 10003-9538; (212) 505-4900

Electronic Learning, published eight times a year, September through June, is a magazine for school administrators and computer-using teachers. An annual subscription is $23.95.

The Latest and Best of Tess,
*EPIE, 103-3 West Montauk
Highway, Hampton Bays, NY
11946; (516) 728-9100*

The EPIE Institute, a nonprofit organization that provides evaluations of instructional and administrative software in electronic form to educators throughout the country, also sells this print version of its reviews. The book costs $49.95 plus $5 for shipping and handling.

Only the Best, *R.R. Bowker Company, P.O. Box 762, New York, NY 10011; (800) 521-8110*

This annual publication is a reference guide to the highest-rated educational software. Reviews are based on evaluations from departments of education, educational magazines, and a number of other school-oriented evaluation groups. Each edition of *Only the Best* costs $29.95.

Technology & Learning, *Peter Li, Inc., 2451 E. River Rd., Dayton, OH 45439; (800) 543-4383*

This magazine for administrators and teachers involved in using technology to improve education is published eight times a year. An annual subscription costs $24.

The 5th Wave

By Rich Tennant

"HOW SHOULD I KNOW WHY THEY TOOK IT OFF THE LIST? MAYBE THERE JUST WASN'T ENOUGH MEMBERS TO SUPPORT AN 'AIREDALES FOR ELVIS' BULLETIN BOARD.'"

CHAPTER TEN

Getting into On-Line Services

■ *What will our family gain by buying a modem and telecommunications software?*

■ *What are the best services for us to subscribe to? Can we telecommunicate without a service?*

■ *If I teach my child about telecommunications, is there a danger that he will be tempted to break into systems he shouldn't be accessing?*

*T*elecommunications, sending and receiving computerized messages over telephone lines, opens up a whole new set of possibilities for your family. At its simplest level, telecommunicating requires a modem (described in Chapter 12 , "Peripherals and Other Options"), telecommunications software, a standard telephone line (it can be your family's regular line or an extra one), and a similarly equipped party on the other end of the line.

Most telecommunications software works with your modem to take care of a few simple tasks: it dials whatever telephone number you enter and, once the connection is made, transmits what you type at the keyboard; it allows you to send files you've already created; it displays messages and files sent to you by other parties; and it saves these files for you. The software required for these tasks is not complex and is often available at a bargain price from public domain exchanges (see Chapter 17, "Public Domain Software") or as part of a much larger program. For example, integrated packages such as *Microsoft Works* and *PFS: First Choice* include a telecommunications module in addition to the word processor, spreadsheet, and database functions provided. In addition, some of the national services described later in this chapter provide their own software for you to use when accessing the service.

Although it's possible to connect directly with another party and "chat" on-line or exchange files on the spot, most people find it more convenient to send and receive messages and files through an intermediate service that will accept the information whenever it is sent and store it until the receiving party "logs on" (dials the service) to collect messages. Such an option is known as *electronic mail* (E-mail) and is provided by a variety of telecommunications services, ranging in size from local *bulletin boards* to large nationwide services.

In addition to leaving personal messages for an individual, E-mail allows you to send public messages that all callers can read. Most bulletin boards and on-line services feature ongoing discussions (also known as *forums*) on a variety of different topics (from politics to writing to how-to ideas on using a specific software package). While many of these forums focus on topics of most interest to adults, certain services have a fairly large group of younger users (teenagers and sometimes even pre-teens) who participate. With public E-mail, it's possible to seek out people you might want to "meet" on-line. For example, you and your kids might post a message indicating that you're looking for other kids under the age of 13, or asking if anyone knows of a good program on a particular topic.

Many systems also provide computer files that you can legally copy from the main system to your system. (This process is known as *downloading*.) These files might be actual programs (public domain games, word processors, and so on) that you can run on your own computer or large documents with information on a particular topic. If you have a program that you've written and want to share, you can send (*upload*) that file to the system's main computer. In both cases, once you give your system a command, the two computers take over and complete the transaction.

From Local to International Service

The smallest on-line systems (known as *bulletin board systems* or *BBSs*) are run on a personal computer. Anyone with a modem, special BBS software, and a phone line can start a bulletin board. These local systems usually accept only one caller at a time and provide a limited number of services, including E-mail and file exchange. Some BBSs are general-purpose; others are formed by a particular organization to meet the needs of a specific group. For example, a school district might offer a BBS that allows parents and kids to exchange messages with teachers and administrators or check on homework assignments and upcoming sports events.

While these services are not fancy, they are an inexpensive way to exchange ideas with other users; in most cases, the service is provided free. A list of BBS numbers in your area is probably available from a local user group or computer store. If you're willing to pay the long-distance phone bills, you can connect with bulletin board systems in other parts of the country as well. Your own local BBS may have a listing of numbers in other areas.

At the other end of the communication spectrum are comprehensive on-line services that run on mainframe computers and handle hundreds of callers at once. In addition to E-mail, such services frequently offer entire reference libraries, on-line shopping, up-to-the-minute news reports, weather and stock quotations, and on-line multiplayer games. Members from all over the world can exchange messages with each other or participate in forums on topics from health to horoscopes. There are even live conferences, publicized ahead of time, that involve numerous people on-line at the same time, typing—instead of talking—to each other.

Deciding which (if any) national telecommunications service to subscribe to can be difficult. One factor you'll want to consider seriously is cost. Some services charge you for the amount of time you spend on-line; others charge a monthly fee; and many combine the two, charging a base amount each month plus an extra charge for extra time you spend using the service. In addition to the fee the telecommunications service charges, you may end up paying the phone company a fair amount for the time spent on-line. Most national services provide a network of local numbers in cities around the United States and Canada that users can dial to connect with the central computer. However, if you live in a rural area, far from the nearest number a service provides, be prepared to run up large phone bills.

The other factors to consider when deciding if a service is worth the cost are: how easy that service is to use; how many features it offers that meet the needs of your family; and how popular it is with other users (this determines how many people you are likely to "meet" on-line). To find out more about some of the most popular on-line services for families, read on.

CompuServe: The Granddaddy of Services

CompuServe has been available for many years and, until recently, boasted more users than any other national service. In fact, many business cards today include a CompuServe ID number. (When you sign up for this or any other national service, you will be given an identification number or name so that other users can send you personal mail.)

Many adults and high school students find CompuServe appealing because it provides more depth than other services. There are numerous forums and conferences to choose from (including a forum for parents of children with disabilities and a number of other family-oriented forums), thousands of downloadable files in various libraries, access to a large number of databases (on news, weather, periodical literature, and more), an on-line encyclopedia (the *Grolier Electronic Encyclopedia*), complete tutorials on a variety of topics, on-line shopping services, and much more.

On the down side, CompuServe can be rather overwhelming to a new user. Cost is also a serious concern. In addition to a start-up fee and a monthly charge, CompuServe bills you for every hour you use. The least-expensive service costs $6.00 an hour and can go much higher if you use certain extra-cost options such as the encyclopedia. To help new users, CompuServe does offer the first hour of on-line time free and also provides free practice areas to help you learn your way around the system.

Traditionally, people have logged onto CompuServe using whatever telecommunications software they owned. You can still use this approach if you wish, but CompuServe now provides special software for MS-DOS and Macintosh computers. This software is worth considering because it can significantly decrease the connect time required to access information or send a message.

To find out more about CompuServe or to sign up, call 800-848-8199.

Prodigy: Plenty of Service at Bargain Prices

Prodigy is a relative newcomer to the world of telecommunications, but according to our figures it has already overtaken CompuServe in terms of national popularity. One of the biggest reasons for Prodigy's success is its affordability: families are charged a flat monthly fee, which covers unlimited time spent on-line and allows you to send up to 30 messages a month. (It's even possible for up to five members in the family to sign on under individual ID numbers, allowing mail to each family member to remain private.) The monthly fee (at the time this book was written) ranges from $8.95 to $12.95, depending on how you pay for the services. There is also a charge of 25 cents for each message over 30 sent per month.

Prodigy also appeals to families and new users because of its attractive and easy-to-use format. At a small initial cost, Prodigy provides new subscribers with telecommunications software (in either MS-DOS or Macintosh format) that they use whenever they access the service. The software is easy to install, takes full advantage of the way Prodigy operates, and provides colorful menu-based screens that allow users to explore the entire system with ease.

Prodigy offers a variety of standard services, including E-mail, forums (including some especially for parents), educational games your kids can play, weather maps and reports, news summaries, and software

reviews. It does not, however, allow you to upload or download files except in a few areas of the system. You can send mail to other users on the system, but you cannot exchange files with them.

Perhaps the most controversial part of this national service is its extensive use of advertising. Prodigy is able to offer such low rates because almost every screen includes an ad for a product or service. You can ignore the message and focus on the other information on the screen. (The ad takes up approximately one fourth of the screen.) Or, if you want to know more about the featured item, you can request additional information on the spot. In some cases, you can even purchase the item through Prodigy by providing a credit card number. Some parents object to the constant sales pitches. Others argue that the ads are relatively unobtrusive and provide information about some products you might not otherwise be able to find.

For more information on signing up for Prodigy, call (800) 822-6922.

America Online: Ease at a Cost

If you're willing to pay more for ad-free service, you might consider *America Online.* Like CompuServe, America Online charges for the amount of time you spend using the service. However, its hourly rate is lower than CompuServe's, especially if you log on after 6 p.m. or on the weekends. (Evening and weekend rates are $4 per hour; prime-time rates, $8 per hour.)

Like Prodigy, America Online requires special software (available for MS-DOS, Macintosh, and Apple II computers) and, with its help, offers a user-friendly interface. Choices are made using windows, pull-down menus, and graphic icons that represent specific options. The software makes it very easy to navigate around the system—especially if you have a mouse.

All the basic services are available from America Online, including E-mail, news, games, educational activities, travel information, on-line shopping, and lots of information about computers and software. In addition, it's possible to upload and download files over the system. A drawback is that there are fewer individuals on the system than on either CompuServe or Prodigy, limiting your E-mail and file-exchange opportunities somewhat.

Probably the biggest danger with this service is that your kids (or you) will get hooked and run up quite a bill. On the positive side, because the software is free and there's no charge for the first hour, you can preview the service before deciding whether to buy—without paying a cent.

Quantum Computer Services, the company that offers America Online, also offers several other services tailored to specific computers or families of computers. For owners of IBM PS/1 models, there's Promenade; for Commodore 64 and 128 owners, Q-Link; and for all MS-DOS computer users, PC-Link (originally started for owners of Tandy computers). All of the services offer the same basic options as America Online but connect you with a narrower group of users.

For information on America Online, call (800) 827-6364. For Quantum's other services, call (800) 545-6572.

Dangers, Exaggerated and Real

Some parents worry that time spent on-line can get their kids into trouble. There has been much in the news in recent years about kids (and adults) "breaking into" large systems (databases responsible for credit ratings, businesses' private systems, and so on) and changing data, reading private files, or generally causing problems. Some of the articles on this sort of abuse would lead one to believe that anyone with a computer, a modem, and telecommunications software can cause that kind of damage. This is far from the truth.

Breaking into a remote computer (also known as *cracking*) takes hours and hours of persistent work. The potential cracker must know the right phone number, passwords, and other communication parameters before he can even log onto a system. Even if he does get past this stage, he has to understand the commands necessary to navigate around the system. As a result of all the publicity about the few successful break-in attempts, most systems have increased security, including multiple passwords and automatic hang-up after three attempts. With help from the phone company, the caller's phone number can also be recorded, providing an easy trace to the attempted access.

These technical barriers aside, it's hard to imagine a typical kid investing time and energy in attempting such illegal acts. Assuming that your kids will want to break into a system just because you have a family computer and modem is like assuming that they will destroy things in your house simply because they can reach the hammer on the tool bench.

There are, however, some issues raised by the stories of break-ins that are interesting to discuss with your children—and that will help prepare them for the electronic world they will face as adults. In particular, it's important to help your kids see that crimes committed electronically without leaving one's house are just as bad as crimes committed by masked bandits. A cracker who excuses his behavior by saying he just wanted to "look around" the system is no different from a potential robber who breaks into a building and then claims that he just wanted to see what was inside.

A more reasonable concern for most parents considering going on-line is how to control costs. If you're just getting started with telecommunications, you might want to begin by contacting local BBSs and seeing how they work. This family project provides a low-cost way of making sure your modem works and becoming familiar with the telecommunications process.

If you do sign up for a national service, you'll want to set some ground rules with your kids to avoid running up large bills. In most cases, this will involve agreeing on how much time can be spent on-line and setting up a system to remind everybody when too much time has elapsed. If you subscribe to Prodigy, it's harder to run up a large bill, but—to avoid extra charges—you might want to put a limit on the number of messages sent by each member of the family.

On-line shopping may also be a concern for you, though it really presents no more of a risk than other forms of shopping. If you trust your child not to call a number listed in a print catalog and use your credit card to order, you can probably trust her not to do the same on-line.

The final precaution to take if you go on-line is to protect yourself against computer *viruses* that can be spread unwittingly by people exchanging files. (See Chapter 13, "Keeping Your Computer Alive and Well," for more about viruses and ways of preventing them.) The good news is that all the major national services do an excellent job of screening for viruses before a file is allowed on the system. However, if you're trying out a local BBS that does not have extensive virus-protection schemes, you'll want to take your own preventive measures.

None of these words of caution are meant to scare you away from spending time on-line. Telecommunications can offer your children many valuable opportunities. They can connect with a vast array of resources to help them with their homework; access reviews and demos of software that will help them (and you) decide whether a program is worth buying; obtain a variety of public domain titles at no extra cost; and "talk with" all sorts of interesting people from all over the world. In fact, once you buy a modem, the biggest problem you may face is scheduling on-line time for everyone in the family.

II

Buying and Maintaining a Computer System

The 5th Wave
By Rich Tennant

"NOT ONLY DID WE GET YOU AN APPLE WITH A MOUSE LIKE YOU ASKED, WE ALSO GOT YOU A BANANA WITH A LIZARD."

CHAPTER ELEVEN

Selecting a Computer for Your Family

Shopping for a computer system is a lot like purchasing a new car. To make sense of all the options and choose the system that best suits your needs, you'll want to visit your local library to read up on the subject, talk to friends who already have computers, and "test drive" several different models at a local computer store. Here are some of the factors you might want to consider when looking for a family computer.

Which Camp Are You in?

The first decision you'll have to make involves choosing a "platform"—a general type of computer. In the early days of personal computing, if you planned to use a computer primarily for your children's education, you chose the Apple II platform because Apple II computers were so popular in K–12 classrooms. If you wanted to use a computer for business, you opted for an IBM PC or an IBM PC-compatible because MS-DOS (the standard operating system for IBM-type computers) dominated the corporate world.

Today, the personal computing scene has changed dramatically. While there is still a large installed base of Apple IIs in K–12 education, schools are now buying MS-DOS and Macintosh computers in large numbers. The Macintosh has also become an acceptable computing alternative to MS-DOS in the business world. Basically, the choice most newcomers are trying to make these days is between the MS-DOS world and the Mac world.

Deciding which of the two is "better" is largely a matter of personal style. On the one hand, new users generally find the Macintosh easier to learn. In part, that's because the user interface of the Macintosh operating system is primarily graphical. While MS-DOS users have traditionally been required to type in text-based commands to perform common computing tasks, such as backing up or formatting disks, Macintosh users have been able to make choices by using a mouse to click on icons (on-screen symbols that represent computing tasks) or by pulling down menus that list possible options. There are no cryptic commands to learn and none of the complicated file-naming conventions used so often in the MS-DOS world.

The Macintosh also appeals to new users because it has a consistent look and feel; after you learn the basics of operating one Macintosh application, it's easy to learn how to operate another. Furthermore, Mac enthusiasts find that the graphical user interface offered by the Mac-intosh makes it easy to perform such tasks as moving graphics on the screen, resizing text, and experi-menting with different text fonts and styles. (Macintosh programs feature a "what-you-see-is-what-you-get," or WYSIWYG (pronounced "wizzy-wig"), approach so that text and graphics on the screen generally look the way they will when they're printed out.)

While the Mac's graphical operating environment may be more intuitive than the interface generally associated with MS-DOS, DOS enthusiasts swear by their machines. They say DOS gives them more

control over their computing environment, and that keyboard commands (single keys or key combinations that, when pressed, summon help, scroll to the end of a document, and so on) are much less cumbersome to use than pull-down menus. They point out that because the Mac uses a graphics-based interface, it tends to run more slowly and require more memory. In addition, they say, MS-DOS has a headstart in education (where the Macintosh has only recently replaced the Apple II as a serious option), as well as a huge lead in the business and home markets, resulting in more software options for owners of IBMs and IBM-compatibles. And finally, they remind Mac fans that it's possible to buy an IBM-compatible machine at bargain prices unheard of in the Macintosh world.

Actually, the differences between the platforms are not as clear-cut as the preceding arguments would make them seem, because the two worlds have moved closer together. The Macintosh has gotten much faster; it has dropped in price; and a number of software developers (especially in the education world) are developing their newest products in Macintosh as well as MS-DOS versions. At the same time, graphical user interfaces, such as *Microsoft Windows,* which offers a

WYSIWYG approach comparable to the Mac's, are becoming increasingly popular in the DOS environment (see the sidebar for more about *Windows*). In fact, a number of MS-DOS computers today, including IBM's PS/1 and many of Tandy's machines, have built-in graphical interfaces that appear automatically on the screen whenever the machine is booted. And while most Mac software now includes keyboard commands for speed users who don't want to be bothered with the mouse, an increasing number of MS-DOS programs support mouse input and pull-down menus.

In the end, your final choice is likely to be based not only on differences in hardware features but on such factors as what platform you are using at work, what your children are using at school, which hardware dealers you find most helpful, and which system runs the software you're most interested in purchasing.

Other Options?

When addressing hardware and software issues in this book, we will focus primarily on MS-DOS and Macintosh computers because those are today's leading platforms. However, we do want to touch briefly on a few other possibilities, in particular the Commodore Amiga and the Apple II line.

In the world of desktop video and computer animation, the Commodore Amiga with its outstanding graphics capabilities is frequently the machine of choice. If, in addition to purchasing a computer for general use with your children, you're also thinking of using the new system for such tasks as video editing, an Amiga is worth considering. Although there are far fewer educational titles available for the Amiga than for the more popular platforms, many basic tools (for word processing, graphics, etc.) and games are available that take advantage of the excellent sound and graphics the machine offers.

And what if you already own an Apple II computer or have the opportunity to acquire one at little or no cost? Are the older machines worth holding on to? Probably. For low-end computing tasks like word processing, financial record-keeping, and personal file management, older software abounds. Furthermore, the large installed base of Apple IIe and IIGS computers in elementary schools means that educational software will continue to be available for at least the next couple of years. However, consider yourself warned: Few new programs are being released for these computers, and you'll have to be prepared to shop by mail or phone for the older Apple II titles. (See Chapter 15, "Where to Buy Software," for information about ordering from mail-order catalogs or directly from the publisher.)

It is also important to realize that most of the best applications for the standard Apple II line (the IIe, IIc, and IIc+) require 128 kilobytes (K) of memory (RAM), while titles for the Apple IIGS could easily require at least 1.25 megabytes (M). If you have a model with less than that amount of RAM, you'll probably have to purchase additional memory to take advantage of what's out there. **Note:** One kilobyte equals approximately one thousand "bytes" (the basic unit of memory required to store a single letter, word, or other item), while one megabyte equals approximately one million bytes.

Choosing a Model... and a Manufacturer

After you've decided on a platform, it's time to choose a specific computer model. Different models within the same line differ in terms of speed, memory, disk storage space, graphics capabilities, and price.

For most of us, the goal is to get the fastest, most powerful, most colorful computer that our budget can afford. Power and speed are related to three factors: the computer's *microprocessor*, the width of its *data bus*, and its overall *clock speed*. The *microprocessor* is a miniature electronic circuit that manipulates data as it interprets and executes a program's instructions. Generally, as a microprocessor's model number increases (for example, from 80286 to 80386 or from 68000 to 68010), so does its processing power and the width of its bus path (both measured in bits), as well as its clock speed (measured in megahertz).

For example, the original IBM PC was built around Intel's 8088 chip, a 16-bit microprocessor (meaning it could process 16 data bits at one time) with an 8-bit data bus (data could only be transferred 8 bits at a time). It could take advantage of no more than one megabyte of RAM. As you can see from Table 11.1, there has been a progression from 16-bit to 32-bit microprocessors accompanied by a steady increase in data bus width, clock speed, and the maximum amount of RAM possible. All of these factors reduce the amount of time the computer requires to complete a given task, change images on the screen, and so on.

Table 11.1 Intel microprocessors.

Micro-processor	Type	Typical Clock Speed Range	Data Bus Width	Maximum RAM
8088	16-bit	4.77–10 MHz	8 bits	1M
8086*	16-bit	6–10 MIIz	16 bits	1M
80286	16-bit	6–20 MHz	16 bits	16M
80386SX	32-bit	16–20 MHz	16 bits	4 gigabytes (4 billion bytes)
80386	32-bit	16–33 MHz	32 bits	4 gigabytes
80486	32-bit	25+ MHz	32 bits	4 gigabytes

This is one of the few examples where the microprocessor number decreases as power and speed increases.

In the Macintosh world, it is less important to know which microprocessor you're considering since options are generally discussed in terms of model numbers (for example, a Mac Plus or a Mac II). However, with the Motorola micro-processors that Apple uses for its Macintosh computers, as with the Intel chips, the processor numbers have been increasing along with the speed and power they offer. For example, the Macintosh Plus, SE, Classic, and original portable are 16-bit machines built around the Motorola 68000 microprocessor. They are less powerful than the 32-bit 68020 Macintosh II and LC, which in turn are less powerful than the 68030

machines (the SE/30, IIfx, Classic II), and so on.

What does all this mean for you as a consumer? As you compare available models, it's important to keep an eye on general trends in the marketplace. For example, the Intel 80286 microprocessor (generally referred to simply as the "286"), considered state-of-the-art in the MS-DOS world a few short years ago, is already on its way out. It still represents an economical entry-level machine that is good for individuals on a tight budget, but the 80386 and 80386SX are rapidly becoming the entry-level microprocessors of choice. (For many consumers, the 386SX seems to be a good compromise; it is slower than the full 386 chip but otherwise offers much of the same power and flexibility at a more economical price.)

If you've decided on a computer with a certain microprocessor, your next question is likely to be: Which manufacturer should I buy from? In the MS-DOS world, there are numerous computer brands available from dealers, at discount stores, and by mail. A number of the less-well-known brands (often referred to as "clones") offer more features for less money. For example, many come configured with Super VGA graphics, larger hard-disk-drive capacity, and increased memory.

All manufacturers of MS-DOS computers claim IBM compatibility at the operating system level. This means that their machines can run the same programs that run on IBM. Before buying, however, you'll want to double-check on the system specs and make sure that the clone manufacturer has a good reputation. (Knowledgeable friends and reviews in industry magazines are two sources to turn to for this sort of help.)

Although you can get incredible deals on mail-order hardware, be sure to check on the mail-order company's return policies. Whether you purchase from a dealer or by mail, it's also very important to have a warranty that guarantees free service and replacement of defective parts (at a location convenient to you) for at least one year.

Finally, ask about the documentation included in the package. A detailed user's manual and technical information about the system's basic components are absolutely crucial when you are purchasing additional peripherals, upgrading, and troubleshooting.

Don't Forget the Memory

Computers are generally sold with a base-level amount of random-access memory (RAM) and the option to add extra memory chips. Most MS-DOS software today assumes that you have a computer with at least 640K of RAM. Newer machines come equipped with 1M, 2M, or 4M of RAM to handle memory-intensive software applications. *Microsoft Windows,* for example, requires a minimum of 1M of RAM and runs better with more memory. (See the sidebar for more information on *Windows.*)

Macintosh computers running under the System 7 operating environment (shipping with all new Macs) require at least 2M of RAM and 4M are recommended. Here again, the more memory the computer has, the better it can handle memory-intensive graphics applications. With increased system RAM, you can have more files open simultaneously and more fonts installed.

Microsoft Windows: What Is It and Will Your Kids Benefit?

If you use computers in your work, you've probably heard plenty about *Microsoft Windows.* Many people see it as Microsoft Corporation's attempt to out-Mac the Macintosh—to bring all the ease of use of the Macintosh operating system to the MS-DOS environment.

Windows (sold as a separate software package or sometimes bundled by computer manufacturers with their machines) works together with DOS to create a graphics-based operating environment. Like Macintosh-compatible software, software designed to run under *Windows* features a consistent system of mouse input, icons, pull-down menus, multiple windows on the screen at once, and other features associated with a state-of-the-art "graphical user interface" (or GUI).

Equally helpful, *Windows* offers software developers and computer owners "device independence." This means that publishers of applications that work with *Windows* no longer have to decide which printers and which graphics cards their programs should support. From the end-user's perspective, it means fewer worries about which add-ons to buy; as long as a printer or card is *Windows*-compatible, *Windows* takes care of making sure that all programs work with it.

Before you rush out to buy *Windows* for your family, however, there are a few things you should know. Current versions of the program require lots of memory (1M is the minimum, but many experienced users recommend closer to 4M), a fast microprocessor (a 386 or 386SX is recommended), and plenty of hard disk space. And because so few schools and homes have had the hardware necessary to take full advantage of *Windows* until recently, there's very little kid-oriented software that runs under *Windows*. (If you have *Windows* installed on your MS-DOS computer, you can still run non-*Windows* programs, but you gain no advantage.)

All of this is likely to change in the not-too-distant future if *Windows* continues to catch on as rapidly as it has so far in the business world. In the meantime, while there might not be much reason to buy *Windows* for your kids today, it's probably a good idea to be prepared with a machine powerful enough to take advantage of educationally oriented *Windows* software as it becomes available.

You will also need to make some decisions about storage devices for your computer. The two most common choices for storage are floppy disks and hard disks. Floppy disks are read and written to when inserted in your computer's disk drive. Hard disks, which are capable of storing many times as much information, generally are mounted inside the computer.

Not too long ago, hard disks were viewed as a luxury for the average home user. Today, more and more people are coming to see them as a necessity. As high-quality graphics and realistic sound are added to children's software, the programs are becoming more memory-intensive, requiring plenty of RAM and working best when loaded onto a hard disk. Without a hard disk, you are likely to find yourself swapping floppy disks in and out of your drive as the program stops and prompts you to "put in disk 3 and press any key." In addition to doing away with such annoying interruptions, hard disks are much faster than floppies, speeding up many other aspects of a program's operation.

If you're getting ready to buy a hard disk, our advice is to get more storage capacity than you can even imagine needing. You'll be amazed at how many megabytes of storage space a single game for young children can

take if it includes color graphics, animation, *and* sound! At the very least, you should buy a 40M hard drive. If you want to splurge, try 60M or 80M.

There are a variety of different floppy disk formats available for microcomputers these days, although if you're buying a new system, you probably won't have that many options to choose from. In the Macintosh world, 3.5-inch disks have always been the standard. If you own or have worked with an older Macintosh, you're probably familiar with the two earlier versions of the 3.5-inch disk: the single-sided disk that holds up to 400K of data, and the double-sided 800K disk. Today's Macintosh computers come with a high-density (1.44M) drive, called a *SuperDrive.* It can read not only Macintosh high-density disks but also most 3.5-inch disks used on IBM PCs and compatibles.

In the MS-DOS world, there are at least four types of disks: the older 5.25-inch disks (the size used by the original PC line), in both a low-density (360K) and high-density (1.2M) format, and the 3.5-inch disks, also in low- (720K) and high-density (1.44M) versions. New MS-DOS computers almost always feature the high-density 3.5-inch drives. However, because so many PC owners still have 5.25-inch drives, publishers continue to produce software in that format as well. (Many of them pack both types of disk in each package they sell, but others offer only one of the disk sizes with a coupon for users who need to make a trade.) In addition, a number of shareware programs (see Chapter 17) are distributed exclusively on 5.25-inch disks. For the next few years at least, it might be convenient to own a 5.25-inch drive as well as the 3.5-inch drive that comes with the newer machines. It is relatively inexpensive to add a second floppy disk drive to most computers.

No matter which disk size you're considering, you should select the drives that can accommodate the higher density disks. These drives can also read, write, and format low-density disks (although, in the case of 5.25-inch disks, sometimes unreliably). Low-density drives, on the other hand, cannot handle the high-density format at all.

Getting the Big Picture: Graphics Cards and Monitors

Historically, MS-DOS users have had to choose among several competing graphics standards when selecting a monitor and the video display card necessary to connect the monitor to the computer. The graphics standards—each identified by an acronym (MDA, CGA, EGA, MCGA, VGA, and so on)—generally differ from one another in terms of display resolution (measured in the number of dots or "pixels" that make up a picture on the screen) and the number of colors or gray shades that can be displayed on the screen at one time. If you own or are considering an older computer, you may still be dealing with such standards as Hercules, CGA, and EGA (all defined in the sidebar "MS-DOS Graphics Standards Defined"). However, for those of you considering a new MS-DOS computer, the choices have narrowed considerably.

VGA, introduced by IBM with its PS/2 computers (the line that has replaced the older PCs), is currently the graphics standard of choice for entry-level MS-DOS systems. In fact, most computer systems are now sold already configured with a VGA monitor and graphics adapter. The high resolution capabilities of VGA make it suitable for both text and graphics applications. While many educational programs and kids' games still support the older CGA and EGA graphics, most are being written to take advantage of VGA graphics on any computer that has the appropriate adapter and monitor.

As of this writing, there is hardly any family-oriented software available for resolutions higher than VGA, but more advanced options do exist. A number of high-end adapters (under names such as Super VGA and XGA) are now on the market, offering more colors and a higher resolution than standard VGA. However, before the average educational software developer begins taking advantage of these new cards, two things need to happen: The industry must agree on an actual higher-level standard (right now, each card manufacturer seems to be attempting to establish its own), and computer memory and disk storage space need to be plentiful enough for the higher resolution screen images (each of which takes a huge amount of memory) to be feasible.

What does this mean for you? Chances are, unless you are planning to invest in a CD-ROM drive to run some of the newest multimedia titles (see the next chapter for a discussion of CD-ROM and what it offers) or want to use the family computer to run some high-end graphics and business packages, you won't have much use for a Super VGA or XGA card for quite some time. However, if you want to leave your options open, you might decide to invest in a monitor that will be able to handle the highest resolution you will need if you eventually

decide to upgrade. This would involve paying a little more for a Super VGA or a multisync monitor (designed to adapt to a variety of graphics standards) with the ability to display higher resolution Super VGA screens (that is, 1,024 by 768 pixels). Note, however, that even a VGA monitor is capable of handling the lower resolution versions of Super VGA—if that turns out to be the route many of the next-generation programs take.

In the early days of Macintosh computing, users had no graphics choices to make: All Macs came with built-in 9-inch monitors for black-and-white viewing. Although newer models such as the Macintosh Classic still follow this "compact" design, the Macintosh LC and all the machines in the Macintosh II line are "modular," offering a choice of monochrome, gray-scale, or color display monitors in a variety of different sizes.

Most of the less-expensive modular Macs (including the LC, IIsi, and IIci) have built-in video circuitry to drive several popular Macintosh monitors, making it unnecessary to purchase a separate video card unless you have the need for unusually high-quality graphics capabilities. Some of the higher-end models require video cards. It takes a 4-bit video card to display 16 colors or gray shades simultaneously, an 8-bit card to display 256 colors or gray levels, and a 24-bit card to display colors from a palette of more than 16 million shades.

When selecting a monitor for use with either an MS-DOS computer or a modular Mac, choose with care. In addition to making sure that the monitor you select works with the

MS-DOS Graphics Standards Defined

CGA (Color Graphics Adapter): This is the lowest resolution possible for color displays on an IBM PC-compatible. CGA can display in two colors at its maximum resolution of 640 dots across by 200 dots up and down. (These dots are referred to as "pixels.") It supports four-color display at a resolution of 200 by 320.

HGC (Hercules Graphics Card): This monochrome graphics adapter, which offers no support for color, provides for a maximum resolution of 720 by 348 pixels. Before the newer color graphics standards became widespread, Hercules was the standard of choice for those using their computers primarily for text-based tasks because the CGA color mode offered too low a resolution to display text crisply.

EGA (Enhanced Graphics Adapter): EGA is rapidly losing place to VGA as the most popular video display technology. At its maximum resolution of 640 by 350 pixels, it displays in 16 colors.

MCGA (MultiColor Graphics Adapter): MCGA is found in older, low-end IBM PS/2 computers, including the original Model 25 (available in many K–12 schools today). It supports 256-color display with a resolution of 320 by 200, which means that it is compatible with most of the VGA software on the market. However, it does not have the higher resolution color mode offered by VGA.

VGA (Video Graphics Array): Like MCGA, VGA can display 256 colors when operating at a resolution of 320 by 200. In addition, it can display 16 colors at a resolution of 640 by 480 pixels.

Super VGA: This graphics adapter has several competing standards. Some cards offer the same resolution as VGA (640 by 480) but with 256 simultaneous colors instead of 16. (You'll also see this described by some developers as VGA Plus.) Others offer resolutions of 1024 by 768 pixels, with either 16 or 256 colors. Still others provide for a maximum resolution of 800 by 600 pixels when displaying 16 colors.

XGA (Extended Graphics Array): XGA, built into the higher-end PS/2 models, is IBM's attempt to set a new standard to succeed VGA. Like Super VGA, it can support 256 simultaneous colors at a maximum resolution of 1024 by 768 pixels. A special 16-bit color mode lets XGA users select from a palette of more than 60,000 colors at standard VGA resolution. It is possible that XGA and Super VGA will eventually merge into a single high-end standard.

graphics adapter you've settled on, you'll want to look for the clearest, crispest display you can afford. The clarity of a screen image is determined not only by the graphics standard selected but also by the monitor's "dot pitch"—the distance between the phosphor dots or lines on the screen. Many people would define a high-quality monitor as one with a dot pitch of .29 mm or less.

It's also helpful to test a monitor under different lighting conditions to make sure that it allows you to adjust the brightness level sufficiently and does not have excessive glare. Finally, it's a good idea to select a monitor that has controls located on the front of the unit where they are easy to reach.

Postponing Obsolescence

When you are shopping for a computer, it's disturbing to realize how quickly today's cutting-edge technology becomes passé. How can you be sure that the model you buy today will not be obsolete in two or three years? The answer is, you can't. But, by weighing your options carefully, you can at least increase the likelihood that the computer you choose will still be useful 5—or maybe even 10—years from now.

The good news is that neither the Macintosh nor the MS-DOS platform

is likely to disappear for a long, long time and that models within each line really are quite compatible in many ways. Furthermore, you can be confident that software publishers will do their best to make sure their products run on a wide range of models—from the older stripped-down machines to the newer high-end entries. After all, it is financially in their best interest to do so. However, eventually you will find yourself being nudged upward by new, enhanced applications that simply cannot run on the older models with the slower microprocessors, the lower resolution graphics, the outdated disk formats, and the lower memory configurations.

Here are some general guidelines to help postpone the day when you finally find yourself with a computer and no new software that will run on it:

- **Splurge on those things that are least easy to upgrade.** For example, while you can generally add memory or a better graphics card to your computer, you usually can't change micro-processors. It's wise, therefore, to spend extra money on a faster, more powerful micro-processor even if it means that you have to put off buying some of the fancier add-ons for a while.

■ **Insist on expandability.** Don't buy a computer unless it offers the ability to increase memory as you need it and has plenty of expansion "slots" (within the computer) or "ports" (on the outside of the computer) for adding such peripherals as printers, sound cards, scanners, etc. It's hard to anticipate exactly what you'll need, but you can be sure that eventually you'll want to build on what you have.

■ **Stick with the crowds.** It's risky to be an "early adopter," the first one on your block to try a new type of system. At best, you'll find yourself waiting around a long time before software developers come out with products that take advantage of the new features you've paid a premium for; at worst, you'll discover that you've invested in something that never really catches on. On the other hand, you don't want to lag behind the crowds once they do decide something is worth investing in. You might be able to get a great bargain on the lowest-end computers on the market (for example, the 286 machines that were so hot yesterday), but that's generally a good sign that everybody else is moving up to the next level—hastening the day that the software publishers will move up as well.

■ **Pay attention to all the markets.** When considering hardware for your family, it's important to watch not only the home but also the school and business markets. Knowing what's hot in the schools is helpful because most of the producers of educational software are interested in developing for the machines that do well in both the home and the school markets. The trends in business indicate which technologies will soon become widespread—and affordable. (In addition, of course, watching the business world helps you find the appropriate computer system if you're planning to use business-oriented titles at home.)

■ **Don't assume that younger kids need less computing power.** Computer manufacturers and educators alike often fall into the trap of assuming that only adults or the most advanced high-school students need fast, powerful computers with extra memory, hard disks, and a variety of peripherals. Sadly, it's often true that K–12 schools in this country can't afford the newest, best computers, but that doesn't mean the kids in these schools would not benefit from them. Young children have a tremendous amount to gain from high-resolution color graphics, appealing animation, and realistic speech—all of which require considerable computing power and memory. Although buying hardware for your family that is not yet supported by educationally oriented software makes little sense, you don't want to sell your kids short by assuming that an older, stripped-down model will be sufficient. By helping your local school district and your friends see the value of powerful technology for kids of all ages, you're increasing the likelihood that ever-more exciting software will follow.

The 5th Wave By Rich Tennant

"IT WAS CLASHING WITH THE SOUTHWESTERN MOTIF."

Peripherals and Other Options

In addition to selecting a computer and a monitor to go with it, families shopping for a complete computer system have several other decisions to think about. A range of peripherals (printers, scanners, CD-ROM drives, and other external devices) must be considered, as well as alternative input devices and various special-purpose add-on cards. Many of these "options" truly are optional. In fact, some people prefer to focus on buying a basic system first and then return (possibly years later) to the subject of peripherals and other add-ons.

On the other hand, after more complete consideration of what's available, you might discover that there are several of these options you simply don't want to do without.

Printers

For family use, a printer is the one peripheral that is an absolute must.

But what type of printer do you want? Although there are several different print technologies available, you are most likely to be choosing among these three printers: *dot-matrix, inkjet,* and *laser.* Which option is right for you will depend on your budget and what you intend to do with the output. No matter which technology you select, stick with a popular brand-name machine, or you may end up with a printer that has few compatible software applications or that will be difficult to service in a few years.

Dot-matrix printers produce text and graphics by firing a vertical row of needle-sized pins (wires) against an inked ribbon, depositing dots of ink on the paper. The more pins per printhead, the better-quality printouts you can expect. Early dot-matrix printers had printheads with 9 pins. Today, 24-pin printheads are quite common. The pins on 24-pin printers are finer and they produce smaller dots, which yield crisper-looking text and graphics. The 24-pin models frequently feature built-in proportional fonts, so that printed output looks more professional.

Dot-matrix printers tend to be very noisy. In addition, generating "letter quality" output is quite slow because the printhead generally has to make multiple passes over a single line. (Most dot-matrix printers also offer a lower-quality draft mode option, which is quicker because fewer passes are made.) On the other hand, dot-matrix printers provide acceptable output for most home uses at a very affordable cost. It's possible to buy a 9-pin printer for less than $200 or a 24-pin model for as little as $300. Color printing, while often painfully slow, is an option on a number of reasonably priced models.

Inkjet printers generate text and graphics by shooting drops of ink onto paper. Inkjet printers, while generally a few hundred dollars more than the average dot-matrix model, still offer a relatively affordable way to produce high-quality printouts in a whisper-quiet environment. Many models generate printouts at a resolution similar to that of a laser printer. On the down side, inkjet printers are considerably slower than laser printers, may require special paper, and can be messy (ink cartridges need

to be changed frequently, and the ink on the printed page tends to bleed into the paper or smear if it gets wet). Color inkjet printers, involving multiple ink cartridges, are offered by some manufacturers.

Laser printers use copier technology to produce superior-quality printouts. They form images by using a laser beam to paint a series of dots on a rotating light-sensitive drum or belt. Toner (ink powder) adheres to any electrostatically charged spot the laser has hit. Eventually, the toner transfers from the drum and fuses to the paper. Laser printers generate hard copy at 300 or more dots per inch, providing users with printouts of near-typeset quality. These printers are typically very quiet, very fast—and are generally more expensive than dot-matrix and inkjet printers. (In addition, toner cartridges, which need to be replaced regularly, are quite expensive.) However, prices on standard laser printers have recently dropped as low as $1,000 and are continuing to fall, increasing the likelihood that you will find a good deal on this technology. Unfortunately, color laser printing continues to cost many times as much as black and white, placing it far beyond the budget of the typical family.

Choosing Input Devices

All computers accept input from a keyboard, and many models are bundled with a stock keyboard. Sometimes, however, a manufacturer expects you to buy the keyboard separately. When this happens, you might as well take advantage of the opportunity to shop around for a version that feels good to you. Factors to consider include: the angle of the keys (some models have adjustable legs that allow users to alter the typing angle for maximum comfort); the availability of a numeric keypad (used in business-oriented programs for numerical tasks); and the existence and location of function keys (some keyboards have functions keys— labeled F1, F2, and so on—along the top row; others have them down the left side; and still others—for non-MS-DOS computers—omit them entirely).

In addition to the keyboard, there are many other input devices that can be useful to a computer user. If you're going to be playing a lot of arcade-style games, you'll probably want a joystick. It plugs into one of the ports on your computer and is used to move objects on the screen. For young children or children with special needs, there is a variety of alternate input devices for you to consider. (See Chapters 6 and 7.)

For art, page layout, and other tasks requiring precise pixel control, the mouse is the input device of choice. A mouse is a standard feature on all Macintoshes, but in much of the MS-DOS world it remains an option. MS-DOS users who elect to buy a mouse have a choice of two types, each available for approximately $100. One type of mouse plugs into a card inserted in an unused computer slot; another connects to an unused serial port at the back of the computer. Both perform cursor-control tasks in exactly the same way. Mice also differ from one another in terms of size, shape, and the number of buttons available for making choices (when there are several buttons, you can decide which one you will use for "clicking on" or dragging objects). These differences do not affect how the computer responds to input from the mouse, but a certain design may feel better to you than others.

Any mouse you purchase should come with mouse-driver software to control device operation and let DOS know that a mouse is attached. Be aware, however, that a mouse will do you no good unless the software you are using is "mouse aware" (has been written to accept certain types of input from the mouse as well as the keyboard).

A trackball is a space-saving alternative to a mouse. The conventional mouse, which works by moving a roller ball located on the underside of the unit across a smooth surface, requires considerable room to maneuver. Trackballs don't take up much desktop space because a trackball's roller ball sits at the top of the case. To move the cursor, you merely roll your fingers across the plastic roller ball while the trackball housing remains stationary. Any Macintosh or MS-DOS program that accepts input from a mouse will respond to a trackball as well. Some users find the trackball easier and less tiring to use than a mouse.

Sound Cards—For Output and Input

Ideally, to produce high-quality sound, including realistic speech, a computer should be equipped with two pieces of hardware: a speaker and a "digital-to-analog-converter" (DAC), which allows prerecorded speech and sound effects included in software programs to be played back through the computer.

A number of computers, including the Apple IIGS, the Commodore Amiga, and the Macintosh, are equipped with such hardware. However, most MS-DOS computers are not. With the exception of Tandy, few manufacturers in the MS-DOS world have chosen to build DACs into their machines, and while most of the PCs do have built-in speakers, they are sometimes quite primitive, all right for simple beeps and buzzes but not capable of much more.

This presents a real dilemma for software developers who know that realistic speech, music, and sound effects add greatly to the appeal of programs for young kids (and old ones, too, for that matter). A few of these publishers have found ways to get around the problem of the missing DAC with the help of special software routines that produce speech and other sounds directly through the computer's speaker. That explains the MS-DOS packages on the retail shelves these days with labels reading "speaks without extra hardware"—or something similar. They do work, but only with a fast enough microprocessor (at least 8 or 10 MHz) and a powerful enough speaker. (Unfortunately, there's no way of telling how good a speaker is from computer specifications on paper; it's advisable when shopping for a computer to ask the dealer to demonstrate some sound-intensive software on the machine to test it out.)

If you really care about having access to high-quality sound on your MS-DOS computer, it clearly is better to invest $100 to $200 in a special sound card. These cards all offer amplification, eliminating the need for a decent computer speaker, and most of them include a DAC. (A few of the older cards, including the older AdLib card and those from Roland, do not have a DAC, only a music synthesis chip, making it possible for the computer to play elaborate music but not to play back actual recorded sounds, such as speech.)

It is unfortunate that the numerous sound cards on the market are not compatible with one another. Because they are not, a software publisher must anticipate which card you are likely to have and write software that will work with that card. The good news is that many publishers now support several of the most popular cards. If you own an AdLib board (especially the newer version with a DAC), a Sound Blaster, IBM's PS/1 sound option, or a Tandy computer with its own built-in sound capabilities, there's a good chance that programs with speech or high-quality sound will work with your hardware. (Other options that are supported by some, but certainly not all, developers include Disney's Sound Source, the COVOX Sound Master, the Roland music cards, the Echo and other speech cards from Street Electronics, and the Digispeech and Speech Adapter cards sold by IBM directly to schools.)

How important are such capabilities? In many cases, the sound board is an option that enhances the entertainment value of a program but is not essential. In a few programs, particularly those written for younger children, sound output in the form of speech is key to the program's value. (See Chapter 6 for more information about computerized speech and what it can offer your child.) Until you know which software programs you plan to use and which cards they support, you may want to put off purchasing a sound card. Eventually, however, if you own an MS-DOS computer, this type of add-on will be worth the investment.

In the Macintosh world, another type of sound card is getting much attention these days. In addition to the sound *output* capabilities built into the standard Macintosh, a number of the newer Macs (the LC, IIsi, and so on) have built-in sound *input* capabilities. These machines ship with a microphone that users can plug into a port in back of the machine in order to record their own voices or other sounds. These recordings are "digitized" by the computer and can be saved on floppy or hard disks just as text or pictures can be saved. An increasing number of Macintosh programs are taking advantage of these sound input capabilities, allowing kids to narrate stories they've created, for example, or to customize the sounds they hear when the program is on the screen. Owners of Macintosh machines that do not have built-in sound input can purchase add-on devices (such as the MacRecorder from Farallon) that bring such features to their computers.

Modems

If you're interested in telecommunications—the ability to exchange computerized messages over telephone lines with other computer users or to access a variety of on-line services that provide everything from on-line shopping to multiuser games—you'll need to purchase an additional piece of equipment: a *modem.* (See Chapter 10, "Getting into On-Line Services," for more information about why and how to go on-line with your family.) Modems, available for as little as $100–$200, translate computer signals into phone line signals that travel long distances over conventional phone lines and then are translated back into computer signals so they can be read and interpreted by your software.

Modems are rated by the speed, or *baud rate,* at which they can send and receive signals. Most modems in use now are 2400 baud, although older, slower modems will still work (if you have the patience to wait for them). Faster 9600-baud modems also exist, but they are considerably more expensive and will only give you an advantage if the party on the other end (an on-line service or an individual with whom you're exchanging data) is set up to receive and send at the faster rate.

Fortunately, when buying a modem, you don't have to worry about compatibility. Virtually every modem sold today is "Hayes-compatible." (Hayes was one of the original modem manufacturers, and the standards set by their modems have since been accepted industrywide.)

Scanning

A peripheral that has gained popularity in the business world in recent years is the *scanner.* Scanners range in size from full-page, flatbed models that resemble hefty printers to palm-sized hand-held devices. All scanners allow a user to capture images and text from a printed page (much as a photocopier or fax machine does) and store them as computerized images, which can then be edited (colored, resized, etc.) and incorporated into other documents. When used with special *optical character recognition* (OCR) software, scanners can translate scanned text into text files that can be edited in a regular word processor.

For the average family, the type of scanner that is most likely to be of interest is the hand-held scanner, used for capturing images more often than character recognition. With such a tool, it's possible to scan photographs (a postcard from a recent trip, a picture of the new baby) and other images (a pen-and-ink drawing your child is particularly proud of, a signature, a school or team logo) and use them in one of the many word processing, desktop publishing, and paint programs that permit you to import graphics. (Basically, scanned images, once saved in the right format, are treated like clip art.)

A number of hand-held scanners are available for under $300. Before picking one, you'll need to be sure that the scanner saves images in a format that the software packages you're planning to use can handle. (Common graphics formats that many programs can read include PICT in the Macintosh world, PCX and GIF in the MS-DOS world, and TIFF in both.) Other features to check out before

buying: the editing software provided with the scanner (some packages allow you to resize, rotate, crop, and alter the sharpness of images); how easy it is to move without wobbling (some models have stabilizing wheels or alignment guides to help with positioning); and, of course, how attractive the final results are.

While a scanner is not a necessity for the average family, it can be fun and will certainly enhance your family's creativity at the computer.

CD-ROM Drives

A final option you might want to consider is the addition of a CD-ROM drive to your system. *CD-ROM* (for Compact Disc-Read-Only Memory) discs are closely related to audio compact discs (CDs), the tiny plastic platters that have taken the music industry by storm. However, CD-ROMs are used to store computer programs, text, graphics, and animation in addition to digitally recorded music.

Users can neither write to a CD-ROM nor alter stored data—unlike conventional floppies or hard disks. However, these limitations are offset by the fact that a computer CD can hold more than 600 megabytes of information. The disc's immense capacity makes it a perfect storage medium for huge technical databases, space-hungry graphics, sounds, and animated sequences.

To take advantage of CD-ROM technology, you must purchase a special CD-ROM drive that attaches to your computer. Many CD-ROM drives today are capable of playing audio CDs. (With speakers or headphones attached, it's possible to play your favorite music in the background while word processing or working with any other software that does not involve the CD-ROM drive.) However, this does not work in reverse: a standard audio CD player *cannot* be hooked up to a computer and used as a CD-ROM drive.

CD-ROM technology is just beginning to gain wide acceptance. In the past, CD-ROM drives were too expensive and CD-ROM titles too esoteric for mass appeal. Now, prices for CD-ROM drives have fallen to as low as $400 or $500, making the technology more attractive to home-based computing enthusiasts, and a number of computer manufacturers have begun offering CD-ROM drives as standard options. If the sorts of titles described in Chapter 26 appeal to you, you may want to buy a CD-ROM drive for your system, in addition to a floppy drive and a hard drive.

When shopping for a drive, you'll want to check on access and data transfer speeds (in general, CD-ROM drives are quite slow compared to hard drives, but some of the drives are better than others). In addition, ask about features such as self-cleaning lenses, sealed drive enclosures, and RCA jacks for connection to external amplified speakers.

If you're thinking of equipping an MS-DOS computer with a CD-ROM drive, you should pay careful attention to a new multimedia standard that has been set by Microsoft and a number of hardware manufacturers. This standard, known as *MPC* (for *Multimedia Personal Computer*), involves the use of a special logo on certain MS-DOS computers to let you know that they are equipped with a CD-ROM drive, a special version of *Windows* known as *Multimedia Windows*, and a sound board that conforms to MPC specifications. In addition, every machine with the MPC trademark has an 80286 or, preferably, 80386 microprocessor with a clock speed of *at least* 10 MHz; a hard disk; VGA or (more likely) Super VGA graphics; and two or more megabytes of RAM.

If you already own an MS-DOS computer with the basic micro-processor, memory, and speed requirements, you can buy an MPC upgrade kit from a hardware dealer or mail-order house. If not, you might consider buying a fully configured Multimedia PC from a company such as Tandy or CompuAdd. Although none of the CD-ROM programs reviewed in this book were designed especially for the MPC platform, you can expect to see an increasing number of titles (all bearing the MPC trademark) that are.

This is not to suggest that an MS-DOS computer is the only way to go if you are interested in CD-ROM. In many ways, the MPC standard brings the sort of consistency to the MS-DOS world that already exists for Macintosh owners. If you do own a Mac, your biggest decision, once you've decided that you're interested in CD-ROM, is whether to buy Apple's own CDSC drive or look for a better bargain from a third-party manufacturer that produces CD-ROM drives which will hook up to a Macintosh. Whichever standard you choose, however, CD-ROM technology is likely to be more and more appealing to you in the years to come.

The 5th Wave By Rich Tennant

"GUESS WHAT DAD - THOSE CHOCOLATE DISKETTES FIT RIGHT INTO YOUR COMPUTER, NO PROBLEM."

Keeping Your Computer Alive and Well

Like all electronic devices, your computer requires some routine maintenance. This "care and feeding" is not very difficult or time-consuming and will add significantly to the life of your computer. From cleaning your computer to taking preventive steps to protect the computer and its software from damage, this is a process that should involve the entire family. Even the youngest child is ready to learn some basic rules about caring for the computer. Older children can take a more active role in maintenance tasks like cleaning the monitor and caring for the disks.

Before you and your kids undertake any cleaning or routine maintenance, check the user's manual provided by the manufacturer. Although such maintenance is neither dangerous nor harmful to your computer, it's always a good idea to follow the advice given by the manufacturer.

Outside Matters

Because your monitor screen generates static electricity, it acts as a magnet for dust. As a result, keeping the screen of your monitor clean is an ongoing challenge. A dirty screen won't hurt the computer but will annoy the living daylights out of the person using it. Almost all screens on monitors made in the last five years can be cleaned with household window cleaners. Spray or pour the liquid on a clean, soft rag or paper towel and clean the screen as you would a window or mirror. Spraying the rag rather than the screen will prevent the cleaner from dripping into the computer or keyboard.

If you have an older monitor, manufactured with a protective coating to cut down on glare, don't use window cleaner. Instead, check the user's manual or consult your computer dealer to learn how to clean your type of monitor. Also, if your monitor has an anti-glare or anti-radiation screen, remove it before you attempt to clean the screen.

Another technique for cleaning your screen is to use a fabric softener sheet created for clothes dryers. A used sheet is probably preferable to a brand-new one because it's softer. Keep the sheet near the computer and wipe the screen whenever necessary. The fabric softener will pick up dust and other loose debris without damaging the screen. By the way, this same technique can be used for your television screen.

If you've owned your computer for more than a few months, you will notice that the cabinet has become smudged. Usually, all you'll need to remove such smudges is a damp, lint-free cloth. If something stronger is required, you can try any nonabrasive soap or window cleaner. Since there are a few computer cases and keyboards that can be discolored or in other ways harmed by cleaning liquids, check your user's manual or test the cleaner on an inconspicuous part of the computer's case before you proceed.

To clean your keyboard and mouse, dip one end of a cotton swab into soapy water or alcohol (Apple's manuals recommend alcohol), and use it to loosen dirt in the nooks and crannies. (Refer to the documentation to find out how to open up your mouse in order to clean it more effectively.) Use the other end to remove the dirt and excess liquid. *Don't spray the keyboard or computer directly with any liquid.* To get the hard-to-reach dust and debris that collects between the keys, try dusting with a small paintbrush or using a puff or two of "canned air" (the compressed air sold in cans at hobby or photography shops). You can also vacuum your keyboard with a special vacuum device made for just this purpose. Kits containing special cleaning materials and tools are also available from many dealers and mail-order houses.

Inside Your Computer

Even in the cleanest environments, dust will collect inside your computer. The electrical components generate enough of a charge to attract dust, and the cooling fan draws dust, hair, and other floating debris into your computer's innards. This debris can create a buildup of heat that will cause chips to fail.

In some cases, dust and hair can actually affect the performance of your floppy disk drive. Debris can build up on the drive's read/write head or other critical parts and cause an increase in the number of input and output errors you experience. Eventually, the disk drive may fail altogether.

To minimize the amount of dust that gets inside your computer, cover the computer when it is not in use. (Computer covers are available from most dealers and mail-order houses.) In addition, locate the computer in an area that is relatively dust free, and try to keep the area as clean as is reasonable.

Even if you are very careful to keep your computer in a clean environment, it's a good idea to take it into a repair center at least once a year for a routine cleaning.

Caring for Floppy Disks and Hard Disks

If you're using 5.25-inch floppy disks with your computer, there are a number of things you should discuss with your children. Make sure that everybody knows *not* to touch the actual storage medium, which is the shiny disk inside the protective jacket; the oil from fingers will attract and hold dust, which can damage the disk

or the disk-drive head and ruin the information stored there. For this reason, it's also important to return disks to their dust jackets as soon as you finish using them.

The 3.5-inch floppy disks are hardier—they can't be bent easily, they provide better protection for the magnetic material inside, and they don't require dust jackets. Nevertheless, it's important to take a few precautions when handling and storing these disks as well.

Here are some basic guidelines for *all* floppy disks:

- Keep them away from heat, cold, dust, and food.

- Don't allow magnetic devices anywhere near the computer or the disks; a simple magnetic toy, an audio speaker, or a refrigerator magnet can wreak havoc with data stored on floppies and even the hard disk.

- Use specially designed disk storage units or other sturdy boxes to store the disks so they don't get damaged or lost.

Hard disks are less temperamental than they used to be, but it's very important to read the manual that comes with your system to find out how to treat your hard disk. With older hard disks, your manual may outline a special procedure to follow to "park" the disk when the computer is being moved from place to place.

Many manuals suggest that you exit the program you are using and return to DOS or the desktop before shutting off the computer. (The Macintosh documentation directs you to use the "shut down" procedure rather than simply turn off the computer.) Such precautions allow the application you are using to remind you to save your current file and to close any temporary files it may have open when you are ready to quit. In the Macintosh world, it is even possible to damage the hard disk if you turn off the computer without giving the system a chance to park the disk and put files back in order.

Be prepared for the fact that hard disks, like floppies and other computer-related devices, do occasionally "crash" (cease working without warning). It's important to "back up" any files you care about (saving them to floppy disks as well as on the hard disk) and to make sure you know where the original program disks are for any application you have installed on the hard disk—just in case.

Computer Viruses

Several years ago, some computer "hackers" discovered that they could write nasty little programs that would duplicate themselves in order to affect hardware and software. Called "viruses," these programs caused a variety of problems. Some were minor, like flashing the programmer's name across the screen with a friendly greeting, but others were more destructive. Thousands of Macintosh users saw their computer's speed slow to a crawl because of the WDEF virus, while another virus caused data transmission and storage problems on the nation's largest research network.

You can contract a virus by exchanging disks or by logging onto an unprotected network or bulletin board. (Most of the larger on-line services these days use protective software to screen out viruses.) Viruses are insidious, hence the name, and you won't know you have one until you experience its effects. (In fact, even then, it's sometimes hard to know whether the problem you're experiencing is caused by a virus, a "bug" in the software, or a hardware problem.) Computer viruses can lie dormant for a period of time before they affect your computer or transmit themselves, making it particularly easy for users to pass them on unintentionally.

Fortunately, it is relatively easy to protect yourself against the most common viruses. Dealers and mail-order houses carry a number of programs that will identify viruses and cure them. Some software now comes with built-in virus detectors that flash a warning and refuse to install if your system is infected. If you are exchanging data by disk or modem with any other user, we urge you to install virus protection at once. Be prepared for the fact that you'll need to update this protection periodically; the existing programs successfully protect against known viruses, but each time a new virus is invented, there is a chance that the protection software will need to be rewritten to deal with the new menace.

Power Surges and Lightning

It's a good idea to buy a *surge suppressor*—a device that plugs into a wall outlet and functions as a power source for your computer. The surge suppressor will keep "spikes" in your electric current from damaging your computer. (A spike typically occurs when the flow of electricity to your home is cut off and then returns suddenly.) Be aware that some surge protectors are more effective than others. Look for a UL marking to indicate approval by the Underwriter's Laboratory and don't assume that the cheapest device available will be sufficient.

Don't expect a surge suppressor to protect your computer against lightning. The only sure protection is to unplug your computer when a storm is approaching (or before you leave on a long trip). Lightning can also damage your computer or modem through the telephone line. There are telephone-line surge suppressors, but like electric surge suppressors, they do not protect against spikes as powerful as those caused by lightning. If you are expecting a storm, you should disconnect the telephone cord between your modem and the telephone outlet on the wall.

Some Final Tips for Keeping Your Computer and Software Healthy

- No coffee, soft drinks, milk, or other liquids should be allowed near the computer. Nothing can gum up a keyboard as effectively as spilled liquids.

■ No paper clips or other small items should be placed on the keyboard. Sooner or later, they will fall and cause a major problem.

■ Keep foreign objects, including pencils, fingers, and paper, out of disk drives.

■ Allow enough room around your computer to keep air circulating. Your computer generates heat, and the fan inside the computer needs space to draw in cool air and blow out hot air. Furthermore, don't put anything on your computer that can block the cooling vents.

■ Don't leave your computer and monitor on for extended periods of time when they're not in use because this can decrease the lifetime of the hard disk. If you do have to step away for a while, turn down the brightness on the monitor (or turn off the monitor entirely) to avoid "burning in" an image on the screen. There are "screen saver" devices available from a number of software suppliers that, once installed, will dim the screen for you if you forget.

III

Building a Software Library

The 5th Wave

By Rich Tennant

"I THOUGHT HE WAS A VACUUM CLEANER SALESMAN. HE CAME IN, SPRINKLED DIRT ON THE CARPET, AND THEN TRIED TO SELL ME A SOFTWARE PROGRAM THAT WOULD SHOW ME HOW TO CLEAN IT UP."

CHAPTER FOURTEEN

Selecting the Best Programs for Your Child

You own a computer system, and you're looking for software to use with your child at home. But how do you decide which of the many titles on the market are worth buying? In Part 4 of this book, we provide you with several recommendations. These include many of our favorite programs (ones that we've seen kids enjoy and return to over and over again), as well as some exciting new titles that, at first try, measure up favorably to the best of what's out there. However, the list is far from comprehensive. There are a number of good programs that were left out, in some cases because they were too narrow in scope, in others because we saw their hardware requirements or price tags as unrealistic for the average home. Other good programs will undoubtedly hit the market after you purchase this book.

Our goal in recommending software, therefore, is not only to get you started with some educationally oriented titles that are likely to be a hit with your son or daughter, but also to provide you with a helpful frame of reference for evaluating future programs for (and with) your children.

What criteria did we use in selecting programs for this book? How did our favorites come to be our favorites? The following is a summary of some of the key factors that we consider important when evaluating software for young people.

Appeal

One of the most important questions to ask about a program is, How much fun is it? Unless your child enjoys the software you buy, it will sit unused—no matter how sound a program you think it is. But what determines a program's appeal? Most young people (and adults, too, for that matter) tend to prefer software that features attractive high-resolution graphics, engaging animation, and entertaining sound effects. Graphics and sound alone, however, are not likely to hold a child's interest indefinitely. When you are evaluating an instructional game or simulation, an equally important factor to consider is the program's *game-playing aspects:* Is the game's premise exciting and motivating? Is the program challenging enough to maintain interest without becoming frustrating? With tools like word processors or paint programs, your child is most likely to enjoy programs that are easy to use, include powerful options, and produce attractive results.

We realize that "appeal" is subjective; clearly, not everyone will find the same things enjoyable. In making our selections, we tried—after watching kids use the programs—to draw some general conclusions about each application's appeal. When looking at software for yourself (or reading our recommendations), you can be more exact about predicting how engaging a program will be for your particular child. After all, you know whether your son or daughter enjoys arcade action, is intrigued by a

good mystery, loves to listen to music, and so on.

Educational Content

In Chapter 3, "Fun, Games, and Learning," we talked about primary and secondary learning and the attitudes that different software promotes. In evaluating educational games and simulations, there are a number of questions for you to ask: Does this program focus on the content or skill areas my child needs to learn? If so, does it appear to do an effective job? How much time is spent "on task" (in other words, on the content area supposedly being taught)? What sort of secondary learning is occurring during the times not on task? Perhaps the program uses arcade-style action, requiring fast reflexes (and in some cases, a love of battle). Or maybe it calls on players to read for clues or use maps to navigate from one place to another. It's important that you and your child be comfortable with these "extra" game-playing elements, as well as with the program's primary content focus—especially since considerable time is usually spent on the former.

In evaluating an entertainment title or a general-purpose tool, such as a word processor or a paint program, don't overlook the program's potential to "educate." An attractive, easy-to-use word processor can do a lot to motivate your child to write. A good strategy game can help with logical thinking and problem solving.

Types of Feedback

In the early days of educational microcomputing, parents and teachers looking for programs to use with young people were often appalled at the insulting feedback they encountered. "No dummy, that's not the answer!" and "You've got to be kidding!" were not uncommon responses to wrong answers. Such insults are practically unheard of in commercial software these days, but programs still vary greatly in the value of the feedback they provide.

"No, try again," a frequent message in many of today's drill programs, can quickly become annoying. It's far more helpful if the program provides young people with hints, help screens that remind them how to approach a problem, the ability to go back and review instructions, and so on. An equally helpful—and generally more enjoyable—type of feedback involves logical consequences. For example, in a simulation that involves estimating distances, a student's "playing piece" might overshoot a target if she overestimates, fall short if she under-estimates, and so on, providing graphic feedback about how far off she is each time and then allowing her to make the necessary corrections.

Lasting Value

A reasonable price tag is important when selecting software for your family, but value for your money is even more crucial. How do you determine a program's lasting value? Questions you might ask include: Are there many different activities or a variety of tasks to be performed so kids won't become bored? If the program is a game, does it have many levels of difficulty that can be set by the user or that increase automatically as your child's playing skills do? (Not only does this help keep a single child interested in the program for a long time, it means that more than one child in the family can use the same game successfully.) If the program is a tool, does it have enough options to keep your family satisfied over time? (For example, if the program includes clip art, there should be numerous pictures to choose from; if it provides "templates" for creating certain types of printouts, there should be a great variety—not just templates for creating calendars or greeting cards.)

Control

Not only do you want a program to have lasting value, you also want to be able to tailor it today to your own child and your home environment. Therefore, in addition to being able to control the level of difficulty, it's also helpful to have control over such variables as sound (if two kids share a room with a computer in it, you'll want to be able to turn off a program's loud music at times) and game duration (some kids are happy to play a single game for hours, while others look for quick results). If your child has special needs, there is a variety of other options you might be seeking, including the ability to control the speed at which action occurs on the screen or to direct the software to read words aloud. (For more information about evaluating software for young people with special needs, see Chapter 7, "Special Solutions for Children with Special Needs.")

Ease of Use

"User friendliness" is highly valued in the computing world. But what exactly does it mean? Some people believe that a program should be so intuitive and easy to learn that one should be able to use it without ever looking at a manual. While that may not be a fair expectation when dealing with a complex tool or game, a user-friendly program makes it easy for its target users to get up and running as quickly as possible. Its *interface* (the way in which choices are made, the appearance of the screens, and so on) is easy for a beginner to understand, and the accompanying documentation is well organized so players know where to turn in the manual or on the screen when they need help. Helpful documentation generally includes some quick tips for getting started (often in an introductory chapter or a handy reference card) and more in-depth information that's easy to find when the user is ready for it.

Representing Diversity

Something that is too frequently overlooked when evaluating educational materials is the question of diversity and the type of world portrayed by the product. While this will be a more relevant issue for some programs than others, it's worth looking closely at every package you are considering to see whether it furthers stereotypes about the typical family, represents only a certain ethnic group, portrays only male characters, and so on. If it's a word processor or graphics tool that ships with clip art, are the faces all white, the religious symbols all Christian, the families all made up of a mother, a father, and one or more kids? If it's a simulation or educational game with a narrator or set of human characters, are there girls as well as boys, African- and Asian-Americans as well as Caucasians, kids with glasses and disabilities as well as "nondisabled" individuals?

If your child is a member of one of the groups underrepresented by a particular program, it's easy to see why you should be concerned: It's important for kids to be able to identify with the families and characters portrayed, to realize that they are not alone or "different." But if your child is a member of a majority group, it's equally important for him to be exposed to cultural diversity—in a way that will help him appreciate individual differences.

Putting It All Together

While some books and evaluation sources offer parents and educators elaborate checklists to use when selecting software, our advice is to focus on several broad questions that will help you determine whether a program is worth buying for your family. When trying out a new program, ask yourself:

- Are the graphics and sound, game-playing elements, and/or program features likely to appeal to my child?

- Does this program appear to be effective at teaching content or encouraging the development of skills and attitudes that will help my son or daughter?

- Does it provide helpful, constructive feedback?

- Is it varied and flexible enough to have lasting value in our household?

- Does it offer control features that allow us to tailor it to our child's and family's needs?

- Is it user-friendly and easy to learn?

- Does it provide a fair and balanced view of the world and the people that inhabit it?

If your answer to most or all of these questions is "yes," there's a good chance you've found a winner.

The 5th Wave

By Rich Tennant

"THERE YOU ARE SIR. ONE MACPAINT, A MACWRITE, A MAC-
ACCOUNTANT, TWO MACSLOTS, A MACPHONE AND A MACDRAW.
WOULD YOU LIKE FRIES WITH THAT?"

Where to Buy Software

When shopping for software for your child, there are many places you can look. The three most common sources of commercial software are retail stores, mail-order catalogs, and the software publishers themselves. Which of these sources is best for you will depend on a variety of factors, including your location, how cost-conscious you are, whether you are in a rush, how much you know about your own computer system, and whether you have already decided which programs to buy.

Your Local Software Store

If you live in the vicinity of a city or large town, you are likely to have access to a number of different retail stores that sell software. Some of these will be computer dealers with a few shelves set aside for the leading software titles. Others might be "ma and pa" stores devoted exclusively to software sales or national software chains, such as Electronics Boutique and Software Etc.

Most of the retail stores (also known as dealers) acquire software from distributors who buy it from the publishers at a discounted rate. (Some of the larger chains serve as both distributors and dealers, purchasing programs for resale directly from the publishers.) This means that all of the stores have access to the same extensive pool of titles. Of course, since each store decides which of these titles to stock based on the amount of shelf space available and the type of customers it hopes to serve, there's no guarantee that you will be able to find a title you're looking for at any one store. However, most stores will be happy to order a program for you as long as the program's publisher is one that the store generally deals with (directly or via a distributor).

There are a number of advantages to shopping in software retail stores. Many people simply enjoy browsing, reading the descriptions on the packages, getting a feel for what's available, and occasionally talking to other customers about their experiences with particular programs. If you are lucky, you will find a retail store that is conveniently located and staffed with knowledgeable salespeople who can make recommendations and help you determine whether a program you are considering will run on your family's computer system.

If you are even luckier, you will find a store that also lets you and your children try out software on the store's computers before you make a purchase. In fact, unless you are already familiar with the program you're thinking of buying, we believe it's worth traveling quite a ways and spending a bit more (if necessary) to deal with a retailer that does allow you to preview. Several of the national chains, including Egghead Software, Software Etc., and Walden Software, have computers set up in each of their stores for this purpose. Often they have "demo" disks available for you to try. Some of these demos are self-running presentations that provide an overview of a program's capabilities; others are more interactive, allowing you to explore a program on your own (but without access to certain features of the full-fledged program, such as the ability to save or print).

If there is no demo available for a program that you're interested in, or if you are not satisfied with the amount of information included in a particular demo, you can ask a salesperson to load the actual program into the computer for you to try. Unless the store is overly crowded or the program too big or time-consuming to install, your request is likely to be granted.

Shopping for Bargains: Locally and by Mail

In addition to the retail stores discussed in the preceding section, you may find yourself with access to a new option: the computer "super store." Super stores such as Comp USA and Computer Super Centers International are appearing at sites throughout the country, offering a huge array of hardware and software in a warehouse-like setting. While not the place to shop if you're looking for advice or the chance to preview, super stores do offer tremendous discounts on the products they carry.

Mail-order catalogs are another way to shop if you're looking for serious discounts. Browse through the popular computer magazines you find on the newsstands, and you'll see pages and pages of ads offering mail-order delivery of hardware and software. (See the sidebar "Some Mail-

Order Suppliers" for a listing of some of the better-known mail-order services.) All of the mail-order houses offer 800 numbers and promise quick delivery (although, in our experience, they're much faster at sending out software than they are at mailing catalogs, which frequently take weeks to arrive). Some of the phone operators at these 800 numbers are surprisingly knowledgeable and friendly, so don't be hesitant to ask for

Whether you're shopping for discounts at a super store or by mail, it's important to find out about return policies. If you're buying a program based simply on recommendations (from us, from friends, or whomever), you'll want some guarantee that you can return it if your child hates it or it doesn't run on your computer. Most suppliers will replace faulty disks that you got from them, but policies vary greatly with regard to other types of

Some Mail-Order Suppliers

For MS-DOS computers
MicroWarehouse: (800) 367-7080
PC Connection: (800) 800-5555
PC Zone: (800) 258-8088

For the Macintosh
MacConnection: (800) 334-4444
MacWarehouse: (800) 255-6227
The Mac Zone: (800) 248-0800

Educational programs for the Apple II and other platforms
Quality Computers: (800) 443-6697
Educational Resources: (800) 624-2926 or (708) 888-8300 in Illinois
Preferred Computing: (800) 327-7234
Programs Plus: (800) 832-3201

help, particularly if you're unsure about the hardware you'll need to run a particular program. If you don't find anybody there who can answer your questions to your satisfaction, try another supplier. By shopping around for the most helpful sources, you'll not only be meeting your family's needs, you'll be rewarding those companies that are committed to helping their customers.

returns. If possible, look for a money-back guarantee that lets you return a program within 30 days if, for any reason, you don't like it. Some mail-order houses offer such an option for all their software; many base their policy on the policy of the software publisher who created the program.

Going to the Source

Most software publishers will take direct orders for their own programs over the phone. Many of them also have catalogs that they mail out periodically to people on their mailing list. Ordering directly from the publisher may be the most convenient route to take if you're having trouble locating a particular program. As we explained, most retailers stock only the better-known titles in the most commonly requested formats. If the program you're looking for is slightly older or a "sleeper" (a slow but steady seller that never gets a lot of press), or if you own a computer other than an IBM-compatible or a Macintosh, you're likely to have to place an order—either directly or through a retail store.

Going directly to the publisher may be faster, can save you a trip to the store, and is particularly helpful if you have lots of questions you want answered about the program, but there is a trade-off: It's likely to be more expensive. In order to maintain a good working relationship with their distributors and dealers, publishers are generally committed to selling their own products at the full suggested retail price. Retailers, on the other hand, buy the programs at a significant discount, some of which they pass on to the customer.

Since a few companies do not sell through the standard retail channels, there will be occasions when you have no choice but to go directly to the publisher. In Chapter 9, "The Home/School Connection," we discussed publishers that sell only to schools (or to parents who choose to order school versions of software directly for use at home). In addition, there are one or two publishers that offer home versions of their products but do not go through distributors. Scholastic Software, for example, sells to families through its "software clubs," which are modeled after the successful Scholastic book clubs. If your child's teacher doesn't participate in the club, you can place orders with Scholastic over the phone.

In the directory contained in the appendix, we have included addresses and phone numbers for the publishers of the programs reviewed in Part 4 in case you choose to order directly—or would just like to be added to a company's mailing list. Those companies that do not take direct orders over the phone will generally help you locate a dealer in your area.

The 5th Wave By Rich Tennant

"I'M AFRAID I DON'T UNDERSTAND ALL THE REPORTS OF OUR UPGRADE HAVING A DELAYED RELEASE DATE, UNLESS,...WAIT A MINUTE – HOW MANY PEOPLE HERE DIDN'T KNOW I WAS SPEAKING IN DOG-MONTHS?"

Staying Informed

Once you've had a few initial successes finding appropriate software for your child, it will become much easier to select additional titles for your family's software library. In the world of literature, once your child has fallen in love with a particular book, she'll generally be anxious to move on to other books in the same series, by the same author, or in the same genre. The same is frequently true of software. As time goes by, you and your children will learn which types of programs and which publishers they like best.

But how similar are programs from a single software publisher? If your kid loved MECC's *Super Munchers,* can you assume he'll love *Oregon Trail,* from the same publisher? Not necessarily. Each publisher works with a variety of software developers/authors, some employed full-time by the publisher and others working on a free-lance basis. Their styles can differ considerably as can the approach taken by different groups within the publishing company. (The people who make decisions about the company's arcade games, for example, probably have little to do with those in charge of producing productivity tools.)

Nevertheless, if you've had great success with one or two programs from a certain publisher, you can feel more confident that future titles, while they won't necessarily meet your child's particular needs, will also be well-conceived and designed. Certainly, new titles in a series (Broderbund's *Carmen,* Learning Company's *Super Solvers,* and so on) are worth looking at if your child loved their predecessors.

It's also helpful to pay attention to who actually designed and developed the programs your child likes best. While this information is rarely on the box, the authors' names (or the development group behind the program) generally appear on the screen when you first load a software package. Often this information will lead you nowhere, but occasionally you'll find yourself following a developer from one publisher to another. For example, Leslie Grimm, who earned fame as the designer of a number of programs for The Learning Company, including the *Reader Rabbit* series, is also one of the developers of *The Playroom* and *The Treehouse*, published by Broderbund. Fans of all these programs will no doubt pay careful attention when future titles by Leslie Grimm appear on the market.

To stay informed about what your favorite publishers are up to, it's helpful to fill out the registration form that comes with a program when you buy it. This will put you on the company's mailing list so that you receive information about *upgrades* (revised versions of the program, often available at a discount for those interested in trading in an older version) and future products. If the publisher has a catalog, you will probably receive that as well. (If not, call and request one; even if you plan to order from a mail-order house or a local dealer, it's helpful to see what the company has produced recently.)

Other Evaluation Sources

We hope that you will find the reviews in this book helpful and that you will return to them as your child grows older or is ready to venture into new subject areas. We also expect that you will find a variety of other valuable sources of information about software programs (friends, magazines, your child's teachers, and so on). Over time, you will learn which of these sources you find most reliable and which recommendations work best for your child.

There are numerous computer-related magazines being published today. The majority of them (including *Macworld, PC World, MacUser, PC Week, and BYTE*) are oriented towards business users. However, it's worth skimming the current issues to see what they include. Occasionally, one of these magazines will have a special section on educational software or other programs for children. In addition, they tend to be valuable sources of information about trends in software and hardware—a good place to turn if you're trying to decide about a new printer, locate a good deal on a computer, or find the telephone numbers of some inexpensive mail-order houses.

There are also a few family-oriented publications on the news-stand, most notably *InCider/A+* (which focuses on the Apple II and, more recently, the Macintosh) and *PC Home Journal* (for owners of MS-DOS computers). If you're looking for a source that focuses primarily on educational products for kids, you might want to consider subscribing to one of the school-oriented magazines listed in Chapter 9, "The Home/School Connection"; they're definitely written with teachers and administrators in mind, but the software they review is frequently as useful in the home as it is in school.

We can't predict which of these publications will be most helpful to you, but we do have some suggestions about how to evaluate a magazine for its usefulness. One of the most important things to look at is the tone of the reviews. Do they read like promotional brochures, packed with superlatives, testimonials from users, and quotes from the developers themselves about how wonderful their programs are? Or are they truly evaluative? There's nothing wrong with an enthusiastic review, but even the best programs have their flaws. So be wary if you read one review after another and they have nothing but good things to say; perhaps they weren't written by neutral, objective reviewers.

Even if a magazine's reviews seem to be balanced and fair, you also need to feel comfortable with the philosophy and approach behind those reviews. The best way to see whether a magazine (or a book like this one) is for you is to read some evaluations it has published of programs you already know. Did your child love the programs the magazine's reviewers loved, has she had trouble with the things they predicted would be troublesome, and so on? If so, you've probably found an evaluation source that's worth investing in.

The 5th Wave

"YES THEY ARE, DID YOU HAVE AN APPOINTMENT?"

CHAPTER SEVENTEEN

Public Domain Software

When you think of software for your computer, big-name publishers and high prices probably come to mind. While there are legions of brand-name programs in the marketplace—some of them with hefty price tags—there is also an abundance of nifty programs available at little or no cost. These programs fall into the category of "public domain software," and they have been a mainstay of personal computing since its early days in the 1970s.

Public domain software is usually written and distributed by a single person. The programmer is an enthusiast, sometimes called a *hacker*, who sees a need for a particular program, creates the program, and then makes it available to other computer users. The programs range from simple desk accessories that display the current time on the computer screen to sophisticated word processing and graphics programs. A number of them are games with an educational flavor. Some popular public domain programs are used by tens of thousands of people; others are eventually acquired by software publishers and end up as mainstream software.

We should explain that the phrase "public domain" is a misnomer. Almost none of the programs labeled "public domain" fit the traditional definition of "a work for which patent or copyright protection has expired." No public domain software has been patented, and almost all of it is copyrighted. The developer or owner of the program has simply made it available at little or no cost. This does not give the person who has obtained a copy the right to resell it or incorporate it in a larger work.

There are two forms of public domain software, *freeware* and *shareware.* Freeware (often referred to simply as public domain) is software for which no payment at all is expected. You can copy it freely, distribute it to your friends, and make it available through on-line services or bulletin boards. Shareware is also distributed freely, but the creator of the program expects a small payment. The opening screen of a shareware program usually includes a request for payment if you like the program and indicates where to send your check.

Public domain software is available from four principal sources:

■ Friends and colleagues.

■ On-line services, such as CompuServe and Prodigy, or electronic bulletin boards.

■ Commercial vendors who will send you copies of shareware for a small fee. (This fee does not include payment to the developer of any shareware product you purchase; you are expected to send that payment directly to the author.)

■ User groups or computer swap meets.

See the directory on the next page for a listing of commercial vendors and user groups who can help you acquire public domain software.

As you can see, public domain software enjoys wide distribution. Because of this, it is easy for exchanged software to carry a virus. If you are planning to acquire some public domain software, we urge you to follow the recommendations in Chapter 13, "Keeping Your Computer Alive and Well."

We also suggest that you pay developers for the right to use their shareware. The prices are low, and you receive both documentation and information about future upgrades. Besides, by paying for shareware, you encourage the programmers to keep up the good work.

Some Commercial Sources of Freeware and Shareware Software

Big Red Computer Club, Norfolk, NB, offers programs for the Apple II and IIGS at a charge of $3.50 per disk. (402) 379-4680

EDUCORP, San Diego, CA , distributes freeware and shareware for the Macintosh (as well as selling many CD-ROM titles). Each disk costs $6.99 (plus $4 for handling). (800) 843-9497 or (619) 536-9999

PC-SIG, Sunnyvale, CA, offers software for IBM and IBM-compatible computers. Prices vary and members receive a discount. (The annual membership fee is $20.) (800) 245-6717

SoftShoppe, Ann Arbor, MI, supports both MS-DOS and Macintosh computers. Prices range from $1.98 to $3.98, depending on disk format and the size of your order. (800) 829-2378) or (313) 761-7638

Some User Groups That Distribute Public Domain Software

A local user group is often a good source of information about public domain software. Some groups distribute such titles. Two well-known user groups that make freeware and shareware available to both members and nonmembers are:

Boston Computer Society (BCS), Boston, MA, (617) 252-0600

Berkeley Macintosh Users' Group (BMUG), Berkeley, CA, (415) 549-2684

The 5th Wave

WHILE SEEKING HER PC-BASED RECIPE INDEX, LORRETTA INADVERTENTLY LOADS A CAD/CAM PROGRAM. INSTEAD OF MAKING CHERRIES JUBILEE, SHE BUILDS A SUBOCEANIC DIVING PROBE.

Reading the Box: Or How to Know If a Program Will Run on Your Computer

For the computer novice, the system requirements listed on a software package or in a catalog can be confusing. Perhaps you've just purchased a Macintosh IIsi or inherited an older Macintosh SE. The software you're considering requires "a Macintosh Plus or later; 1Mb for monochrome, 2Mb for color; System 6.0.4 or higher; supports System 7.0." Will it run on your computer? If you own an IBM-compatible computer, you may find yourself wading through an even longer set of system requirements: "512K required (640K for VGA); DOS 2.1 or better; CGA, EGA, Tandy 16-color, or MCGA/VGA required; 5.25-inch disks enclosed; supports AdLib, SoundBlaster."

If this computerese makes perfect sense to you, you can skip this chapter. If not, here's some help. At the back of this book is a worksheet for you to fill out with the information about your system. After you read each section of this chapter, you may want to turn to the worksheet and fill in the corresponding lines. When you're finished, you should be better prepared to shop for software—and have the cheat sheet to prove it.

Two notes before you begin: First, you might want to start by looking at Chapter 11, "Selecting a Computer for Your Family," which includes some hardware-related definitions and explanations that will be helpful to you. Second, *do not worry if you cannot fill out every line on the worksheet!* Some of the categories may be irrelevant to you. Others may be hard for you to find right away in the manual or shipping materials. ("Where is that manual anyway?" you might be asking if you own an older computer.) Basically, fill in what you can with our assistance and then add more information as you find it.

Got a pencil? Here goes....

Your Model and Its Operating System

The most important thing you need to know is the brand and model number of your computer and the basic operating system on which it runs. Chances are, if you've recently bought a new computer, it is either a Macintosh or a machine that uses Microsoft's Disk Operating System, known as *MS-DOS*. (The version of MS-DOS that IBM sells for its own computers is actually known as PC-DOS, but it is fully compatible with other versions of MS-DOS.)

Once you know your basic platform (for example, MS-DOS, Macintosh, Apple II, or Amiga), you've narrowed down your software-shopping choices considerably. Almost all software stores and catalogs separate their titles by operating system. That means there's no need

for you to linger in the IBM and compatibles section if you own a Macintosh (or vice versa). (The box in your hand may read "requires 3.5-inch disk drive," but even though your Mac is equipped with that drive, the MS-DOS software won't work on it.)

The version number of your operating system is also important when you're shopping for software. If you can find the floppy disks containing the operating system you're currently using, the version number will probably be clearly labeled on the outside of the disks. If not, owners of MS-DOS computers can get this information by watching the messages that appear on the screen when they first "boot" (turn on) the computer. Macintosh users can find the Macintosh System number by selecting "About the Finder" or "About this Macintosh" from the Apple menu when they are on the "desktop" (the main menu area that appears each time you turn on your Mac or quit a program).

The higher the operating system number, the more recent the version, and the more features you can expect. If the software package indicates that you need a certain version of DOS or a certain Macintosh System number and the version you have is too low, you'll need to visit your dealer for an upgrade before you can use that software. The dealer may provide the upgrade for free or, if the new system has been greatly enhanced, may charge a fee. (For example, an upgrade kit for Macintosh owners interested in moving from a version of System 6 to System 7 costs approximately $100.) Other common sources of upgrades—almost always for free—are user groups (see Chapter 2, "Getting Up to Speed Yourself") and on-line services such as CompuServe (see Chapter 10, "Getting into On-Line Services"). In some cases, however, it may be necessary to add extra memory or upgrade your hardware in some other way to allow it to run the new operating system.

Sometimes, in addition to the basic operating system software that comes with the computer, programs are designed to run with the help of an extra software tool. For example, you may come across *HyperCard* programs (known as "stacks") that will only run if the correct version of *HyperCard* has been installed on the hard disk of your Macintosh, or *Windows*-based software that requires Microsoft's *Windows* operating environment (in addition to MS-DOS) in order to run. If you're planning to purchase such software, it's important to note which version of *HyperCard*, *Windows*, or other relevant program you own, and to be prepared to

upgrade as software comes along that requires newer versions of these programs.

Microprocessors and Speed

As we discussed in Chapter 11, "Selecting a Computer for Your Family," each computer model is built around a specific microprocessor, operating at a certain speed (measured in megahertz or MHz). Your computer's manual or shipping materials should indicate which microprocessor you've purchased and at what speed it operates. MS-DOS computers almost always use the Intel chips (8088, 8086, or—more recently—80286, 80386, and 80486); Macintosh computers use the Motorola 68000 series (68000, 68020, 68030, and so on).

Until recently most MS-DOS packages have been labeled in terms of the IBM models required to run the software. For example, a package might read, "Requires an IBM PC XT, AT or compatible," meaning that the software will run on an MS-DOS computer with an 8086 or 8088 microprocessor (the chips associated with the IBM PC XT) or an 80286 (the chip introduced with IBM's PC AT). With the newer, faster chips, such as the 80386 microprocessor, the industry has switched over to using the microprocessor number rather than an IBM model. If you see a label that reads, "Runs on XT, AT, 386 and 486 machines," you know that this product will work with any well-known Intel microprocessor from the old 8088 up to the high-end 80486. Since the same microprocessor can often operate at a wide range of clock speeds, many recent programs that require speed for features like computerized speech or animation will include a message on the box such as "8MHz or faster required" or "10MHz recommended."

Memory—RAM and Storage

You'll definitely need to know how much random-access memory (RAM) your computer has. Keep in mind that RAM is not the same as hard disk capacity or storage space, although all three are measured in kilobytes (K) or megabytes (M). If you have a fairly recent MS-DOS computer, it is likely to have at least 512K of RAM—probably 640K or more. Recent Macintosh models have shipped with two or more megabytes of RAM.

If you don't know how much memory your system is equipped with, it should be pretty easy to find out. Most MS-DOS computers list the amount of RAM on the screen when you first turn on the computer. If you miss the information there, type "CHKDSK" (for "check disk") at the DOS prompt (>) and a screen will appear that includes information about the total amount of RAM in your system. Find the line that refers to "total bytes free" and divide by 1,000 to figure out approximately how many *kilobytes* are free. For example, if there are 654,336 bytes free, that's approximately 654K, indicating that your computer has 640K of RAM. (The amount of RAM in the system will no doubt be a multiple of 64: 128K, 256K, 512K, 640K, 1024K—referred to as one megabyte since it's approximately 1000K—and so on.) On the Macintosh, "About the Finder" or "About this Macintosh" (mentioned earlier in this chapter) will tell you how much memory (how many kilobytes of RAM) there is in your system.

If you purchased a hard disk with your computer, you'll need to know how much capacity it has for storing data. It might offer 10M, 20M, 30M, 40M, or more. If you need to double-check on the size of your hard disk, use the CHKDSK command on an MS-DOS computer, or look at the top of the window that appears when you double-click the hard disk icon on a Macintosh (as long as the window is set to "view by" icon or small icon).

Because there are so many floppy disk options for computers these days, we've provided a checklist for you to indicate which types of disk drives you have, in what quantities. Keep in mind that if you have a high-density drive (or the double-sided instead of single-sided Mac drive), it will frequently read disks created in the older lower-capacity formats but not vice versa. If a software package doesn't say anything about high-density disks (very few entry-level packages do), you can assume that low-density disk drives are fine. Then (if you have an MS-DOS computer), you'll just have to pay attention to whether the package includes 5.25-inch disks, 3.5-inch disks, or both formats.

Video Display—Cards and Monitors

In the MS-DOS world, it's important to know what graphics standard your system supports. (See Chapter 11, "Selecting a Computer for Your Family," for an explanation of graphics standards.) It's possible that a video display card came already installed in your computer, or you may have had to purchase it separately. In either case, your dealer should have let you know which graphics standard you were buying into. On older machines, it might have been a Monochrome Display Adapter (no graphics), a Hercules (monochrome graphics adapter), a Color Graphics Adapter (CGA), an Enhanced Graphics Adapter (EGA), or the MCGA standard (built into the original PS/2 Models 25 and 30). With newer purchases, you're more likely to have a Video Graphics Array (VGA) or something even higher (SVGA or XGA). For higher end Macintosh computers, you might also be called on to buy a graphics adapter. If so, it will probably be a 4-bit or an 8-bit card.

The same basic terminology is frequently used to describe monitors. You may have an EGA monitor, a VGA monitor, a multisync monitor (which supports many different standards), and so on.

Printer

Most software packages support a wide range of printers—so many, in fact, that printers are rarely mentioned on software packages or ordering forms. However, when you get down to the detailed information in a program's manual, you may find a list of the actual printers that the program supports or some recommendations about the general type of printer (dot-matrix, laser, etc.) that will work best with the software you have selected.

If you purchase a printer made by a manufacturer that is less well known, you should make a note not only of the model name and number but also of compatibility with better-known brands, such as Epson, IBM, Apple, or Hewlett-Packard. (If your printer does offer such compatibility—the ability to substitute this printer for a better-known model without affecting the way software runs—the documentation that shipped with the printer should say so.) Then, if your printer isn't on a menu of choices presented to you by the program, you can select an equivalent model that *is* on the list.

Sound Cards

If you purchased a board to enhance the sound output on your MS-DOS computer, it's important to remember which board you purchased since the many cards on the market are not compatible. A software package or ordering form will generally indicate which sound boards—if any—the product supports. Although sound output is built into the Macintosh, you may have a different sort of sound add-on to record on this line of the worksheet: If you've purchased a device such as Farallon's MacRecorder to give you the sorts of sound input capabilities that are built into some of the newer Macs, you'll want to add that information to the sheet.

Other Options

Whenever you purchase an optional mouse for your MS-DOS computer, a CD-ROM drive, a scanner, or some other add-on to your system, make a note of the brand, the model, and (when applicable) the type.

IV

Software Reviews

A Word About Program Versions

In describing software packages in this section of the book, we have included only the most general information about the hardware required to run the programs. As you read, you will learn whether a program has been released in MS-DOS, Macintosh, Apple II, or various other formats. However, information on exact memory requirements, disk formats, operating system version needed, and so on would not only have taken up a tremendous amount of space (some programs are available in several different configurations for each computer they support), it would probably be out of date in a matter of months. For example, while some of the 1989 and 1990 titles were not yet available in color format for the Macintosh when we finished the book, color versions were generally in the works.

In general, you will find some indication in our comments that a product has "unusual" requirements.

Here's what appears to be "usual" these days in the world of consumer-oriented educational software: Most of the MS-DOS programs we looked at will still run with a range of graphics cards/monitors, including EGA, VGA, and (in some but not all cases) the lower resolution CGA. (See Chapter 11, "Selecting a Computer for Your Family," for definitions of these and other hardware-related terms.) Usually, they have two or even three separate sets of graphics screens so that users with the higher resolution monitors see more attractive output. A few of the newest titles require VGA, although they're still not the majority.

Many of the MS-DOS programs support add-on sound cards—almost always the Sound Blaster and AdLib cards, plus assorted others. We've commented when we think such a card is important to have; otherwise, you can assume that it will enhance the program but not make a significant difference to its value. If you have

640K of memory, almost all of the programs reviewed here will run on your MS-DOS computer. Most of the products contain both 3.5- and 5.25-inch disks. And only a few require hard disks, although most work better with one.

In the Macintosh world, most of the products we reviewed have (or soon will have) both black-and-white and color graphics, and will run under System 7 but do not require it. Although a number of the older titles (with copyright dates before 1990) will run on a Mac Plus or better with 512K, most of the newer programs require one megabyte of memory for black-and-white and two megabytes for color. And a number of them are beginning to require hard disks.

If you read here about a program that looks interesting but is not yet available for the computer you own, don't rule it out. If it's relatively new and only available on one platform, there's a good chance that other versions are planned but haven't been released yet. (For example, it's common these days for educational software developers to publish an MS-DOS version and then follow up with one for the Macintosh later.)

When several different versions of a single title were available, we tried to spend time with both the MS-DOS and Macintosh versions before writing the reviews. Keep in mind that features do vary from version to version. So, for example, if you have an Apple II or Commodore 64 computer, the program that runs on your computer might not match our product description exactly.

Publishing Programs for Kids

I f you're in search of one or two titles to start a family software library, we recommend that you begin by looking at the programs described in this chapter. They are designed to help kids (and the adults they live with) create a variety of interesting printouts and publications.

If this were a chapter on printing and publishing tools for adults, we might have divided it into the categories traditionally used to describe such programs: tools for creating text-based documents would be classified as *word processors*; those for handling page layout (placing text in columns, adding headlines, graphics, borders, etc.) as *desktop publishers*; and programs for creating artwork as *graphics tools*. However, the lines between the different types of programs—which are becoming fuzzier even in the adult world—are very hard to draw when looking at publishing programs for kids.

Most of the titles reviewed here are easy-to-use packages that support both graphics (in the form of ready-to-use clip art) and text and allow users to create such printouts as posters, picture books, calendars, and greeting cards. A few are tools that come closer to meeting the traditional definition of a word processor or paint program.

In looking for the best titles to include in this chapter, we found one disappointing hole in the market. There is a surprising lack of simple word processors for very young kids, complete with large text, graphic images, and the capability to read aloud whatever a child types. There are some older tools of this sort, in school-oriented Apple II and MS-DOS versions, available from IBM, Sunburst (both described in Chapter 9, "The Home/School Connection") and Scholastic (listed in the appendix). And Macintosh users can get a scaled-down talking word processor (also a few years old) as part of Great Wave's *KidsTime* package (reviewed in Chapter 20, "Software for Preschoolers"). But at the time this book went to press, little was available in the retail stores for MS-DOS computers. Fortunately, if Davidson's new *KidWorks* package (see Chapter 27, "Sneak Peeks") does all it promises to do, this gap might soon be filled.

If you're a parent of a teenager or a sophisticated pre-teen, you might be wondering about adult word processors, desktop publishing tools, and graphics packages that would work well for your kid. There are several tools designed for adults that are perfectly appropriate for kids as young as 10 years of age—as long as you're around to get them started and help occasionally when they get stuck. In deciding which program of this sort to buy, you should pay attention to which tools your child's school is using, or planning to use in the grades he will soon enter, or you might choose the tool that you yourself already use for your own work. With your expert help, there's a good chance your kid will catch on quickly.

If neither of these methods leads you anywhere, there are a few adult-oriented programs we think are worth

considering for the whole family. For word processing, we recommend investing in a complete integrated package that offers several extras—a spreadsheet, a database, and telecommunications—in addition to basic word processing capabilities. Two such packages that are very popular with beginning users are *Microsoft Works* (available in MS-DOS, Windows and Macintosh formats) and *PFS: First Choice*, from Spinnaker (in MS-DOS format).

Desktop publishing tends to be quite complicated for new users, but we've found that most people do quite well with the *Publish It!* series from Timeworks, especially with *Publish It! Easy* for the Macintosh and *Publish It! Light* for MS-DOS computers. Finally, most "paint" programs (with simple tools for creating pictures on the screen) are quite easy for young people to get going with. A few popular paint programs you might want to check out are *MacPaint* (for the Macintosh) from Claris, *Easy Color Paint* (also for the Mac) from Creative Software, and *DeluxePaint* (for MS-DOS computers) from Electronic Arts.

 For other programs related to publishing, see also KidsTime *(Chapter 20)*, Mickey's Crossword Puzzle Maker *(Chapter 22), and* KidWorks *(Chapter 27)*.

BannerMania (1989)

Publisher: Broderbund Software   **Ages:** 8 and up

MS-DOS, Macintosh, Apple II

MS-DOS
$34.95

Apple II
$34.95

Mac
$59.95

This program lets you and your child create attractive-looking banners plus a number of other printouts. *BannerMania* is very easy to learn and to use, offering a set of predesigned banners plus simple editing tools to design your own. You can create both horizontal and vertical banners with one or two lines of up to 63 characters, a choice of 19 fonts and 20 special effects (shadows, 3-D lettering, etc.), any of 27 shapes, and 68 different colors. You can adjust the scale and the layout of your banner, enlarging it to a variety of different sizes or reducing it to use the printouts as bumper stickers, small signs, or labels. It's even possible to print a design in reverse so that it can be transferred to a T-shirt or used as a window decal.

As you work, you can preview what your banner will look like. Finally, *BannerMania* has the capability to "transmogrify" or automatically modify your design in hundreds of ways. Select this option before printing, and the program will generate numerous versions of the banner—some with unusual colors or shadowing effects, others stretched or reshaped in interesting ways, still others with added graphic elements, such as balloons. When you see a version you like, you can choose it and send it off to your printer.

Comments

This is a valuable program to own if you and your kids want to create banners to celebrate birthdays,

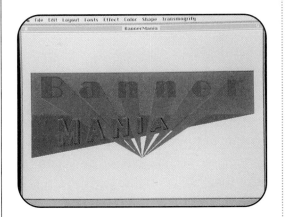

BannerMania, from Broderbund Software

welcome people home, or cheer on the team. Your children will undoubtedly come up with plenty of uses for the scaled-down options as well. In addition to creating eye-pleasing results, *BannerMania* is lots of fun to use. We've seen kids spend hours experimenting with options on the screen and watching the computer transmogrify their results. In the process, the young designers are involved in estimating (in order to space and size words correctly) and planning.

Unlike some older banner-making programs, this one creates smooth-looking letters in a variety of sizes. Color banners take quite a while to print if you use a color dot-matrix printer—but you can't blame the software for that. If you're in need of a banner, set aside a few minutes to design a beautiful one with *BannerMania*'s help and then an hour or more to print it out.

The Children's Writing and Publishing Center (1989) Ages: 7 to 14

The Writing Center (1991) Ages: 7 and up

Publisher: The Learning Company

CWPC: **MS-DOS and Apple II;** *Writing Center:* **Macintosh**

MS-DOS $69.95

Apple II $59.95

Mac $89.95

The Children's Writing and Publishing Center is an introductory word processor with a number of desktop publishing features. Using a set of steps that are easy for even young kids

to learn, the program allows users to create and illustrate documents such as reports, stories, letters, newsletters, and fliers. It's possible to choose between a single-column report format and a two-column newsletter, and to decide whether or not to include a heading.

This program features a simple interface with pull-down menus, on-screen prompts, and help menus. Its tools include basic word processing capabilities (typing, editing, and cutting and pasting, a choice of type styles and sizes, etc.), a 150-picture graphics library, and the capability to import clip art from other libraries. As graphics are inserted, the text automatically wraps to fit around them. It's possible to print in color if a color printer is available.

In converting *The Children's Writing and Publishing Center* to the Macintosh, The Learning Company added many new features— including a spell checker, additional fonts, the capability to resize, crop, rotate and flip graphics, plus an increased number of formatting choices—and renamed the program to reflect the changes. *The Writing Center* features over 200 color and black-and-white pictures of higher quality than those offered by the older versions, supports all of the standard Macintosh fonts and sizes, and will even print text in color.

Like its predecessor, *The Writing Center* is extremely easy to use. For the beginner, predesigned layouts are

still available, but each can be modified in a variety of ways. There is also a page-preview mode, which allows you to view the whole document before printing. A thesaurus may be purchased from The Learning Company and added to the program.

Comments

These may be the simplest tools around for creating short newsletters, stories, and other publications involving one or more columns, graphics, and a major headline. Young kids love both programs and the results they can create with them, as do many parents who are new to computers. It's possible to get up and running in a few minutes and to complete a two- or three-page document, including graphics from the library, in less than an hour.

The Children's Writing and Publishing Center, from The Learning Company

Older kids will eventually outgrow *The Children's Writing and Publishing Center* because it limits the length of the documents that can be created, does not allow kids to combine different word processing files (making it difficult, for example, to take two or more stories written at different times and combine them into a "literary magazine"), offers neither a spell checker nor a thesaurus, and does not have very sophisticated-looking fonts.

Mac owners will appreciate the improved features in *The Writing Center*, although by billing this program as a publishing tool for the whole family, The Learning Company might be setting up some users for disappointment. Teenagers and adults looking for more choices in terms of layout, graphics editing features, or advanced import capabilities will undoubtedly want to move on to a real desktop publishing package.

For younger kids and computer novices, however, there are few programs that can beat these two. The printouts MS-DOS and Apple II

owners can create with *The Children's Writing and Publishing Center* may not be as sophisticated-looking as those created with a more adult-oriented package, but they're attractive and more than adequate for most kids of elementary-school age. With *The Writing Center*, the results will be even more striking—without taking much more time to create. School projects, newsletters, and fliers have rarely looked so good or been so easy to make.

The Writing Center, from The Learning Company

Electric Crayon Deluxe Series (1989, 1991)

Publisher: Merit Software   **Ages:** 3 and up

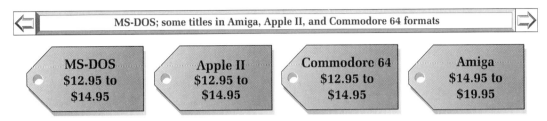

MS-DOS; some titles in Amiga, Apple II, and Commodore 64 formats

MS-DOS
$12.95 to
$14.95

Apple II
$12.95 to
$14.95

Commodore 64
$12.95 to
$14.95

Amiga
$14.95 to
$19.95

Coloring pictures is easy and fun when you have an electronic crayon. Boot up any of the programs in this series (*At the Zoo, All Dogs Go to Heaven, Teenage Mutant Ninja Turtles, Inspector Gadget: Safety Patrol,* and *Super Mario Brothers: When I Grow Up*) and the bold outlines of a coloring book will appear on the screen. Point to the area to color and press the mouse button or the Enter key. The area is immediately filled in with the color of your choice. If you don't like the way that color works, simply select another one and try again.

Anyone three years old and up can enjoy this computerized version of the classic coloring book. The pointer, shaped like a crayon, controls everything, including selecting colors and new pictures. The menu across the top of the screen contains buttons that you use to move to another picture, clean the colors off the screen, or undo the last color choice. There's also a button that allows you to pull up a page of text related to each picture.

There are several choices when it comes time to print. You can add a personalized message to any of the images and print them out as stand-ard pictures, banners, posters, or calendars. The MS-DOS programs print in black and white, while the Apple II and Amiga versions support color printing.

Comments

If you hate the idea of coloring books, you may not appreciate this electronic version. Like any coloring book, it severely limits a child's creative possibilities. However, this approach to coloring does have its appeal: it helps a newcomer learn how to use a mouse (in the DOS version the mouse is optional, but we strongly recommend it) and develop hand-eye coordination, teaches very young children about cause and effect, and is lots of fun. We've seen little kids (and even some older brothers and sisters) play with these programs for hours, experimenting with different images and colors, inserting messages with adult assistance, and printing out pictures for everyone in the family.

Some of the titles also have messages to convey. For example, *Inspector Gadget*'s 30 pictures all relate to the topic of safety and are accompanied by written advice, available at the touch of a button. Unfortunately, none of the text is read aloud, making it necessary for an adult or older sibling to help nonreaders.

Once the program has been started and the few basics demonstrated, most young children will be able to use the software to create multicolored images on the screen. Selecting the various printer options before printing an image may require some help. Older children (7 to 10) may enjoy the programs initially but will lose interest before long.

Kid Pix (1991)

Publisher: Broderbund Software   **Ages:** 3 to 12

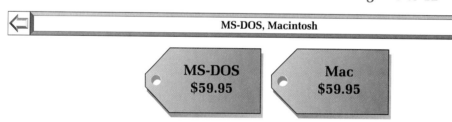

MS-DOS, Macintosh

MS-DOS
$59.95

Mac
$59.95

Hand a kid a crayon and he'll draw (with or without paper). Put even the youngest child in front of *Kid Pix* and he'll draw, listen and laugh, then draw some more. This graphics package is designed for even the youngest user. It offers the normal array of "painting" tools—including lines, rectangles, ovals, erasers, pens, and text—plus many unusual offerings.

The rubber-stamp icon allows children to choose from a menu of dozens of small pictures and stamp them on the screen again and again. With the "wacky paintbrush," you can paint in 32 different patterns. The electric mixer changes the drawing in a variety of fun and silly ways. Even the erasers are fun: watch your picture disappear into the black hole or explode like a firecracker! If you choose the "?" eraser, you can erase your picture and discover another picture underneath.

Your family will also love listening to the sounds that accompany each action. If you make a mistake, you can undo it while listening to a little voice saying "uh oh!" or "oops!" You'll hear a "cur-chunk" each time you use the rubber stamp and the "glug-glug" of paint being poured each time you use the paint-can icon to fill a shape with color. When you decide to move part of an image from here to there, select the moving van and listen as it starts its engine, races along as you move the pointer, and screeches to a halt when you finish.

Using text is easy, too. Point to the letter tool on the screen, and it pops up the letters of the alphabet. No more hunt and peck at the keyboard. The letters are pronounced (in a choice of Spanish or English) as you click on them. On Macintosh computers that support sound input, you can even add your own spoken commentary to each picture you create.

Comments

Although *Kid Pix* is designed for users between the ages of 3 and 12, many kids will find themselves fighting with

their parents for a chance to use it. On the other end of the spectrum, this program is a favorite with some two-year-olds we know. In fact, we've rarely seen a user of any age who wasn't captivated at first by the program's sounds and many fun visual options.

If your child is quite young, you'll probably want to use the "Little Kids" option and hide the menu bar so that your child doesn't accidentally exit the program or alter files. Once the few basics of tool selection are demonstrated, any kid old enough to control the mouse can use the program. While many preschoolers will enjoy choosing letters on the menu and hearing them said aloud, some may find using the mouse to select and place several letters together in order to form words more difficult than hunting and pecking at

Kid Pix, from Broderbund Software

the keyboard. There is an option that allows you to enter text directly from the keyboard and to control its font and color as you work, although, unfortunately, your child no longer hears the letters spoken aloud.

Although everybody seems to agree that *Kid Pix* is great fun to use, not everyone agrees on how valuable a tool it is for creating printouts. Some 11- and 12-year-olds who tested it were frustrated that it didn't have

many of the more sophisticated editing tools (the ability to zoom in and make small changes, for example) offered by standard paint programs. On the other hand, we've seen some pretty amazing printouts created by young kids and adult artists. Whatever the end-results, there's little doubt that your family's first pictures will look like scribbles—the result of trying out each and every tool and listening to all the sounds.

The New Print Shop (1989)

Publisher: Broderbund Software   **Ages:** 5 and up

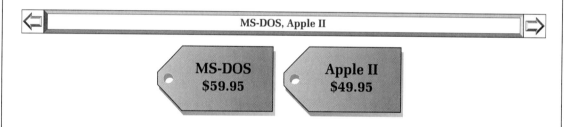

MS-DOS, Apple II

MS-DOS
$59.95

Apple II
$49.95

This classic program allows the entire family to create signs, banners, greeting cards, calendars, letterheads, and certificates. An easy-to-follow split screen allows you to see your menu options and preview the screen you're creating at the same time. You can make selections and choices by using either the mouse or the arrow keys.

The New Print Shop offers over 100 clip-art graphics and the capability to import others. Multiple graphics can be placed anywhere on a page and then moved, resized, flipped, or centered. Ten print fonts can be further modified by using one of the five style options. Multiple fonts and sizes can also be used on a single page.

There are many other options as well. A name file can be created ahead of time, allowing you to print a batch of certificates, each with a different name. Calendars can be made for daily, weekly, monthly, or yearly use. Posters and signs can be enlarged up to nine feet by six-and-a-half feet! If a color printer is available, some of the graphics can be printed in color. The program also contains a set of premade signs, banners, and certificates that you can modify and print out.

Comments

The original *Print Shop*, first published in 1984, was a runaway success in schools and homes alike. *The New Print Shop* has built on the previous version's strengths, offering even more options and ease of use. This may be one of your family's favorite programs, spurring you to generate attractive printouts for practically every occasion. Eventually, you may want to buy an extra graphics library to complement the clip art provided with *The New Print Shop*.

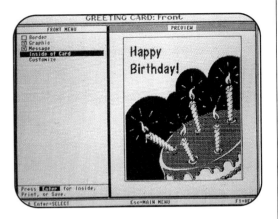

The New Print Shop, from Broderbund Software

(Broderbund sells a school and business library, a party collection, and a sampler library with a little bit of everything.)

The only frustrating part of the program is the text editing: to change what you've written, you need to backspace, erase, and then retype. The large-scale results created with *The New Print Shop* aren't as smooth-looking as those printed with *BannerMania* or *SuperPrint*, but overall it's one of the most flexible tools around.

SuperPrint II (1989)
SuperPrint for the Macintosh (1991)

Publisher: Scholastic Software   **Ages:** 5 and up

SuperPrint II: MS-DOS and Apple II; *SuperPrint for the...:* Macintosh

**MS-DOS
$39.95**

**Apple II
$39.95**

**Mac
$89.95**

SuperPrint II is another graphics program that allows kids to create posters, signs, calendars, reports, banners, and more. It is best known for its ability to create giant posters, although it can also be used to create regular-sized personalized stationery and greeting cards. *SuperPrint II* offers over 200 graphics that you can mix or match in any manner that you choose. For example, you can start with a large picture of a witch and add spiders, pumpkins, and bats to create a Halloween printout. It has options that allow you to erase, flip, or invert your clip art, and a painting tool you can use to create your own masterpieces. Also available at additional cost are clip-art libraries that include such things as maps, famous places, and holiday art.

And of course, you can also incorporate text in your designs. *SuperPrint II* is a great program for producing "big books" using your preschooler's own words. If a color printer is available, you can use this program to print your creations in color, although, as with most color printing, this is a very slow process.

Scholastic's new *SuperPrint for the Macintosh* takes the basic features of *SuperPrint II* and expands upon them. The Mac program offers several types of printouts (poster, banner, calendar, and card) plus many variations that allow you to print any number of newsletters, Super Posters, book reports, Big Books, greeting cards, extra-long banners, invitations, and more. The clip art is more upbeat than in the previous versions, and there are additional choices. There is also a variety of new tools, including a more sophisticated painting program, a "fun tool" that allows you to stamp designs around the screen, and editing tools that help you cut, copy, move, or resize different parts of your drawing. Text options include 15 different fonts, several different type styles, and the capacity to scale each letter down to as small as 8 points or up to a gigantic 720 points.

Comments

SuperPrint was one of the first programs to allow users to create giant posters up to six feet tall. Now, a number of other programs have this option, so you'll need to compare other program features to decide which tool is best for you. Overall, we find *The New Print Shop* more user-friendly and flexible than *SuperPrint II* and appreciate *Print Shop*'s ability to preview an entire image before printing. (With *SuperPrint II*, you need to use arrow keys to move from screen to screen when previewing a poster-size printout on the screen.) However, *SuperPrint* does have a few advantages. In particular, it is more flexible in its ability to move text and multiple clip-art graphics around on the page.

For Macintosh owners, the story is different. Assuming you're not deterred by its higher price tag,

SuperPrint for the Macintosh might be your best bet for this sort of printing. In addition to its flexibility and attractive results, we particularly appreciate its varied clip art.

For both programs, the developers have done an excellent job of providing playful, believable images (people look natural, not as if they posed for the drawings, and there are plenty of options) and of representing ethnic, cultural, and physical differences (there are children in wheelchairs, with glasses, and so on, in addition to a multi-ethnic cast of characters).

SuperPrint for the Macintosh, from Scholastic Software

CHAPTER TWENTY

Software for Preschoolers

"Are there many good programs for young children?" parents often ask. No, we haven't found *many*, but the good ones we know of are real gems. In evaluating early childhood software, we used the guidelines outlined in Chapter 6 to find programs that were in many ways "developmentally appropriate." While no program we know of meets all the criteria established as ideal by early childhood educators, each of the titles reviewed here does quite well in a number of areas.

In particular, they all are playful and positive in their approach, offer appealing graphics, and have age-appropriate expectations. While several of the programs focus on traditional skills (letters, numbers, etc.), and some even offer problems with "correct" answers to be found, none of them tell children they are "wrong." Instead, the computer provides helpful guidance or simply allows kids to explore until the results on the screen make it clear that they've found the right answer.

There are many software packages on the market labeled as appropriate for "ages 3–7." The ones that we considered for inclusion in this chapter focus on the younger end of that age range, stressing "readiness" rather than reading, arithmetic, and other primary-grade skills. They are all designed to be used effectively by nonreaders (sometimes with, sometimes without parental help).

 For other programs of interest to parents of preschoolers, see also Electric Crayon Deluxe *and* Kid Pix *(Chapter 19);* Reader Rabbit *and* ReadingMaze *(Chapter 22); and* Edmark's early childhood series, KidWorks, *and* Living Books *(Chapter 27).*

Dinosaur Discovery Kit (1989)
Puzzle Story Book (1989)

Publisher: First Byte   **Ages:** 3 to 8

 Versions: MS-DOS, Macintosh, Amiga

$39.95 each

These two programs use charming and colorful graphics and computerized speech to help young children develop prereading skills. In *Dinosaur Discovery Kit*, Zug the Megasaur introduces your child to three activities. In one game, the user fills in the blanks in an unfinished story by choosing graphic icons. With each choice, the picture and sentence on the screen change to reflect the child's input. When the story is complete, Zug reads it aloud. In the coloring book, children choose colors and use them to fill in different parts of a prehistoric scene. The computer names each color and part as the child works and presents a fact about the dinosaur in the picture once it's all colored in. The final activity is a Concentration-style game that requires the child to match identical pictures.

In *Puzzle Story Book*, children select a picture from the program's library and then personalize this scene by picking a friend, a moving object, and a building from a menu of choices. They then have the option to change this scene into a jigsaw-type puzzle or to write a short story to accompany it. The child decides whether the puzzle should be "easy" or "hard" and then reassembles the picture by responding to prompts (both oral and visual) given by the program. If your child chooses to write a story to accompany the picture, your help might be needed at the keyboard. Then Zug will read the story aloud.

Comments

Computerized speech is essential to these programs. It allows younger children to work fairly independently on the activities and reinforces early reading skills. If you have an MS-DOS computer, you'll want to make sure that the programs will actually speak on your machine. Although they promise to work without extra hardware, this is only true if you have a fast enough microprocessor (at least 8 MHz) and a loud enough speaker (or if you have a Tandy computer with built-in sound). With older MS-DOS machines, you might have to purchase a special speech card to take advantage of what the programs offer.

The speech used here is "synthesized," meaning that the computer sounds out each word, allowing it to read back any word entered from the keyboard. Compared to the "digitized" speech (prerecorded words played back through the computer) that you hear on some programs these days, Zug's speech will sound somewhat robotic. However, most children don't seem to mind, especially when Zug says their names (entered by you at the beginning of the program) or reads

back the stories they've created themselves.

The activities don't leave as much room for creativity and free play as they might (there are a limited number of choices within each game, leading to rather uniform results), and your child might be disappointed if he tries to print out the pictures (the results are in black and white and reduced in size). However, children play an active role in the activities, have plenty of opportunities to experience success, and generally love playing with Zug and his friends.

Dinosaur Discovery Kit, from First Byte

KidsTime (1986, 1987, 1988)

Publisher: Great Wave Software   **Ages:** 3 to 8

Macintosh (Apple IIGS and MS-DOS versions including *some* of the activities are also available)

MS-DOS
$34.95

Mac
$49.95

Apple IIGS
$34.95

While adults frequently want the computer to be a learning tool for their children, your kid's goal, no doubt, is to have fun. With *KidsTime* children play freely—clicking here and there, watching and listening for the computer's response as they search for letters, connect dots, match objects, write stories, and play music.

The program features five activities, each with several levels of difficulty. In *ABKey*, a letter or picture appears on the screen. When the child presses the appropriate letter, it is spoken aloud. In *Dot-to-Dot*, a completed picture appears when players succeed in connecting all the dots on the screen in the correct order. (Each dot in this traditional connect-the-dots game can be marked with an upper- or lowercase letter so your child can work on the alphabet or with a number so he can practice counting.) In addition to the dot puzzles provided by the program, you can create your own by importing simple pictures and using the *KidsTime* editor to add dots.

Children play a variety of matching games by moving objects on the screen in *Match-It* (Macintosh version only). *Story Writer* (Macintosh version only) is an introductory word processor that allows you or your child to enter stories, complete with little pictures (rebus style), and hear the stories read aloud by the computer. And *KidsNotes* turns your computer into a musical instrument. Kids play music by pressing keys on the keyboard or clicking on piano keys displayed on the screen. The songs they create in this manner can be played back or edited in a variety of ways.

Comments

KidsTime is appropriate for children of many different ages, at many levels of development. If you're the parent of a two- or three-year-old, you can alter the *ABKey* game so that your child can press any letter and hear it read aloud, or turn off the recording feature in *KidsNotes* so children can press and listen to their hearts' content. Almost all of the activities are well suited for older preschoolers, but at their harder levels, many will challenge a six- or seven-year-old as well.

The simple talking word processor will delight most kids—whether the story is typed in by you for your little one or entered by a young reader in the family. Older kids will also enjoy composing music and creating their own dot-to-dot puzzles.

The program's one drawback is that its interface feels a little dated. For example, to go from one game to another, you select Quit from the File menu and are returned to the desktop—a less user-friendly approach than the large graphic menus used by many kids' programs today. Other choices that you might want your child to handle independently (for example, deciding whether to play *ABKey* in its exploratory or quiz mode) are buried in pull-down menus that little ones will not understand how to use. Nevertheless, owners of Macintosh computers will find plenty to love about this program. MS-DOS and Apple IIGS users will miss out on one of the best parts of the program—the *Story Writer*—but still may enjoy three of these five entertaining activities.

McGee Series

McGee (1989)   Katie's Farm (1990)
McGee at the Fun Fair (1991)

Publisher: Lawrence Productions, distributed by Broderbund   **Ages:** Ages 2 to 6

 MS-DOS, Macintosh, Apple IIGS, Amiga

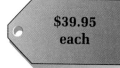
$39.95 each

With this "no words" software, even a two-year-old can experience success at the computer. Each story allows your child to explore a rich environment accompanied by little McGee, a fun-loving and slightly mischievous preschooler.

If you've ever opened your eyes early in the morning to find yourself staring straight into the face of your eager little son or daughter, the opening screen of *McGee* will feel like déjà vu. McGee wanders around the house investigating everything. He uses the telephone to call for a weather report, feeds the dog, and goes outside in the yard to swing. Your child chooses what McGee should do next by using a simple menu consisting of four large pictures at the bottom of the screen. Want to see McGee ride on his hobby horse? Go into Mom's room? Head downstairs to play? Simply select the appropriate picture. The program is set up so that a child using a mouse never strays from the menu; one of the menu choices is always lit.

In *Katie's Farm*, McGee visits his cousin Katie in the country. There are all sorts of new places to explore and new things to try. Your child can feed the chickens, sail a boat, play with a

Katie's Farm, from Lawrence Productions

turtle, and even sit on the back of a horse. Then it's on to a third adventure: *McGee at the Fun Fair*. In this program, McGee and his friend Tony take McGee's parents to a park where a fair is taking place. They watch a clown, play on the playground, squirt Dad with water from a fountain, listen to guitar music, and more.

Comments

The *McGee* programs are a great choice for the very young child. They allow youngsters to experience independence and success. There are no time limits, no winning or losing, and the average three-year-old will have no trouble guiding McGee and his pals from place to place.

These titles are also valuable as tools for you to use together with your child. Even a very young child can play with your help; you can take requests, highlight the choice your child has indicated, and then let him press the mouse button or Enter key. Older preschoolers might also enjoy your company while playing the game. This would give you a chance to discuss some "do's and don'ts" related to McGee's behavior. (Some parents have expressed concerns over scenes in which McGee turns on the water in the bathroom by himself, wanders outside while Mom is asleep,

or heads out to a dock with Katie and a fishing pole.)

The speech and sound effects in this program are not essential but do add to its appeal. On some MS-DOS machines, you'll find the sound difficult to understand unless you have an add-on card.

Which *McGee* program should you choose? You might decide based on content (does your child love animals? clowns?) or the main characters portrayed (*McGee* shows a child at home with one parent, *Katie's Farm* features a female main character, and *McGee at the Fun Fair* introduces Tony, an African-American). None of the titles will keep your child interested forever. By the time the average kid is four, a program like *The Playroom* will offer more challenges and have more lasting value. But for a two- or three-year-old, the *McGee*

McGee, from Lawrence Productions

series provides a delightful introduction to the computer. Parents will be charmed and touched by McGee, Katie, and Tony, and children will love going exploring with their new friends.

Walt Disney's Premium Preschool Line

Mickey's 1,2,3's (1991) Mickey's ABC's (1991)
Mickey's Colors & Shapes (1991)

Publisher: Walt Disney Computer Software **Ages:** 2 to 5

MS-DOS

$49.95 each

In Walt Disney's *premium* line of preschool software, Mickey Mouse and his friends introduce young children to numbers, letters, colors, and shapes with help from colorful animations, high-quality sound, and interactive environments that allow children to explore relatively freely. (Note: Disney also offers a "value-priced" line with titles available for less than $15 each; we don't recommend them, however.)

Mickey's 1,2,3's: The Big Surprise Party opens with Mickey asleep in his living room. He awakens to remember that he has things to do before the surprise party he is planning. He must send out invitations, buy food and party decorations for the guests, and make a present. With your child's help, he hops into any of the vehicles at his disposal (there are nine) and heads for the post office, grocery store, or toy factory. The program emphasizes problem solving and early math skills, asking children to make such decisions as how many balloons to buy, which box of toy parts to select, and how much food to serve each guest. (All choices in this program are made by typing in a number.)

Mickey's A,B,C's: A Day at the Fair introduces your child to the alphabet and the initial sounds of words. Mickey travels from spot to spot, within his house and at the fair. Each letter on the keyboard corresponds to an item or activity on the screen. For example, type the letter *W* when Mickey is at the fair and you're transported to a part of the fairground where a watermelon-eating contest is taking place; enter *A* and an airplane flies overhead.

In *Mickey's Colors & Shapes: The Dazzling Magic Show*, Mickey is a magician who performs wonderful tricks in a three-act show. The program comes with a flexible overlay to place on your keyboard, allowing children to select the shapes and colors they would like Mickey to use for his tricks. In Act I, Mickey works with five shapes and eight colors, juggling whatever the child selects. In the second act, Mickey creates a magic picture using the shapes and colors your child chooses. For example, a circle becomes a pumpkin, a rectangle is transformed into the car of a train, and so on. Finally, players help Mickey locate a missing animal that is hidden behind an object on the screen. They can peek behind each object by selecting its shape on the overlay.

Comments

If you have the right hardware setup, these programs are very appealing. The graphics and animations are beautiful, especially when displayed on a VGA monitor. Although the box reads "compatible with" The Sound Source, this add-on (Disney's own) is not really optional; rather it's *crucial* to the success of the programs. With its help, your child has access to high-quality sound effects and music (which add to the software's entertainment value) plus speech (which allows the programs to give instructions and to reinforce content by counting aloud, naming letters, reading words, and so on).

You'll have to be careful not to lose the sheet of Mickey characters that comes in the box since the

Mickey's 1,2,3's, from Walt Disney Computer Software

program requires you to match the proper Mickey picture to a number displayed on the screen before you can play. This copy-protection scheme is time-consuming and frustrating for parents (we found the pictures hard to see and easy to misplace) and too difficult for young children to handle on their own.

Together, these three programs provide a rich array of exploratory activities and learning experiences for your child, although each program individually lacks the variety offered by some other early childhood titles. If you're thinking of trying just one title in the series, our favorite is *Mickey's 1,2,3's*. It does the best job of balancing free play with a mission that motivates kids. (They enjoy seeing the results of their work at the surprise party that culminates the game.)

Mixed-Up Mother Goose (1990)

Publisher: Sierra On-Line   **Ages:** 4 and up

MS-DOS, Macintosh, Apple II series, Apple IIGS, Amiga

MS-DOS $39.95   **Mac $29.95**   **Apple II, IIGS $29.95**   **Amiga $29.95**

Nursery rhymes have never been so much fun! Your child enters fantasy land on the back of Mother Goose and proceeds to help her find 20 characters and items that have been misplaced. Old King Cole has lost his pipe, Mary Quite Contrary has lost her watering can, Peter Pumpkin Eater his wife, Little Bo-Peep her sheep, and so on.

There are over 40 colorful and beautiful graphic screens to search. Along the way, players meet and interact with personalities from 18 popular Mother Goose nursery rhymes. To win the game, children must remember where these characters live because after they find a lost item, they have to pick it up and return it to its rightful owner.

A colorful poster and map included in the package help them on their way.

Comments

This program has been a favorite with young kids for years. It has been through several revisions during that time, and the versions available today vary greatly in terms of technical quality. The version for the Apple IIe and IIc is slower and much more awkward to operate than the others. On the other end of the spectrum is the high-quality CD-ROM version for MS-DOS computers (see Chapter 26). Although a sound card is really wonderful with this game, the lack of one does not inhibit a player's success.

Mixed Up Mother Goose is a first-rate electronic puzzle for the pre-school set. A combination of pictures and words are used so prereaders

have no problem playing. A friendly graphical interface encourages exploration. And as they explore, kids are called upon to think, use maps, and remember the location of important objects. If you're looking for a fun way to introduce young children to computers, *Mixed-Up Mother Goose* is a great choice.

Mixed-Up Mother Goose, from Sierra On-Line

The Playroom (1989)

Publisher: Broderbund Software   **Ages:** 3-7

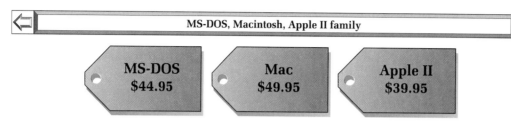

MS-DOS, Macintosh, Apple II family

MS-DOS	Mac	Apple II
$44.95	$49.95	$39.95

The Playroom is an entertaining collection of activities for your preschooler. The program's main menu is a playroom filled with objects that come to life when your child "clicks" on them. Young users will spend plenty of time on the main screen, watching and listening as the fish does somersaults in its bowl, drawers fly open to release balloons, parrots squawk, and much more. If you own a Macintosh computer with sound input capabilities, it's possible to add one more element of fun to this activity by recording your own sounds for each of the objects in the playroom.

Six of the toys, when selected, take your children to other rooms, where they play games that reinforce reading and math readiness skills, keyboarding, time telling, problem solving, and creativity. In one room, children select a time on the face of a clock and see the program's friendly guide, Pepper Mouse, perform a task appropriate to the time chosen. In another room, they select a number from one spinner and an object from another, and watch as the requested number of objects appear on the screen. Other activities in this collection involve locating letters on the keyboard, creating "mixed-up" toys from a choice of interchangeable parts, playing a multilevel board game involving counting and strategy, and creating pictures by entering the first letter of each picture component to be included.

The Playroom, from Broderbund Software

Most of the activities provide a balance of free play and structured learning. For example, in addition to experimenting with the number/object spinners, children can click on Pepper and he'll give them a problem to solve. (Several objects are displayed and the child must count them; when the right number is chosen, the objects on the screen become animated.) Most of the games have multiple difficulty levels, which you or your child can adjust.

Comments

The Playroom is easy for even the youngest users to operate. The interface is consistent throughout the program, and no reading ability is required. However, the method used by Broderbund to prevent illegal copying might cause you and your children some problems if you're not prepared for it. Every fifth time you boot the program, it's necessary to match a code that appears on the screen with one on the back of the reference manual; you'll have to keep careful track of the manual and help your child respond appropriately. (The matching activity can be treated as a game, but it needs explaining and may be difficult for the youngest users to master.)

This caution aside, *The Playroom* is one of the best preschool programs we've seen. It presents a variety of traditional "readiness" skills in a colorful and dynamic manner and provides a delightful introduction to the computer. It offers children plenty of positive reinforcement while allowing them to explore, create, and solve problems. *The Playroom*'s appealing music and sound effects (when enhanced by a sound card), attractive graphics and animation, and playful style will charm both you and your children—and lead to hours of educational fun.

Reading Magic Library

Jack and the Beanstalk (1988)
Flodd, the Bad Guy (1989)

Publisher: Tom Snyder Productions   **Ages**: 2 to 6

MS-DOS, Apple II family, Apple IIGS

$34.95
each

"Lapware" is Tom Snyder's name for this approach to software for young kids. These two programs are meant to be used by a parent or other adult working with a child. Each program tells a story, stopping at numerous points to allow the viewers to make choices about what should happen next. The first title in the series takes the familiar fairy tale, *Jack and the Beanstalk,* and transports it into the future. Jack travels in a spaceship accompanied by his robotic cow, encountering many challenges that you and your child must help him solve.

In the second title, *Flodd, the Bad Guy*, King Alex and his dog, Ollie, take on the meanest bad guy, Flodd. Alex and Ollie encounter many difficult problems, but they have the help of a genie, three magic wishes—and your child.

Comments

The *Reading Magic* programs provide an excellent opportunity for you to work closely with your child, building problem-solving and decision-making skills. The software also reinforces directional concepts, such as up and down and around and through, and introduces simple phonics in the form of initial sounds. (Each choice is entered by pressing the first letter of the choice—*D* for down, *U* for up, and so on.)

The stories are humorous on levels that both a child and a parent will appreciate. While the graphics aren't as dramatic as those in some of today's VGA programs, they are charming and appealing—as are the stories they tell.

Math

A large percentage of the educational software packages produced over the years have been math programs. In part this is because computing and other mathematical tasks have historically been what computers handle best. Long before microcomputers were capable of displaying detailed maps, animated demonstrations of difficult concepts, or documents with multiple fonts, they were being used to drill kids on math facts.

Although some of the historical reasons for favoring math software have disappeared, it remains true that mathematics is well-covered by software producers and that parents and teachers frequently think of math first when looking for software for their kids. We've looked through many of the most popular math titles and selected those that we think you should know about.

Some of our favorites are programs that focus on problem solving and thinking skills. The developers of such programs recognize that knowing how to add, subtract, multiply, and divide is of no use to a child unless she also knows when and how to apply these computational skills. A few of the programs even offer on-screen calculators, shifting the emphasis almost entirely from computation to strategy.

In spite of the growing priority placed by leading math educators on problem-solving skills, in most elementary and middle schools, kids still spend a huge amount of time learning and practicing the four basic operations. Because there's a good chance that your child will need (or simply enjoy) practice in these areas, we have also included several of the best drill-and-practice programs on the market.

For other programs related to math, see also The Playroom, Mickey's 1,2,3's, *and* Mickey's Colors & Shapes *(Chapter 20);* Super Solvers Treasure Mountain! *and* The Treehouse *(Chapter 24);* Mutanoid Math Challenge *(Chapter 27); and all the programs in Chapter 25.*

KidsMath (1989)

Publisher: Great Wave Software   **Ages:** 3 to 8

 Macintosh

**Mac
$49.95**

KidsMath features eight short games that focus on premath and primary-grade math concepts. The two simplest games use a space theme to introduce children to the mouse and to counting: click on a rocket and you see it take off; count the asteroids correctly and they explode before your eyes. *Paddle Ball,* an addition and subtraction game that involves hitting a ball to eliminate objects from the screen, will bring back memories of one of the earliest of computer games: *Pong.* This and several of the other

KidsMath, from Great Wave Software

games in the program help your child develop hand-eye coordination while they practice math skills. For example, in *Shuffleboard,* kids shoot pucks at numbered targets as they practice addition and simple multiplication.

In other *KidsMath* activities, children practice "greater than and less than" by moving balloons up and down; work on introductory addition, multiplication, and division by filling up trucks with scoops of sand; and practice unit measures and beginning fractions by controlling the weather (for example, they select the thunderstorm icon and watch while the water line moves up on a rain gauge they've been told to fill to three-quarters). As players complete activities correctly, the program cheers and applauds and rock-and-roll music plays in the background.

Comments

KidsMath provides an entertaining introduction to math for young children. The games are easy to complete in a short sitting, making them appealing to many parents who have only a little time to sit down and play with their children at the computer. But watch out: your four-year-old might beat you at some of the games!

The documentation is easy to understand and full of helpful hints on how to customize the program for your own child. Because the eight activities span such a wide range of math skills and several of the games have multiple difficulty levels, this is the sort of program that can be used effectively by both your preschooler and your second grader. On the down side, a three- or four-year-old will only be able to handle some of the activities; if he tries the harder games, he'll quickly become frustrated. Parents of preschoolers will also wish that the written directions had been read aloud.

The varied activities and entertaining graphics and sound all add to the program's appeal. This is drill at its best. While a few of the activities use the more old-fashioned drill approach, interrupting play to ask math questions and responding to incorrect answers with "No, try again," most of the activities are very entertaining and involving. Kids definitely feel as if they're playing, not just practicing math.

New Math Blaster Plus! (1990)

Publisher: Davidson & Associates   **Ages:** 6 to 12

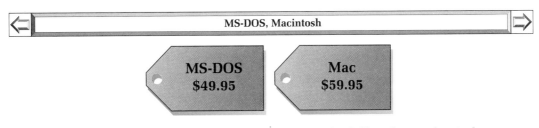

MS-DOS, Macintosh

MS-DOS
$49.95

Mac
$59.95

New Math Blaster Plus!, an enhanced version of Davidson's best-selling *Math Blaster* program, features four space-oriented activities that drill kids on math skills. Players begin by building themselves a rocket: each time they correctly solve a set of math problems, a piece of the rocket appears. When all the problems have been answered correctly, the rocket blasts off!

In outer space, the children are again called upon to help out by completing math problems. In the *Trash Zapper* activity, they fill in the blanks on different equations and, once they've completed a certain number successfully, have the chance to help clean up space by "zapping" trash that is floating around. In *Number Recycler*, they attempt to rearrange equations correctly in a window. Careful planning is needed so that numbers not used in the current equation are recycled, not thrown away; players may need them later.

The final activity, *Math Blaster*, is an arcade-style math game. A math problem is displayed at the top of the screen with four possible answers displayed in space stations immediately below the problem. Players need to answer each question fast enough to get the Blasternaut to fly to the correct space station in the time allowed—without hitting any flying objects. If they do well, they get to play in the bonus round.

Comments

Whether you love or hate this program will have a lot to do with how you feel about drill. *New Math*

Blaster Plus! is classic drill-and-practice that is well implemented. Although the program uses a single motif throughout, there is little connection between the math content and the games played; instead, games are used primarily as a reward for completing math problems successfully. And only one of the four activities (*Number Recycler*) focuses on problem solving in addition to straight computation.

If your goal is to help your child practice basic math facts and simple computation in an entertaining way, this may be the program for you. Davidson does a particularly good job of designing software programs that grow with your child's ability. *New Math Blaster Plus!* covers addition, subtraction, multiplication, division, decimals, fractions, and percentages at six levels of difficulty. In addition,

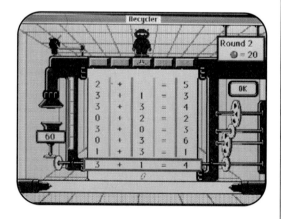

New Math Blaster Plus!, from Davidson & Associates

you can add your own problems. This program won't teach your kids to love math, but arcade-loving kids will get better at math just because they enjoy playing the games.

Math Blaster Mystery (1989)

Publisher: Davidson & Associates   **Ages:** 10 and up

MS-DOS, Macintosh, Apple II

MS-DOS $49.95

Mac $49.95

Apple II $49.95

Are story problems "a problem" for your child? *Math Blaster Mystery* takes the mystery out of solving math word problems by breaking the problems down into steps that are easy to understand. There are four separate activities, each of which focuses on a separate type of problem solving.

Follow the Steps leads kids through story problems using a four-step process that helps them understand and solve the problems successfully. In *Weigh the Evidence*, players are presented with a target weight and challenged to figure out a strategy to match that amount by moving and stacking the weights in ascending order. *Decipher the Code* is a real challenge. The goal is to figure out a mystery equation at the bottom of the screen using trial and error and deductive reasoning. At the lower levels, only the operators $(+, -, \times, /$ and $=)$ have been filled in; at higher levels, all the spaces are blank. In the final activity, the computer picks a secret number and hides clues in different places on the screen. A clue might read "$N > 4$" or "N is odd." If children have trouble figuring out the value of N from the clues, they can request hints that help them analyze the information they've been given.

Each activity can be set to one of four levels of difficulty. *Math Blaster Mystery* has "user-friendly" extras such as pull-down menus, a pop-up calculator, certificate printouts, and an editor that allows personalized problems to be added.

Comments

In naming this program, Davidson was clearly trying to build on the success of its *Math Blaster* program. However, the similarity in names can be misleading. While *Math Blaster* (or *New Math Blaster Plus!*, as it's currently known) emphasizes computational drill, *Math Blaster Mystery* focuses on problem solving. The two programs do not even share common graphics or game-playing elements.

Math teachers and parents concerned about helping kids to reason and solve problems involving mathematics generally prefer this program. On the other hand, your child may prefer the arcade-style drill approach used in *Math Blaster*. Before dismissing *Math Blaster Mystery* as too serious, however, try it out. The approach, while definitely educational, is also quite a bit of fun—especially for the kid who suddenly "gets it" with the software's help. The activities are so varied that the program does not get stale. With four levels of difficulty, *Math Blaster Mystery* has lasting power and continues to challenge users as they become more skilled.

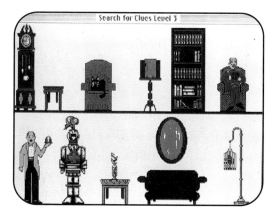

Math Blaster Mystery, from Davidson & Associates

Math Shop (1986) **Ages:** 10 and up
Math Shop Jr. (1989) **Ages:** 6 to 9

Publisher: Scholastic Software

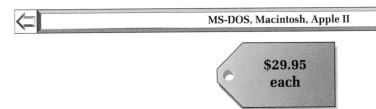

MS-DOS, Macintosh, Apple II

$29.95 each

Help Wanted! The shopkeepers at the Math Mall need your help waiting on customers. You can take a job in any one shop in the mall, or you can try all 10 of them at once, hopping back and forth as you are needed. Each store offers a different set of challenges. In *Math Shop*'s pharmacy, use percentages to fill prescriptions; in the donut shop, your knowledge of fractions helps you determine how many of the donuts coming out of the donut machine should be glazed. The other shops in the same mall cover everything from basic computation (addition, subtraction, multiplication, and division) to the use of decimals, ratios, and introductory algebra.

Math Shop Jr. uses the same mall environment with different shops. In the *Small Change Bank,* for example, kids break down the money they receive from customers into quarters, dimes, nickels, and pennies. Other math skills practiced in this mall include simple addition, subtraction, multiplication, and division; odd and even numbers; and estimation.

If you choose to play the *All Shops* version of the game, you'll have to be careful not to let too many customers build up in one store or they will leave. The game ends when 50 customers have left the mall without being helped. If you do well, you may make the "Top Employees" list. Whichever version of the game you play, when you are done, the program lists the number of customers waited on per store. Kids can use these lists to measure their own progress or compete with friends and family members.

Comments

This program, excellent in a school setting, also has a place in many homes. The Math Mall is a wonderful learning environment that not only helps children practice math skills, but also helps them see how math is used in everyday life. It's this strong connection between on-screen math practice and real-life experiences that has so many teachers excited about the *Math Shop* series.

Whether your child will be equally excited depends a lot on his expectations. The make-believe aspects of the program will appeal to many kids as will the variety, the easy-to-follow directions, and the ability to choose which shops to visit and which to ignore. On the other hand, a kid used to Nintendo-like action may find the program too slow-paced. One frustration for some kids is the length of time it takes before they receive any sort of reward for performing well. (They receive feedback that lets them know if their input is right or wrong, but then the game continues as before.) In fact, in the *All Shops* game, it's only when they do *poorly* enough to lose 50 customers that the game finally ends and lets them know how their score compares to that of other high scorers.

Before your child starts using this program, it's a good idea to sit down with her and discuss the skills

required for each shop. Then, the two of you can decide together which stores to start with and which ones to build up to with time.

Note: There are other programs in the *Math Shop* series you might want to look for as well. *Advanced Math Shop* is targeted to kids over the age of 12 and includes shops where players focus on such areas as decimals, squares and square roots, negative numbers, and simultaneous equations. *Math Shop Spotlights* is for the same audience as *Math Shop* but allows kids to focus on a certain subject in each of the shops. (One spotlight title concentrates on weights and measures; another on fractions and decimals.)

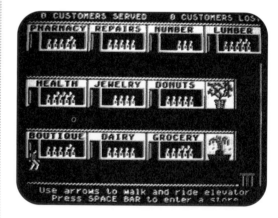

Math Shop, from Scholastic Software

NumberMaze (1988) **Ages:** 5 to 12
NumberMaze Decimals & Fractions (1990)
Ages: 8 to 13

Publisher: Great Wave Software

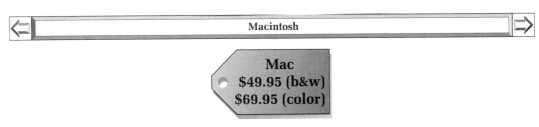

Macintosh

Mac
$49.95 (b&w)
$69.95 (color)

In *NumberMaze*, the object is to solve your way through a variety of different mazes. You move your playing piece (a horse, a mouse, or a car) from the start all the way to the castle at the end of the maze by answering basic math questions. When you reach a barrier that blocks the way, the screen fades into a close-up view. It might be a ladder with no rungs, a doorway blocked by a pile of rocks, or any of a number of other obstacles. In order to remove the barrier, you have to solve two or three math problems (problems range from simple counting to multiplication, division, and word problems). You can point and click on the numeric answers or use the keyboard.

The graphics and sound effects are highly entertaining. Doors scrape open, and the mouse makes little mouse noises. Once a maze is solved,

the castle drawbridge is lowered and players enter the great hall, accompanied by appropriate fanfare. Players are then automatically moved up to the next level.

There are 36 mazes that grow progressively more difficult, adding extra paths, invisible walls that appear only occasionally, and locked doors that can be opened only with the help of keys that players must collect. A child who enjoys the challenge of harder mazes can actually control most of these variables rather than leave it up to the program to decide how difficult the maze will be.

NumberMaze Decimals & Fractions takes a similar approach to practice with fractions and decimals. In this program, the maze is a house in which players pick up items such as newspapers, milk bottles, apple cores, and soda cans. The player piece is either a bumble bee, a panda, or a bird, and as each one moves, it is accompanied by realistic sound effects. (The bee buzzes as it follows a flower around the maze, you can hear the panda shuffling around as it tries to nibble on the bamboo shoot, and so on.) When a maze has been completed, an item is placed in the attic of the house.

The math problems encountered in *NumberMaze Decimals & Fractions* cover number comparison, rounding, converting decimals to fractions and fractions to decimals, reducing and comparing fractions, and improper and mixed fractions.

Comments

A particularly impressive feature of both of these programs is how easily they can be customized to meet an individual child's needs. Children who are good at mazes can increase the difficulty level for themselves; others will gradually be led into more difficult mazes. Frustration is

minimized because there is no time clock or negative responses to incorrect answers. If the going gets too tough, hints are available or the player can ask for a different problem.

While the maze navigation is totally unrelated to the math skills being practiced, both sets of activities contribute to the learning value of the program. The mazes will challenge your child to watch carefully and use strategy and problem-solving skills. Any kid who loves mazes should respond well to this software—and learn a fair amount of math at the same time.

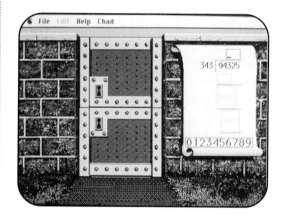

NumberMaze, from Great Wave Software

Number Munchers (1986, 1990)

Publisher: MECC   **Ages:** 8 and up

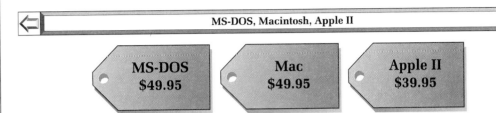

MS-DOS, Macintosh, Apple II

MS-DOS
$49.95

Mac
$49.95

Apple II
$39.95

Number Munchers, a long-standing favorite of students in the classroom, is a drill-and-practice game reminiscent of *Pac Man*. The object is to guide a "Muncher" through a grid of numbers eating only those that match the given specifications (multiples of 3, factors of 12, numbers greater than 10, and so on).

When the game begins, you have four Munchers, one on the grid and three waiting on the sidelines. If your Muncher happens to munch an incorrect number or be caught by a Troggle, you lose it and have to use one of the others. With each correct answer, you are awarded points. You can earn more Munchers at the 1,000 and 10,000 point levels. When a level is finished successfully, there is a graphic cartoon confrontation between a muncher and one of the Troggles. Of course, the Muncher wins.

On the higher levels, you run into more Troggles. There are five different types of Troggles, and each has a different pattern of movement. Some travel in straight lines and change the numbers in the spaces as they move over them; others move randomly and fill in empty spaces with numbers. Beware of the Smarties Troggle because it travels in an unpredictable way and its sole purpose is to destroy your Muncher. Earn a high enough score, and you will be entered in the Hall of Fame.

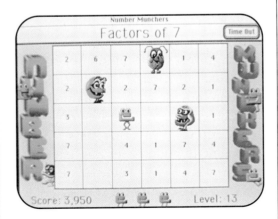

Number Munchers, from MECC

Comments

If asked to choose only one math drill program for use with their students, many elementary school teachers would pick this one. The game is simple, and may even seem repetitive to adults, but we've seen kids stick with it for hours. It definitely appeals to the child who enjoys a fast pace.

In addition to providing a motivating environment in which to practice computation skills, *Number Munchers* forces players to think about each set of problems a little differently. Not only must kids solve individual problems (for example, 3 x 8= ?), they need to apply their results to the criteria at hand, determining if the answer is greater than 22, a multiple of 6, a factor of 32, and so on. Parents can also tailor the game to the abilities of their own children.

Operation Neptune (1991)

Publisher: The Learning Company   **Ages:** 10 and up

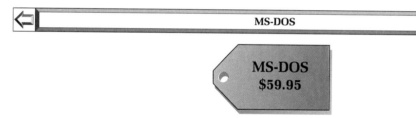

MS-DOS

MS-DOS
$59.95

Your help is needed to save planet earth from a serious disaster. On its return from a secret mission in space, the unmanned space capsule, *Galaxy*, crashed into the ocean, dropping data canisters containing vital information. In addition to recovering these canisters, it will be your mission to retrieve the capsule before it spills a toxic substance capable of destroying all life.

Players set off in a small submarine—navigating through an underwater maze of trenches and obstacles, steering clear of dangerous sea creatures, and being careful not to run out of oxygen. As the submarine travels along, it receives periodic requests for help from its command ship. Each of these requests takes the form of a math problem to be solved. For example, you might be told that an unidentified obstacle has been detected 16 miles ahead and that your sub is approaching at 8 miles per hour and then asked to indicate how many hours till you reach the obstacle. Other problems focus on measurement (distance, area, perimeter, volume, etc.); reading and interpreting graphs and charts; estimation; and performing operations with whole numbers, fractions, decimals, and percents. A calculator is available to solve many of the problems. Incorrect answers decrease your oxygen supply.

When you reach a supply station, there's another problem to be solved before you can open the lock and refuel. Breaking the access code in order to read the message in every canister you find requires yet another kind of problem solving: players are asked to complete a number pattern that appears on the screen.

To complete your mission, you must travel through five separate zones, each with three sectors. (Sectors are separated by supply stations.) There are two levels of game play—voyager and expert—each with a separate set of underwater mazes. As players progress, the math problems become increasingly difficult to solve and the mazes increasingly complex to navigate.

Comments

While some adults (or the rare kid who hates Nintendo games) may find the navigation challenges frustrating, most kids in the target age range (or even younger) will figure out what to do immediately—and will then refuse to turn off the computer for hours. The underwater scenes, especially when displayed on a VGA monitor, are gorgeous and quite realistic (although the scale is definitely off and some elements of fantasy have been added). The music and sound effects are entertaining even without a sound card; with an AdLib, Sound Blaster, or Roland add-on card they sound even better.

In addition to being extremely entertaining, *Operation Neptune* is quite educational as well. The math

Operation Neptune, from The Learning Company

problems are interesting and relevant to the task at hand. When players have difficulty, the program provides hints that help with the process without giving away the answer. Although a fair amount of time is spent on underwater navigation, this process is far more educational than most arcade games. Speed and fast reflexes are not the most important skills here; instead, children learn to watch for patterns (this fish always moves up and down, so I have to time my move so I go above him as he drops down) and plan strategically.

The mazes and math problems are varied and become much harder with time, making this a game with lasting value. It might not appeal to every child, but those who *do* get hooked are likely to stay hooked for quite some time.

Super Solvers Outnumbered! (1990)

Publisher: The Learning Company   **Ages:** 7 to 14

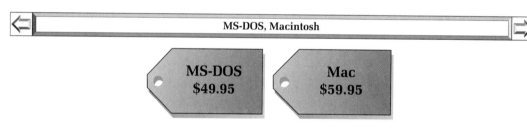

MS-DOS, Macintosh

MS-DOS $49.95   **Mac $59.95**

The Master of Mischief is trying to take over Shady Glen's TV station and only you can save the television viewers from the Master's boring programs. You have until midnight to find the Master's hideout. To do this, you have to search each of the five rooms—solving math problems and collecting clues. Telly, the robot, and LiveWire, the hot electric wire, will try to prevent you from finding their Master. You may have to zap them with your Zapper! Telly has clues you need, so be sure and answer all his math problems correctly.

Once you have searched all the rooms and collected all the clues, you can find the Master. Each time you find him, your rank improves and the next round of the game becomes more difficult. Maybe you can be the first one to reach the rank of Champion.

Comments

Like all the *Super Solvers* programs, *Super Solvers Outnumbered!* provides an entertaining environment for kids. Many educators criticize the program for its overemphasis on arcade-type skills. It's true that kids spend at least as much time jumping wires and zapping enemies (neither of which requires much in the way of thinking skills) as they do answering math problems. When they do get a story problem, it is generally challenging and relevant to the story at hand; but, unfortunately, many more of the math problems are straight computational drill and tend to be unrelated to the rest of the game.

In a home setting, you might not be so concerned with these criticisms. If you're looking for an arcade game that provides some math practice on the side, this program is an appealing choice. There is an on-screen calculator available for some of the word problems, and you can customize the drills to include any combination of addition, subtraction, multiplication, or division.

Although some users may find the program difficult to understand at first, the messages in the opening round help the typical beginner. Once kids get going, there is generally a healthy rivalry to be the first to reach the title of Champion.

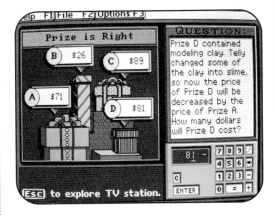

Super Solvers Outnumbered!, from The Learning Company

CHAPTER TWENTY-TWO

Language Arts Software

L ooking for a program to help your children improve their reading skills, build vocabulary, improve spelling, or become better writers? The titles that follow are ideal for these purposes. It's important to note, however, that many equally valuable programs for improving language skills are included in other chapters of this book. In fact, many educators would argue that the best way to teach writing is to give kids a good word processor, and the best way to teach reading is to give kids something they really want to read—a fun game in any subject area, for example, that motivates them to read for clues or other information necessary to complete the exciting activity.

For these reasons, we have cross-referenced many programs in other chapters that you might want to consider when looking for language arts software. In this chapter, though, we have identified some valuable programs that focus *primarily* on improving language arts skills. Many of them focus on individual words (their meaning, sound, or spelling), others deal with entire sentences, and one of the programs reviewed here takes a broader approach to reading comprehension.

For other programs related to language arts, see also KidsTime, Dinosaur Discovery Kit, Puzzle Story Book, Mickey's A,B,C's, *and* The Playroom *(Chapter 20);* Super Munchers, Super Solvers Treasure Mountain, The Treehouse, *and* Cartooners *(Chapter 24);* WordTris *(Chapter 25);* Discis Books *and all the reference tools in Chapter 26;* KidWorks, Living Books, *and* Macmillan Multimedia Dictionary for Children *(Chapter 27); and all the programs in Chapters 19 and 23.*

For Beginning Readers (under 8)

Mickey's Crossword Puzzle Maker (1990)

Publisher: Walt Disney Computer Software   **Ages:** 5 to 8

MS-DOS

**MS-DOS
$49.95**

This crossword puzzle program can be used by you or your child to create personalized, kid-oriented puzzles. It also ships with ready-made puzzles that have three different levels of difficulty. The clues pop up on the screen as players select the words they relate to. The program will even give players hints if they come across a word they can't figure out from the clue.

Kids can play on their own or against a Disney character. When the game is played in this competitive mode, players earn points for correct spellings and are penalized for incorrect spellings. When the game is finished, the sky lights up over Cinderella's castle and the winner's name appears in fireworks.

When creating puzzles, you can use words or pictures (from the program's clip-art libraries) as clues. Background graphics can also be selected for each puzzle. Three types of printouts are possible: a standard blank crossword puzzle with word and picture clues printed below; a blank puzzle accompanied by a list of the words, in incorrect order, for younger or learning-disabled children who need to see the word in order to be able to spell it; and a completed puzzle to be used as an answer sheet. In addition, it's possible to have the program fill in some of the letters before printing out the puzzle (all of the vowels, every other letter, and so on).

Comments

This program is fairly simple to use, although kids at the lower end of the recommended age range might need your help. The range of possibilities is impressive, making it fun and challenging at many different ability levels. Kids will enjoy playing at the computer or solving printed-out puzzles created especially for them. Designing their own puzzles to give to friends or to use for school projects challenges their intellect while boosting confidence and creativity.

Older children (eight- or nine-year-olds) will probably see the Disney graphics as too "babyish." If you want to create personalized puzzles for them or encourage them to design their own, you'll probably end up bypassing all the graphics options. Aside from the commercial graphics,

the most annoying feature of this program is the copy-protection scheme it uses. Like Disney's early childhood titles (see Chapter 20, "Software for Preschoolers"), this program ships with a single, hard-to-see sheet of Mickey Mouse images that you must keep on hand and decipher each time you want to use the program. Once you've gotten over this hurdle, however, *Mickey's Crossword Puzzle Maker* is probably the easiest, most versatile tool of its kind for young kids.

Reader Rabbit (1) (1984, 1989, 1991) **Ages:** 3-7

Reader Rabbit 2 (1991) **Ages:** 5 to 8

Publisher: The Learning Company

RR1: MS-DOS, Apple IIGS, and Macintosh; *RR2:* MS-DOS

MS-DOS
$49.95 (RR1)
$59.95 (RR2)

Mac
$49.95

Apple IIGS
$49.95

Reader Rabbit (renamed *Reader Rabbit 1* in its newest incarnation, which includes enhanced graphics and sound) works on both prereading and early reading skills. One of the games offered by the program can be used by kids as young as three to match shapes and images, as well as

by older kids to match simple words. Most of the other activities involve practice with three-letter words.

A variety of pictures and moving graphics helps keep children's attention as they play. In one game, kids place words on shelves of a sorting machine that moves if they have a letter in the same place as a target word and throw them in a trash can if they don't. The two other games involve unscrambling words and building a word train in which each word differs from the previous word in the train by a single letter. Animated effects and music are used to celebrate players' successes.

Reader Rabbit 2 overlaps the first program, beginning with three-letter words and building to harder second-grade-level words. Like *Reader Rabbit 1*, this sequel provides four language-oriented games. In *Word Mine*, players build compound words or complete words involving consonant clusters (*st, ck,* and so on). At the *Vowel Pond*, they identify and sort words with specific long and short vowel sounds. Rhymes, homonyms, and antonyms are the focus in *Match Patch*. And the *Alphabet Dance* has kids moving animal characters around on the screen in order to place their names in alphabetical order.

Each of the games offers multiple difficulty levels. Both *Reader Rabbit 2* and the new *Reader Rabbit 1* track each child's activities, returning players to the same level at which they left off the last time they played.

Comments

The reading content of the two

programs is quite "school-like," although the kids they're designed for are unlikely to see that as a problem. (The typical six-year-old does not yet think of learning as "work.") This is especially true because the activities are presented in such an entertaining way. Both programs use a lively set of games and animated characters to spice up the learning. Trains move across the screen, rabbits dance, and groundhogs applaud tasks well done. Although the programs will run with no more than CGA graphics, the new 256-color VGA graphics add greatly to their appeal.

Unlike much of the early childhood software on the market, these programs definitely focus on problems with right and wrong answers (rather than on free exploration), but they do so in a gentle way without overemphasizing

Reader Rabbit 2, from The Learning Company

incorrect responses. In fact, some kids might find the feedback *too* subtle; for example, in the sorter game, not all players will notice that the words they place incorrectly (while remaining where they were put) light up or change color to indicate that they should be relocated.

Reader Rabbit has been a favorite of children and parents for years. The revisions and new additions have made a good program even better.

ReadingMaze (1991)

Publisher: Great Wave Software   **Ages:** 3 to 7

 Macintosh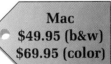

Mac
$49.95 (b&w)
$69.95 (color)

A large unfamiliar house can be fun to explore. The computer version of this activity provides the mystery—without being too scary. With *ReadingMaze,* the child moves easily from room to room in an amazing house. Each door opened, each corner turned provides a new view of a room filled with interesting items—some of which players need to solve problems. Hints are given about each item and other language arts challenges are posed, requiring kids to test their skills in letter and word recognition.

The program helps kids practice a great range of reading skills, including recognizing easy words, matching letters and words, and identifying complete sentences. Particularly interesting are the activities in which kids move objects around on the screen based on written directions they receive or reassemble scrambled sentences by dragging words. There are dozens of levels, with mastery of one level necessary to move on to the next. Once a level has been completed, a "Certificate of Achievement" can be printed.

The program includes over 300 words, 70 problem levels, and 26 mazes. At all points, the program can provide statistics for the eight latest problem levels the student has worked in. Designed for school as well as home, the program can track the progress of up to 50 students. The material can be customized by selecting specific graphic images and beginning letters.

Comments

This program definitely feels quite "serious." The language challenges aren't really games; they're practice exercises. Nevertheless, the maze house will appeal to many kids as will the graphics (in color on Macs that support it). And the exercises are so varied that they don't immediately get boring. Once the basics of pointer movement have been demonstrated, most children can use this program on their own. You may want to watch for the first few minutes to make sure that your child has started at the appropriate skill level and doesn't need your help.

If you're looking for a rich environment on the Macintosh that provides your child with plenty of reading and language practice at many difficulty levels, this is a program to consider. It's probably most useful for kids near the top of the suggested age range (six and seven) because the most interesting reading problems are geared to them.

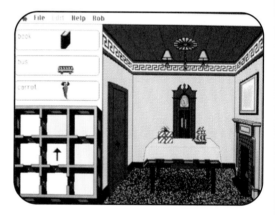

ReadingMaze, from Great Wave Software

For Older Kids (8 and Up)

Spell It Plus! (1989, 1990, 1991)

Publisher: Davidson & Associates   **Ages:** 6 and up

MS-DOS, Macintosh, Apple II

MS-DOS
$49.95

Mac
$49.95

Apple II
$49.95

Learning to spell is not always fun, but *Spell It Plus!* can make the process a little easier. With the help of several different activities, kids can study and use their own spelling words or work with lists provided by the program. The games include a version of tic-tac-toe in which a player claims each square by unscrambling a word; a decoding game in which players complete a mystery message at the bottom of the screen as they fill in missing letters from their spelling words; and a game in which kids direct frogs to leap over hurdles while eating all the words that are (or, in some rounds of the game, are not) spelled correctly.

In addition to these games, kids practice their words by typing them into blanks in sentences (after seeing the correct word flashed on the screen) and using computer-editing techniques to fix misspellings within a sentence. In each activity, the computer provides helpful visual feedback. For example, in the tic-tac-toe game, players actually see the words being scrambled (the letters move around the screen for a while, scrambling in different ways before finally coming to rest). Then, as the child attempts to unscramble a word, each letter entered at the keyboard disappears from the scramble above, providing graphic feedback about whether the correct letters are actually being used.

Children can choose from several levels of difficulty and many word lists. There's also an editor that makes it possible to enter your own words.

Comments

This program offers a varied set of activities that make good use of the computer yet stick closely to the approach taken in traditional spelling lessons. Many of the program's word lists follow specific rules or patterns that the computer explains to the kids. This approach is very popular with many elementary school teachers, although other teachers feel that it's not the best way to teach spelling because so many words in English do not follow the rules. Some educators might also be concerned about the amount of time kids spend in this program looking at words spelled *incorrectly*—although that's a problem with most spelling-oriented games both on and off the computer.

In addition to the lists that come with the program, parents may want to insert the spelling lists that their children bring home from school. Better yet, the kids can enter their own. (Your help will probably be needed because not only must they enter each word correctly, they are encouraged to divide each word into syllables and write sentences that include the words.)

It's possible to have the spelling words read aloud through the internal speaker on the Apple IIGS or on many MS-DOS computers. The speech

sounds reasonably good on most MS-DOS machines *if* you can hear it. However, many internal speakers are too soft, requiring the user to have headphones or a special speech card (for example, Street Electronics' Echo board or IBM's speech adapter) to take advantage of this feature.

This is not necessarily a program your kid will play for its pure entertainment value. But if kids are called upon by their teachers to practice spelling words at home anyhow, *Spell It Plus!* is a great program to make the task more enjoyable.

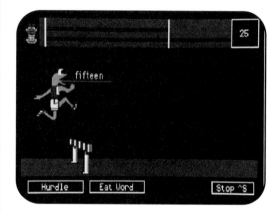

Spell It Plus!, from Davidson & Associates

Super Solvers Midnight Rescue! (1990)

Publisher: The Learning Company **Ages:** 7 to 14

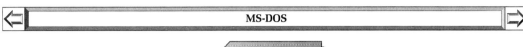

MS-DOS

**MS-DOS
$49.95**

Five robots are painting Shady Glen School with disappearing paint. Morty Maxwell, the Master of Mischief, is disguised as one of the robots. You have until midnight to explore the school, read the clues, and stop Morty. The clues provide information about the robots. You must use your deductive reasoning skills to decide which robot is actually Morty Maxwell and then stop the plot to make the entire school disappear.

As you be-bop around the school, the robots harass you. You must take a picture of each robot as part of your investigation. The combination of clues and robot pictures helps you determine which robot is actually Morty Maxwell. Once you guess successfully, you add points to your total score and begin again. Each new level requires more reading and careful thinking to find the Master of Mischief.

Comments

Midnight Rescue!, the first title in the *Super Solvers* series, is a real favorite with educators. It does a great job of balancing fantasy and game playing (navigating through the school, catching up with robots to take their pictures, and so on) with reading skills. Furthermore, the reading relates to the rest of the game, making the whole experience truly educational.

Super Solvers Midnight Rescue!, from The Learning Company

Almost everyone in the family—even those outside of the recommended age range—will enjoy playing. Because the program keeps scores on multiple players, everyone can play at different times and compare scores. This is also a good game for a group to play cooperatively. Everyone can help read and gather clues as they attempt a midnight rescue.

Super Solvers Spellbound! (1991)

Publisher: The Learning Company   **Ages:** 7 to 12

MS-DOS

MS-DOS
$44.95

The Master of Mischief is at it again. This time he has challenged you to a spelling bee. Beat him at his game, and you may make it to the White House! In spite of the opening premise, this latest entry in the *Super Solvers* series has an entirely different feel from the others. It's not really an exploratory adventure in the *Super Solvers* style; it's a straight spelling program—and a good spelling program at that.

In order to make it to the spelling bee, you must first play three different practice games to accumulate enough points. There's a word search activity that has you finding spelling words on a grid—horizontally, vertically, or (as you get better) at a variety of angles. In the flash game, words appear on the screen for a period of time (brought on by a modern-looking machine) but disappear when you begin to type them in. *Criss Cross* presents blank spaces in crossword fashion and challenges you to place the correct spelling words in the correct boxes.

Words can be selected from dozens of word lists, each related to a topic (food, sports, parts of the body, etc.). It's also possible for you or your kids to create new word lists. When enough points have been accumulated, players progress to the spelling bee. There they compete against two computerized opponents. Each word is either spoken aloud or flashed on the screen before the contestant begins spelling.

Comments

Spellbound! gives *Spell It Plus!* a run for its money. While both programs are varied and make good use of the computer to enhance the value of traditional spelling exercises, *Spellbound!* has the edge when it comes to user-friendliness. Each of the activities is easy to complete even without instructions, and the program is extremely flexible in the way it allows kids to edit what they have done and request help as they play.

Unlike many other spelling programs, this one organizes words by subject rather than by spelling patterns. As a result, each list presents a wide range of difficulty levels. Kids might like this because it allows them to relax on certain words, or they may complain that too few of the words are challenging enough. Organizing by subject ties in well with the popular "whole language" approach, which focuses on teaching kids words in a broader context (as part of real reading and writing projects they're involved in), although the games' use of words totally out of context certainly does not fit with such a philosophy. A definite advantage of the fact that no fill-in-the-blank sentences are used is that it's very easy for kids to enter their own words and see them instantly transformed into criss-crosses, word searches, and other fun games.

If your child is going to work on spelling at home, *Spellbound!*'s ease of use and general appeal are hard to beat.

Super Solvers Spellbound!, from The Learning Company

CHAPTER TWENTY - THREE

Learning About the World: Social Studies and Science Programs

I n the past year or two, there has been a flood of new titles designed to teach kids about geography, history, and the environment. Fortunately, many of these programs are excellent, taking an entertaining approach to teaching subjects that American children have traditionally known far too little about.

Most of the programs we know of in this area are geared towards kids in the upper elementary or junior high grades. In addition, however, we've included a few titles for children who are just starting school, as well as two programs that will challenge the typical 12- or 13-year-old.

Unfortunately, we have not found many state-of-the-art programs that focus on scientific topics other than the environment. Now that so many programs that take advantage of high-quality graphics and sound are hitting the market, perhaps we'll see more new titles focused on science for kids—titles that teach about animals, volcanoes, astronomy, and many other subjects that, when taught effectively, are fascinating to young people. Keep your eyes open.

For other programs related to social studies and science, see also Super Munchers *and* The Treehouse *(Chapter 24) and all the reference tools in Chapter 26.*

Programs for the Younger Set (Under 9)

Eco-Saurus (1991)

Publisher: First Byte, available from Davidson & Associates   **Ages:** 4 to 9

MS-DOS

MS-DOS
$39.95

Eco Island suffers from too much trash and too few Environmental Conservation Officials (ECOs). Players join Zug the Megasaurus in his mission to clean up the island. They move around the island with the point and click of a mouse or by typing at the keyboard. Each place they visit is strewn with trash that must be added to the proper recycling bin— aluminum, plastic, organic waste, glass, or paper. As they wander around, they also learn to conserve electricity and water by turning off switches and faucets. For each item recycled or turned off, players earn energy points.

Inhabitants of the island provide tips on recycling and fun facts about the island. You can stop Floyd, the Tubularsaurus dude, as he flies by on his skateboard; approach Mr. Bronto the loud-mouthed polluter who lives in Fashions a la Bronto castle; or chat with Tyrone A. Saurus, the famous

Shakespesaurian actor. Even the rocks and trees will have something to say if your child clicks on them. Their comments (and the program instructions) appear in written form on the screen and are read aloud through the system speaker or an optional sound board.

Comments

This program is part of the series that began with *Dinosaur Discovery Kit* and *Puzzle Story Book* (see Chapter 20, "Software for Preschoolers"). Zug the Megasaurus will be familiar to graduates of the older programs as will the use of First Byte's synthesized speech (words are sounded out by the computer and played back through the PC speaker as long as you have a machine with a clock speed of 8 MHz or faster and a powerful enough speaker). However, this new program reflects the changes in hardware that have occurred in the past few years. It requires a hard disk and EGA or VGA graphics, offers improved speech quality, and supports the best-known sound cards, such as AdLib and Sound Blaster. A mouse is optional but makes playing the game much easier.

After a few minutes of demonstration, most children will understand how to use the program. Although the graphics are attractive, they are not always detailed enough to make it clear what each trash item represents. (Is that a can or some crumpled-up paper?) It sometimes takes two or more tries to get the item into the proper bin.

Young kids will undoubtedly have fun exploring the island and talking with its zany inhabitants. Some may tire of the game eventually (filling the bins can take several days, but after that, kids may not be so

interested in starting all over—even though the trash items change location from game to game). On the other hand, the program reinforces important concepts—recycling packaging materials and saving energy—in an entertaining way. Your child is likely to get the message from playing with this program and want to begin recycling in your home.

Eco-Saurus, from First Byte

Nigel's World (1991)

Publisher: Lawrence Productions, distributed by Broderbund   **Ages:** 7 to 12

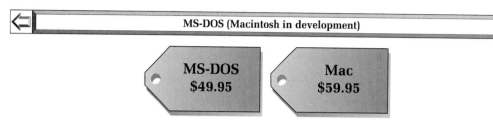

MS-DOS (Macintosh in development)

MS-DOS
$49.95

Mac
$59.95

This geography game is targeted at children as young as seven, although its high-quality VGA graphics will fascinate even a teenager. As Nigel, you travel all over the world to take pictures for your boss, Roxy. You receive your photo assignments over the fax machine in your home office. For beginners ("shutterbugs"), assignments involve traveling to a specified continent and bringing back a photo. As you advance, you are given several countries to visit in a single trip. When you finally reach level four and become a "master," you are required to apply what you have learned in previous levels to locate and take pictures of specific landmarks.

Children use unlabeled, on-screen maps to select continents and then countries. When they arrive at their destination, they choose whether to take a picture of a person, animal, or landmark. The pictures are breathtaking; after clicking on the camera icon, players watch as a real photograph (over 90 digitized photos are included) develops before their eyes.

As with most photo assignments, the young photographers are working under a deadline. Once they have taken the pictures, they return to Roxy's office. If they have taken the pictures from the assigned location, she is happy; otherwise, she sends them back out to find the right location and shoot again.

Comments

Compared with much of the educational software on the market, this program's hardware requirements are quite high. In addition to VGA or MCGA graphics, you will need a hard disk (the photographs, music, speech, and over 100 animated scenes require over 3 megabytes of disk space). A mouse and a sound board are both recommended, though not required.

If you have the right hardware, you will be pleased with what the program provides. Because the VGA/MCGA screens can display 256 colors at one time, the photographs are truly recognizable. If you have a sound board such as the AdLib or Sound Blaster, your experience will be enhanced with music from many of the different countries. By listening closely, you can win extra points later when Roxy becomes game host and challenges you to guess which of three countries has a particular musical selection. Owners of the Sound Blaster card will even hear a spoken welcome as they arrive in many of the countries.

It's refreshing to find a geography program for young kids. The game is easy to learn and play, and the first few photo assignments can be accomplished in a few minutes. Even nonreaders can enjoy the program as tourists. In this mode, they roam around the globe, taking pictures where they wish. The program won't hold older kids' interest as long as many of the other programs described in this chapter, but the stunning graphics and the fact that the higher level assignments are reasonably challenging will draw the over-10 crowd in for at least a little while.

Nigel's World provides an enjoyable way to "travel" around the world and learn something about many countries. World geography, map reading, critical thinking, and reading are all reinforced in the process. The program even contains a small booklet: *Helping Your Child Learn Geography*. Whether as tourists or globe-trotting photojournalists, everyone in the family can participate.

Nigel's World, from Lawrence Productions

Intermediate-Level Programs (Ages 10-14)

Bushbuck Charms, Viking Ships and Dodo Eggs (1991)

Publisher: PC Globe   **Ages:** 12 and up

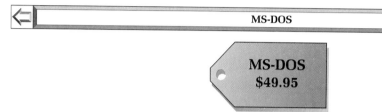

MS-DOS

**MS-DOS
$49.95**

Are you and your kids ready to embark on a worldwide scavenger hunt? *Bushbuck Charms, Viking Ships and Dodo Eggs* begins by presenting you with a list of items to search for and a handful of airplane tickets. Then you're off, hopping from city to city in search of clues. You can compete with another player or with Pierre, your computer opponent, as you hunt for such items as a poda-poda tire, a mooncake, a rubber warthog nose, avocado ice cream, and a bouzouki.

Each airplane trip depletes your ticket allowance, and periodic electrical storms cost both time and tickets. Even with the occasional bonus tickets, you'll struggle to find the items and return to your home city for an additional 500 bonus points. If all this sounds too hard, you do have some resources available to you. The software package includes a large world map with all the air routes and cities. Descriptions that appear as you arrive in a new city sometimes provide clues for later searches. The beginner mode even provides a cold-to-hot scale to show you when you are close to an item on the list.

Comments

While the typical adult might feel impatient with the amount of time spent dealing with electrical storms and wandering in search of clues that appear only occasionally, most youngsters seem content to explore until they stumble upon clues and items. An important role you can play is to help with reference materials. Keep a dictionary near the computer so players can look up some of the more exotic items. For example, the dictionary will tell your children that a "bouzouki" is a stringed instrument from Greece—an important clue to get them started in the right direction. Remind them that careful study of the world map saves precious airplane tickets, while reading the city descriptions helps locate items on later hunts.

The sounds that you'll hear if you have the AdLib sound card are entertaining, but not at all necessary to use the program. A mouse speeds up selections, although complete keyboard commands are available. You'll experience a few delays if you don't have a hard disk.

This is a challenging game, best for kids 12 and up who enjoy solving puzzles and are willing to use reference materials occasionally. Many kids will love the fact that it allows them to play against one another—something that few of the other geography programs do. It's even possible that the adults in the family will find themselves engaging in a little friendly, after-hours competition.

The Carmen Sandiego Series

Where in the World Is Carmen Sandiego?
Where in the U.S.A.?...
Where in Europe?...   Where in Time?...
Where in America's Past?...

Publisher: Broderbund Software

Ages: *World, USA,* and *Europe*: 8 and up; *Time* and *Past*: 12 and up

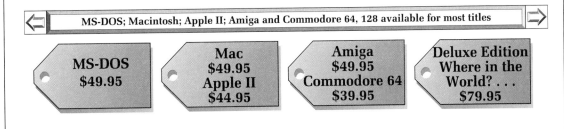

MS-DOS; Macintosh; Apple II; Amiga and Commodore 64, 128 available for most titles

MS-DOS
$49.95

Mac
$49.95
Apple II
$44.95

Amiga
$49.95
Commodore 64
$39.95

Deluxe Edition
Where in the
World? . . .
$79.95

Each of the five *Carmen Sandiego* programs places your child in the role of super detective. Carmen and her V.I.L.E. agents are causing trouble, and it's up to the young detectives to gather clues using the tools provided in the program. They conduct interviews and searches, and take notes as they piece together the information they need.

Each program provides a different "territory" players must travel in order to arrest the criminals. *Where in the World Is Carmen Sandiego?* includes dozens of cities around the globe. *Where in Europe?...* focuses on a single continent, and *Where in the U.S.A.?...* on a single country. The two newest programs in the series add an extra element of challenge to the game: players must travel in time as well as geographically. *Where in Time?...* ranges from A.D. 400 to the mid 1950s, while *Where in America's Past?...* focuses on American history.

Most of the clues require some research on the part of kids. Local residents might inform players that the criminal traded in her money for drachmas, that she told them she wanted to climb the highest mountain in the world, or that she was off in search of llama wool. The reference books included in each software package can provide the links your child needs to take the next step. For

example, *Where in the World?...* includes *The World Almanac and Book of Facts* and *Where in America's Past?...* contains *What Happened When*. All these references are useful books on their own. To solve the many *Carmen* mysteries, they're essential reference tools.

In addition to deciphering clues about the criminal's destination, players must figure out what route to take (they are presented with a choice of cities but may need to pull out a map to find out which state or country is represented by each one). Also, they must identify which one of Carmen's agents they're chasing. Based on clues they receive from informants (about the suspect's appearance, likes and dislikes, etc.) and a database of information about each member of Carmen's ring, they are able to deduce which criminal is causing the problem and issue a warrant for his or her arrest. (Without such a warrant, the criminal will get away.)

The *Carmen* series provides an exciting adventure based on fact. Regardless of the time or place, players have to learn a great deal as they search for Carmen and her agents. Once your child understands how to use the program, he may be able to find each agent in a half hour or less. But since every game has at least 12 agents and clues and locations that are randomly generated, there's plenty to do before mastering the game.

Comments

These programs are practically classics in the world of educational computing, and have led to all sorts of spin-offs, including a national television show. A number of teachers and parents report that *Carmen* has inspired a new interest in geography on the part of their children.

The *Carmen* programs are great games for the whole family. Most kids 12 and older will be able to use the clues on their own to capture the bad guys, while younger users may need some help piecing the facts together. No matter how old they are, your kids will probably need encouragement from you before they begin using the reference tools. If you participate in some of their first games and show them how to locate the information they need in the books, they will be more likely to realize how easy-to-use and helpful these resources are.

The sleuthing motif, complete with trench-coated individuals who sneak across the screen and mysterious music that intensifies as you get closer to your suspect (DOS users might want a sound card to experience the mood fully), adds greatly to the appeal of these programs

for young people. While there are many criminals to catch, the mood is playful and humorous, not violent. (None of the crimes, graphics, or clues involve injuries or bloodshed.) It's also refreshing to see so many characters that contradict the stereotypes your child might have about male versus female behavior.

If your kids are new to *Carmen*, you'll probably want to start off with one of the three programs that challenge them to travel only in space, not in time. *Where in the World?...* is a good first choice, especially if you have VGA graphics. (The deluxe edition of *Where in the World Is Carmen Sandiego?* offers stunning graphics to owners of systems with VGA cards and monitors.) When they're ready for a harder challenge, they can move on to *Where in Time?...* or *Where in America's Past?...*

***Where in the U.S.A. Is Carmen Sandiego?,
from Broderbund Software***

Headline Harry and the Great Paper Race (1991)

Publisher: Davidson & Associates   **Ages:** 10 and up

MS-DOS (Macintosh in development)

MS-DOS
$49.95 (16 colors)
$59.95 (256 colors)

As the cub reporter of the *U.S. Daily Star*, your mission is to find the key elements of the lead story. You'll have to travel all over the country (and through time), conduct interviews, "listen to" (read) the radio, and check references about each event in order to piece together the story and get back in time to meet your deadline. You can also use the phone to call your office, your mother, or Mr. Know for information. As you gather parts of the story, you save this information in a notebook. Questions involving geography and history pop up occasionally, allowing you to earn extra time if you answer correctly.

For each story you report on successfully, you are promoted and earn a new area of the country to cover. But your boss also has another goal. He wants to put the rival paper, the *Diabolical Daily*, out of business. You help in this mission by reporting honestly, accurately, and promptly.

The faster you turn in accurate stories, the more the circulation figures shift to the *U.S. Daily Star*.

Getting all the facts straight is no easy task. In each round of the game, you receive clues related to three different historical events, making it necessary to read carefully in order to determine which clues are relevant to the particular story you're pursuing. In addition, the "sleazeball" reporters from the *Diabolical Daily* constantly get in your way as you try to get the facts straight.

Comments

Headline Harry and the Great Paper Race is another one of those programs that will motivate users of older machines to upgrade their systems. The program requires a hard disk, and while the screens look good on an EGA monitor, they are beautiful in VGA. The sounds produced with an optional sound board, although not essential, are very entertaining. (You'll reach for your telephone more than once when you hear the on-screen phone ring, and cringe when the taxi driver "stops" by crashing into the car ahead of him.)

This program has high educational value. It challenges kids to read carefully and sort out the facts. Because most of the stories are based on actual historical events and require travel to different locations in the United States, players are also exposed to U.S. history and geography. Some kids may find this a little daunting, dismissing *Headline Harry* as "harder work" than the *Carmen* programs. On the other hand, many other kids will be drawn into the story and learn plenty in spite of themselves. One weakness of the program is that each time you restart the game, the same sets of clues appear, making it very difficult for kids to enjoy playing after they've successfully completed the game once.

A small group of kids can enjoy the program at the same time. If you find yourself called on frequently to help with history and geography questions, you might want to provide some reference tools for players to refer to. Reading the manual will also provide a number of clues to help your kids race to get the story in on time. If they don't, they'll have lost Headline Harry's great paper race.

Headline Harry and the Great Paper Race, from Davidson & Associates

The Oregon Trail (1985, 1990, 1991)

Publisher: MECC   **Ages:** 10 and up

MS-DOS, Macintosh, Apple II

MS-DOS
$49.95

Mac
$49.95

Apple II
$39.95

You begin your journey in 1848. But first, in order to survive the 2,000-mile Oregon Trail, you have to purchase provisions. The role you take (banker, carpenter, or farmer) determines how much money you start off with and how well you are likely to fare on the trip. You must decide how many oxen, how much food, and what quantity of other supplies you'll need. Because you can't carry everything, you'll need to supplement what you begin with by hunting or trading along the trail.

You and your four companions must cross rivers, aim and fire a rifle, and keep up a good traveling pace. If you make a mistake while crossing a river, the wagon may capsize and lose food. If you run out of food, you must hunt (assuming you have ammunition left and the skill to bring down the deer or buffalo). Without enough food, everyone's health deteriorates and someone in your party is likely to die from typhoid. Eventually, you, too, may succumb—and be memorialized with an epitaph that appears on a tombstone on the screen.

Comments

The Oregon Trail has been around—and a favorite with kids—for years. With each revision, more sophisticated graphics, sounds, and game-playing elements have been added. Still, when compared with some of the most recent programs on the market, this one feels more "serious" and less visually appealing. It's much more of a true *simulation* than an entertaining game. Younger players (6 to 9) will probably lose interest quickly unless they are playing with an adult who can help them get into the mood. On the other hand, many kids within the recommended age range are drawn to the challenge of crossing the open prairie and will play for hours.

This is a great program for those with less powerful computers. It runs easily from a floppy disk, supports CGA and EGA graphics (in the DOS world), and uses the internal speaker to play "Yankee Doodle," "Skip to My Lou," and over a dozen other recognizable songs.

Every trip on the Oregon Trail is different. It takes several attempts before kids begin to understand all the variables necessary to complete the trip. With careful planning, and by paying attention to other travelers' tales, it is possible to complete the arduous journey successfully. This simulation works very well for a small

group and can easily inspire drawings and stories about the time period.

The Oregon Trail, from MECC

Challenges for Kids Over 12

Castles (1991)

Publisher: Interplay   **Ages:** 12 and up

MS-DOS (Mac and Amiga in development)

**MS-DOS
$59.95**

Becoming the ruler of Albion is easy. You simply select your title from the beginning menu. However, remaining in power is very difficult. It is A.D. 1280, and you must consolidate and defend your conquests. This requires dealing with hostile neighbors, labor

accidents, and treacherous family members. Your ability to control your territory is determined by your success at designing and building castles.

Based on historical facts, the game creates an alternate world, carefully described in the 64-page manual. After picking a site for your castle; locating the towers, walls, and doors; and deciding how high to build the battlements, you must hire the right number and kinds of laborers to complete the project. As you watch them build your castle, you must make sure you have enough food and troops for defense. When attacked, you deploy your troops and hope your castle can withstand the onslaught of the enemy. You can only hope that you are not attacked before the castle is finished. If you run out of money, you'll have to raise taxes, provoking even more unrest among the populace.

The measure of your success is the castle's ability to withstand an enemy attack. Once you succeed at the Peasant level (the castle is partially built and you have unlimited funds), you are ready to progress to harder and harder levels. You can begin your campaign with one, three, or even eight castles. If you do not succeed, the program provides a brief synopsis of your efforts and returns you to the land of DOS. Sessions can last as little as 15 minutes if you fail, hours if you succeed. You can save and resume sessions.

Comments

This is a relatively sophisticated program, even for the 12- and 13-year-olds at the lower end of the recommended age range. Although typing is minimal, a lot of reading is required to understand what is happening during the game. (The lengthy manual is important reading but beyond the patience of most kids.) On the other hand, the subject of this game is likely to appeal to everyone in the family with an interest in medieval history and castles, and the easiest level provides a good chance for younger players to succeed.

The program supports CGA and EGA graphics but provides beautiful 256-color graphics for those with MCGA or VGA capabilities. Even though keyboard commands are provided, a mouse is essential for ease of use. The most popular MS-DOS sound boards are supported, bringing owners a variety of music and sounds (galloping horses, for example) that add to the excitement of the game.

This is a good program for family play—with the kids controlling the action and everyone deciding on next steps. The MCGA/VGA screens provide details even the younger kids can appreciate. The older kids and adults are likely to sneak back later and see just how well they can build and defend their own castles.

SimCity: The City Simulator (1989)

Publisher: Maxis, distributed by Broderbund   **Ages:** 12 and up

| MS-DOS; Macintosh; Amiga; Commodore 64, 128 |

MS-DOS
$49.95

Mac
$49.95

Commodore 64, 128
$29.95

Amiga
$29.95

SimCity places you in the role of mayor about to design a new city. You begin by zoning the land and building roads. Then you build power plants, connect zones with utility lines, and place police and fire stations in order to control crime and fires.

Your city grows only if the simulated citizens (Sims) like your city's design. The Sims move in and pay taxes. They build homes, stores, and factories in the designated zones and call upon you to build more roads to support their traffic needs. The Sims complain if they don't like what you are doing. As mayor, you may (or may not) add zones or services to respond to your citizens' requests.

The program can be completely controlled with a mouse or joystick, which you use to place items on a city map on the screen. Each placement depletes the city budget. You have to be sensitive to all sorts of costs and plan the city growth based on the tax income as well as the Sims' demands. The simulation provides a number of maps and charts that show how the city is doing (and what the Sims think of their mayor).

SimCity has several add-on products, including a Terrain Editor and two graphics sets, to change the images to ancient or future cities.

Comments

While kids drawn to fast action and dramatic graphics may lose interest in this game before giving it a real chance, those who stick with it generally get hooked. Although it takes only a few moments to learn how to place zones and build roads, designing a prosperous city is likely to require several attempts, with each attempt taking anywhere from 30 minutes to many hours. Every city is unique, based on randomly generated terrain, your design, and the Sims' response to your efforts.

SimCity can be played by some 10-year-olds, yet the simulation has enough city planning theory to provide an educational base for high school or college courses. Younger members of the family can participate in a group game, helping to place roads and watching as the Sims construct buildings and clog the freeways. Most kids under 14 will need help learning to design effective cities. Older players will enjoy the challenge of determining the growth rate and the placement of city services as the Sims move in (or out) of the simulated city.

Note: If your kids love *SimCity*, there are two Maxis programs you should be aware of. *SimEarth*, a simulation that involves controlling the evolution of life on this and other planets, is far more complex than *SimCity* but tends to appeal to *SimCity* graduates. *SimAnt*, just reaching the market as this book went to press, introduces kids to the behavior of ants through a simulation game that involves following the patterns of two teams of ants traveling around in a complex ant hill.

SimCity: The City Simulator, from Maxis

CHAPTER TWENTY-FOUR

Other Subject Areas

In this chapter, we bring you information about some of the software packages on the market that don't fit neatly into a single subject area. The first set of titles takes a decidedly multidisciplinary approach; these programs present themselves as tools for practicing everything from math computation to reading to scientific reasoning. The other two titles are programs we've classified as tools for "creative arts." One furthers creativity by encouraging students to create animated stories on the screen; the other, by turning students into accomplished musicians.

 For other programs related to creative arts, see all of Chapter 19.

Multidisciplinary

Super Munchers (1991)

Publisher: MECC   **Ages:** 8 and up

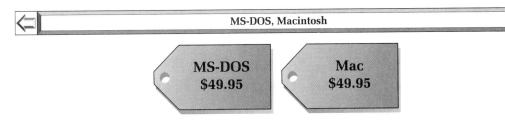

MS-DOS, Macintosh

MS-DOS
$49.95

Mac
$49.95

In the latest of MECC's "Muncher" games, children work on a variety of skills and subject areas as they attempt to munch words and escape Troggles. The chase is played out on a grid of words. At the top of the screen is a rule for selecting the right words. For example, the rule might be "animals that fly" and the words on the grid might include *duck, bee, snake,* and *ant.*

As you attempt to munch the right words, you'll have to watch out for the Troggle who is trying to munch you. You do have some defenses: certain cells are safe zones; and if you munch 20 correct words in a row, you can become Super Muncher and chase the Troggles.

The rule categories include Animals, Famous Americans, Food and Health, Geography, Music, and so on. Within each category, there are a number of subsets from which to choose. For example, Famous Americans includes sports, politicians, and basketball greats. The difficulty of the rule is based on the skill level that you select when the program begins. You can choose from five skill levels, ranging from a third/fourth-grade level to a level meant to challenge bright high school students.

Comments

Number Munchers has been a favorite with young kids for years. Now even older kids can get into the act. While we're not sure about the typical high school senior, we have seen several sophisticated 14-year-olds get seriously hooked. At the easier levels, the program remains comfortable for an eight- or nine-year-old.

Super Munchers feels like play to your kids. But as they munch their way around the screen, their word recognition, categorization, and vocabulary skills improve. Although some of the information covered can be thought of as "trivia," many of the categories challenge players to learn scientific terminology and acquire factual information concerning history, geography, science, and music.

Super Munchers, from MECC

Super Solvers Treasure Mountain! (1990)

Publisher: The Learning Company   **Ages:** 5 to 9

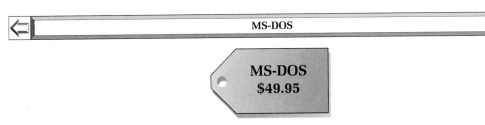

MS-DOS

MS-DOS
$49.95

The Master of Mischief has stolen a magic crown and is using its powers to steal all the gold from Treasure Mountain. You must search the mountain for hidden treasures and lock them away safely in the mountaintop castle. As you explore, little elves play tricks on you. But if you catch one with your net and answer its question, you are rewarded with clues and magic coins to help you uncover the secrets of Treasure Mountain.

Reading, math, and thinking skills are required to answer the elves' questions. Each clue leads you closer to the location of the hidden treasures. The magic coins provide additional clues (when dropped) and allow you to purchase new nets to catch the elves.

Comments

This is definitely a program for the home market. While some of the other *Super Solvers* programs fit neatly into specific curriculum areas, this one dabbles in many. Its educational strengths are that it requires kids to sharpen their thinking skills and problem-solving abilities and to read carefully. On the other hand, the problems are not focused or frequent enough to provide extensive practice in either math or reading.

After a brief demonstration, most children five and up can learn to move the character and locate coins. The youngest players may need some strategy tips from you at first. (For example, your child might attempt to catch all the elves at first and need to be reminded that only elves carrying scrolls have clues and can be caught.) If your five-year-old is not yet a comfortable reader, she may find the questions frustrating. On the other hand, since even kids over nine will be drawn to the program's game-playing elements, it's a great program to help older kids who have reading problems get extra practice in an environment that is fun and affords them plenty of success. The variety of challenges makes it an excellent program for you and your kids to play together.

As always, the *Super Solver* graphics are attractive, especially on a VGA system. A mouse is very helpful for movement. Finishing a game may take an hour or more, but games can be saved under several names to be resumed later.

Super Solvers Treasure Mountain!, from The Learning Company

The Treehouse (1991)

Publisher: Broderbund Software   **Ages:** 5 to 9

MS-DOS (Macintosh and Apple II in development)

MS-DOS
$59.95

This sequel to *The Playroom* will provide your child with countless hours of enjoyment. Everywhere kids look in the opening scene there are things to discover and explore. They can write or draw on the chalkboard in six different colors; look through the telescope and see a different view each time; or click on the cloud outside the window and watch it take

on different shapes. Cans of worms, spider webs, and a variety of "inanimate" objects all come to life when your child selects them.

There are also six separate games that can be reached by clicking on objects in the treehouse. In the puppet theatre, kids create animated sentences by piecing together phrases offered by the program. They can also make the stage setting more interesting by adding extra props or view silly sentences by clicking on "mix up." Two of the games focus on animals. One has children exploring the world outside of the treehouse while using clues about animal traits to guess the mystery animal. The second game involves creating animal scenes while classifying, sorting, and matching.

A road-rally game helps kids practice their math skills while moving around a game board, trading chips or coins. Finally, for music lovers, there are several entertaining musical activities. In *Musical Keys*, you can play an assortment of recognizable songs, such as "London Bridge," "Itsy Bitsy Spider," or "Yankee Doodle," or write your own. You can store your songs in a songbook and/or print them out. There is also a musical maze game to test musical recognition. You navigate through the maze by matching note sequences played aloud with their written representation. With each correct answer, you earn a note in the sequence. Eventually, you can guess what popular tune the sequence is from.

As kids return to the treehouse after playing games, they sometimes bring prizes with them. When players click on these prizes, they offer yet another entertaining activity. Kids are guided through the program by one or two "awesome possums" (your kid can choose the boy or the girl possum) with distinct personalities and needs of their own. Periodically, your child's possum friend will interrupt with comments or requests for food, a nap, or a particular game.

Comments

It's hard to believe how many different activities Broderbund has packed into a single program. Kids play and play and play while they learn about music, animals, mathematics, sentence structure, and more. Not only are there many different activities, each game becomes harder as your child plays.

You need a sound card such as Sound Blaster or AdLib to really

The Treehouse, from Broderbund Software

appreciate the program's musical games. Printouts can be created from most of the activities. If you have a color printer, the results are fantastic.

The program's "Even Steven" feature is great for families with more than one child. It allows children to play a number of the games against one another but to adjust the difficulty levels separately so that the younger player is playing at an easier level. You'll be glad to have this feature when it comes time to settle the inevitable battles over who gets to play with *The Treehouse* next!

Creative Arts

Cartooners (1988, 1989)

Publisher: Electronic Arts   **Ages:** 10 and up

MS-DOS, Apple IIGS

MS-DOS
$49.95

Apple IIGS
$59.95

Which is better—to watch or to create? *Cartooners* may lure your kids away from Saturday morning cartoons to get involved in hours of creative cartoon making of their own. With features designed for even the youngest reader, *Cartooners* provides the building blocks to create animated plays. Backgrounds, moving characters, and even music can be combined into entertaining scenes performed on the computer screen.

Children add dialog by typing text into the characters' "balloons." These balloons can be shaped in several ways to indicate shouts, thoughts, and so on.

All elements needed to create a cartoon sequence are selected from simple pull-down menus. Once they've selected a character and placed it on the screen, kids can make the characters walk, hop, dance, or move in a variety of ways. The movie controls operate like a VCR with play, record, fast forward, and reverse buttons. Once finished, the animation can be saved to a disk to be viewed or edited again. Six movies can be placed on the marquee so even a young user can select and watch movies others have created.

Comments

The beauty of this program is how easy it is to use. Once your kids learn how to use the mouse (required by the program) to make choices, small scenes can be created in minutes. Children as young as seven can have a good time moving characters across the screen and experimenting with different sound effects. Kids in the target age range will plunge right into creating entire stories with words and action. For those who need extra practice in reading and writing, creating dialogue for the characters provides a rewarding way to work on these skills.

A few tips: An adult may have to demonstrate how to "clean up" the final version. (Kids tend to leave their mistakes and just keep adding frames as they experiment; deleting some of them brings the story together.) The music and sound effects in the MS-DOS version work with the computer's internal speaker but sound

much better with an add-on board. Although a hard disk is not required, it makes program operation much quicker.

If your kids are expecting vivid graphics or Disney-like animated effects, they may be disappointed. The "animation" in this program involves moving the characters across the screen in a number of different ways. Some kids will complain about the fact that they can't alter the characters to look at one another or take on different poses. (As a result, the scenes look rather stiff.)

Nevertheless, the ability to tell stories with the help of moving cartoons will captivate the interest of many young people. In the process, they will learn fundamental principles of story creation and graphic composition.

Cartooners, from Electronic Arts

The Miracle Piano Teaching System (1990, 1991)

Publisher: The Software Toolworks   **Ages:** 10 and up

 MS-DOS (Macintosh and Amiga in development)

**MS-DOS
$479.95**

If you've never played a music synthesizer—a piano-like keyboard that allows you to simulate a number of instruments as you play—the Miracle Keyboard that ships as part of this package will amaze you. Even if you have had plenty of practice with such keyboards, the software that accompanies this particular synthesizer will hold many surprises.

The Miracle Piano Teaching System is designed to teach just about anyone how to play the piano. Plug the Miracle Keyboard into a serial port on your computer, install the software, and you're ready to begin playing. In the *Classroom,* you are led through interactive lessons that begin with how to play single notes with your right hand and how to follow a metronome and progress to levels that will challenge some intermediate piano players. The lessons are presented using text with highlighted words that can be selected to learn more about specific topics and plenty

of visual and auditory demonstrations. At the end of each page, you are given a task to perform, such as playing certain chords.

The main menu shows several rooms that players can visit at any time. In addition to the classroom, there's a practice room you can visit to review what you've learned in a lesson or to practice any of the 40 songs provided with the program. When you feel confident about your abilities, you can go to the performance hall and play along with a full orchestra or head for the recording studio to record and play back your own performance. An arcade room offers three arcade-style practice games plus a "jukebox" that plays pre-recorded songs.

Comments

This is a powerful teaching tool for a beginner or a slightly more advanced player who wants to brush up on existing skills at the piano. It can be used by kids and adults alike, although it's probably best suited to kids between 10 and 14. (Younger kids may have trouble reading all the lessons; adults may be put off by the musical arrangements—tending to elevator music.) The fact that the music is transposed to a simple key—no matter how it was originally written—and that the synthesizer keyboard has far fewer octaves than a piano, limits the program's usefulness for intermediate and advanced players.

A strength of the system is the huge array of valuable options and types of feedback it offers. In the beginning lessons, the program guides you closely, not allowing you to continue playing until you've hit the right note, keeping time with a metronome, displaying numbers on the screen to indicate which finger to use, and providing visual feedback via an animated keyboard on the screen. During practice and performance, players can easily control variables such as tempo, the type of instrument they want to play, the type of accompaniment desired, whether to use one or two hands, and the difficulty level of the songs.

The program has a few annoying features. It takes a long time to move from one screen to the next, and the function keys involved for users without a mouse are quite cumbersome. Even with a mouse, constantly having to go back and forth between the synthesizer keyboard and the mouse buttons might frustrate some users.

Our final concern involves the arcade games, two of which are relatively violent. In one, players shoot ducks by hitting the appropriate notes. Each correct shot is accompanied by a duck's plaintive quack as it disappears from view. In another, players control parachutes attached to figures about to jump from an airplane: hit the correct chord and the chute opens; miss and the little men go splat. Given your individual child's sensibilities, you'll have to decide whether this approach bothers you enough to rule out an otherwise excellent program.

Games

Don't be too quick to dismiss entertainment software as a waste of time. Whether we're talking about Nintendo or the personal computer, there are indeed plenty of mindless electronic "shoot-em-ups" available for those who want them. But there are also many programs designed with entertainment in mind that help children develop valuable thinking skills.

Electronic strategy games and computerized adventure games help young people learn to solve difficult problems. Audio-visual reinforcement encourages players to strengthen their powers of observation and deductive thinking. And kids who don't normally like to read find themselves reading manuals to learn the rules and strategies of the games.

There are hundreds of entertainment titles from which to choose. To help you get started, we've provided a sampling of our favorites. These programs promote thinking while they entertain, provide a flexible supportive atmosphere, minimize the amount of violence young people are exposed to, and—on top of all that—hold the interest of kids for a long time.

The first category of programs reviewed here includes board games and jigsaw puzzles—electronic versions of the noncomputerized activities that we and our parents enjoyed as kids. Some people wonder why one should use the computer to do something that can be done much less expensively off-line. We've found that the best electronic board games add great value to the experience. By providing interesting feedback (animation and sound effects, for example), they motivate kids to stick with the problem-solving tasks, and they provide a flexibility not possible away from the computer (for example, kids can frequently play alone or against an opponent, or can choose to add variety by altering the gameboard or other graphic elements). Children who lack confidence in their own problem-solving abilities find themselves attracted to electronic board games and jigsaw puzzles that allow them to control the difficulty level and get help from the computer.

We've also included a group of games that would not be part of our kids' lives if it weren't for computers, Nintendo, and other game machines. These entertainment programs involve action on the screen, requiring kids to respond quickly, practice spatial relations, and use strategic thinking. Some have an "arcade game" feel, requiring quick reflexes to hit some sort of a target. But most go beyond that to provide a richer environment that involves thinking as well as reflexes.

Finally, we've included just a few of the many electronic "adventure games" on the market today. We've ruled out some because of their high level of violence or their adult orientation (many of the latest titles, targeted primarily at young adult males, tend to feature scantily clothed females and plenty of sexual innuendo). Of those that are appropriate for the typical 10-year-old, we selected programs that have appeal, that challenge without frustrating, and that can be enjoyed by many members of the family. No doubt, if your child is interested in adventure games, you will find a number of others that fit the bill as well.

Electronic Jigsaw Puzzles and Board Games

Mickey's Jigsaw Puzzles (1991)

Publisher: Walt Disney Computer Software   **Ages:** 5 and up

MS-DOS

MS-DOS
$49.95
$69.95 (combo with Sound Source)

Popular Disney cartoon characters come to life on the computer screen in this innovative jigsaw puzzle package from Disney Software. Kids keep company with Mickey Mouse and his friends, Minnie Mouse, Goofy, and Donald Duck, as they solve 15 different colorful puzzles. A point-and-click icon-based interface lets youngsters view pictures before selecting one to solve. Puzzles may be cut into seven different sizes (ranging from 4 to 64 pieces) to accommodate a wide range of skills.

Mickey's Jigsaw Puzzles features three levels of difficulty in addition to puzzles of different-size pieces. Young children can select the silhouette option (easiest), which enables them to solve puzzles by dropping puzzle shapes onto picture outlines. Older children can work with either jigsaw-shaped (harder) or square (hardest) puzzle pieces. If the "grid option" is turned on, kids see outlines of all the jigsaw-shaped puzzle pieces.

Puzzles may be solved with or without a timer. Puzzle-solving help is available if needed. If the "text message" option is active, dialogue spoken by Disney characters appears on-screen in written form. When a puzzle is complete, youngsters may animate the whole screen (by selecting the movie camera icon) or just a particular puzzle portion. Wacky sound effects often accompany the animation.

Comments

Of the electronic jigsaw programs on the market, we think that *Mickey's Jigsaw Puzzles* is the most flexible and easiest to use. It provides several options not found in other puzzle programs. First, it lets kids print line-art drawings of each puzzle screen that they can then color in. Second, for those users with the Sound Source or other support sound cards, it offers high-quality background music and entertaining speech. Finally, the software features spectacular 256-color graphics.

Our main complaints are the same ones we expressed when reviewing *Mickey's Crossword Puzzle Maker* (Chapter 22, "Language Arts Software"). We find the copy-protection scheme (involving deciphering pictures on a hard-to-read, easy-to-lose sheet of paper) annoying, and we wish there were additional graphics options beyond the Disney characters. Otherwise, we think this is a good choice, because it helps young kids feel comfortable at

Mickey's Jigsaw Puzzles, from Walt Disney Computer Software

the computer and practice visual skills. If your child does not do well

under pressure, be sure to run the program with the timer turned off.

Shanghai II: Dragon's Eye (1990)

Publisher: Activision   **Ages:** 6 and up

MS-DOS (Macintosh in development)

MS-DOS
$49.95

Shanghai II consists of two games: *Shanghai* and *Dragon's Eye. Shanghai* is a game of strategy, memory, and chance. Challengers play alone (in Solitaire mode) or compete against a friend. When a round begins, 144 tiles are arranged in one of 13 possible layouts. Some tiles are in plain view. Others are hidden. The object of the game is to clear matching tiles from the board by removing one pair at a time.

A point-and-click user interface makes it easy for even young children to select and remove tiles. Customizing options allow challengers to use one of eight picture tile sets, including playing cards, flags of the world, animals, numbers/letters, and colorful mah-jongg symbols (with

images of dragons, winds, seasons, and flowers). You can control the game-board layout by choosing an Easy, Advanced, or Master layout, or by constructing one of your own. The game automatically tells you when there are no moves left, but a "shuffle remaining tiles option" rearranges available tiles in random order, so that new matching possibilities emerge.

Dragon's Eye is a more challenging variation of the basic *Shanghai* game. Players compete as Dragon Masters or Dragon Slayers. Dragon Masters place tiles on the board, trying to fill it up. Dragon Slayers must clear the board by removing matching pairs of tiles. The game ends when a Dragon Slayer cannot make another move.

Comments

Both *Shanghai* and *Dragon's Eye* encourage players to observe carefully (searching for matching pairs among tiles that block the most moves) and to plan ahead. They are terrific programs for the whole family because they offer so many different levels of difficulty. Preschoolers will enjoy playing *Shanghai* with alphabet/number tiles. (To make them feel more comfortable, have them play the game without activating the timer.) The truly daring members of the family can try their skill in Tournament mode (one round of *Dragon's Eye*, plus three rounds of *Shanghai*) either alone or against a friend.

Shanghai II offers hours of entertainment for even the most discerning game enthusiast. Music, sound effects, and animated tile movements capture the mystique of the Orient, and the program's many options keep players coming back for more. If you're looking for a fun computer game to play with your kids, this one is a strong candidate.

Spot: The Computer Game (1990)

Publisher: Virgin Games   **Ages:** 5 and up

MS-DOS; Amiga; Commodore 64, 128

MS-DOS
$19.99

Amiga
$19.99

Commodore 64, 128
$19.99

Spot: The Computer Game is a contest of strategy for one to four players. The hero of the program is Spot, 7-Up's shade-sporting, animated cartoon figure. Spot's acrobatic antics and the software's toe-tapping musical score make this mind-puzzling board game lots of fun.

Each challenger starts a round with only two pieces on the board. The player with the most pieces by game's end wins. Contestants earn extra pieces in two different ways. If they move a piece by advancing it to an adjacent square, the piece "clones" and becomes two. Pieces also clone when they land on a square that borders a square with an opponent's piece. If pieces move by skipping a square, they merely shift location and do not clone, but they still capture all bordering pieces.

Comments

Spot is a fast-paced strategy game at a price that's hard to beat. Customizing options make it suitable for a wide range of ages and developmental levels. Kids will play it again and

again because it's so easy to learn. Even young children will have fun because they can select a board layout (there are 512 options) or configure a computer opponent to play at a skill level they can easily beat. Encourage youngsters who do not do well under pressure to play without the clock. Kids who thrive on competition will enjoy playing with a timer and matching wits against a tough computer adversary.

Tesserae (1990)

Publisher: Inline Design   **Ages:** 8 and up

Macintosh

**Mac
$49.95**

Tesserae, from the Latin word meaning cube or die, is a simple game of strategy played on an electronic board covered in tiles. The goal is to clear the board of all tiles but one, in as few moves as possible. The program caters to a wide range of skills and abilities, offering nine game boards (each one harder to solve than the next) and three levels of play

(Beginner, Intermediate, Advanced). Challengers who opt to compete in Tournament mode must solve all nine game boards in order to win.

Challengers remove tiles from the board by having one piece jump another in a vertical, horizontal, or diagonal direction. Strategy comes into play because not all *Tesserae* tiles are created equal. Each square on a *Tesserae* board may be occupied by one (primary), two (secondary), or three (tertiary) tiles. Secondary and tertiary tiles frequently require more than one jump to clear.

While there are many ways to solve the puzzle, some strategies work better than others. For example, players register fewer moves when a secondary tile jumps another secondary, or a tertiary jumps a tertiary. Players do better if they avoid leaving orphan tiles strewn around the board.

Comments

Kids who enjoy cerebral aerobics without the pressure of competition will find *Tesserae* very appealing. There are no clocks to beat. And an "Undo" command lets players "take back" as many moves as they wish, allowing young strategists to try out different play options to see which one registers the fewest moves.

Tesserae is an easy game to learn. In addition, it offers many types of help that will appeal to beginners. For example, the software highlights all legal-move positions whenever players select a tile for maneuvering. And players can call up interactive on-line help that provides complete game instructions using detailed illustrations. Even relatively young children can master the game quickly.

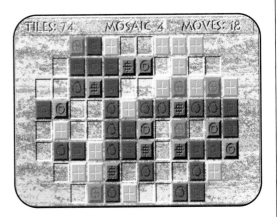

Tesserae, from Inline Design

Strategy, Reflexes, and Spatial Relations

PipeDream (1989)

Publisher: LucasFilm Games   **Ages:** 10 and up

MS-DOS; Macintosh; Apple II; Amiga; Commodore 64, 128; Atari ST

MS-DOS $29.95

Mac, Apple II $5.95...

PipeDream starts out as a simple strategy game involving spatial relationships, but challengers end up testing their wits as well as their reflexes. The object of the game is to build a pipeline using randomly shaped plumbing parts that come from a dispenser at the left side of the screen.

The game becomes more complicated after eight seconds of play. A viscous fluid starts to ooze through the pipe. If players don't find the right parts to stay ahead of the "flooz," the flow spills out the end of the pipeline and the game ends.

Players earn points for every piece of pipe they place, but their pipeline must meet or exceed a specified target length if they wish to advance to the next level. Each round of play requires challengers to build a longer pipeline. Players score double points for each piece of pipe the flooz

flows through beyond the target distance.

PipeDream can be played by one or two players. Single players compete in Basic (one-pipe dispenser) or Expert (dual dispenser) modes. A special Trainer mode is available for all novices who wish more control over the speed of flow. At higher levels of play (there are 36 levels in all), the game becomes even more challenging: Obstacles appear on board to block pipeline construction; flooz flows through the pipeline at a faster rate; and would-be plumbers must build pipelines using more complicated pipe shapes.

Comments

Whether you and your kids love or hate this program depends largely on how you feel about working under time pressure. Even though there's a slower Trainer mode for novices, kids have to think quickly in order to succeed. It is definitely not a game for those who are easily frustrated.

If your kid does get hooked, however, you can feel confident that he is working on his reflexes, visual perception, and problem-solving skills. Players do well (that is, obtain higher scores or advance levels) only if they position pieces in places that anticipate future connections.

PipeDream, from LucasFilm Games

Super Solvers Challenge of the Ancient Empires (1990)

Publisher: The Learning Company   **Ages:** 10 and up

MS-DOS

**MS-DOS
$49.95**

Challenge of the Ancient Empires is the one *Super Solvers* program that does not focus, at least in part, on academic subject areas. Instead, it pits enterprising sleuths against the infamous Morty Maxwell, Master of Doom, in a game that has them navigating through cavernous underground chambers with hidden passageways and many death-defying obstacles to overcome. The goal is to find the buried treasures (artifacts of ancient civilizations) before Maxwell grabs them for his private collection.

While the story line for this software makes the program sound like a plot from a Hollywood B movie,

Challenge of the Ancient Empires is actually a powerful thinking game. Activities combine arcadelike thrills with challenges requiring logical reasoning. There are numerous puzzles to solve, offering several hours of engaging play. Games can be played at the Explorer (easy) or Expert (difficult) level. Each rank features different logic problems.

Super Solvers collect artifact pieces as they explore the chambers. High-tech gadgets (turbo tennis shoes, a miner's hat, a force-field beam, and so on) help them work through cavern challenges and find their way through locked underground passageways. There are ropes to climb, sliding panels to unlock, conveyor belts to master, and menacing cavern creatures to overcome. Once all artifact pieces have been collected, enterprising detectives use the power of logical thinking to put the artifact together.

Comments

Challenge of the Ancient Empires is a game designed for older children (though not necessarily for their non-Nintendo-literate parents). It requires a certain degree of hand-eye

coordination and a lot of persistence to master. It can also be quite unforgiving, sending players all the way back to the beginning of a difficult chamber if they don't succeed the first time. For many kids, however, this challenge is what makes the program so appealing.

Parents or teachers who buy this software thinking it will teach children about ancient culture will be disappointed. Although the artifacts gathered by players do come from the ancient civilizations of China, India, Egypt, and so on, they do not play a major role in the game. On the other hand, the program does encourage logical thinking and puzzle solving — and will keep some kids playing for hours.

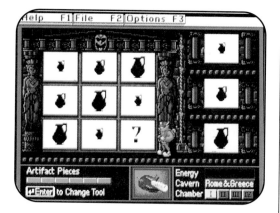

Super Solvers Challenge of the Ancient Empires, from The Learning Company

The 'Tris Series

Tetris (1987) *WellTris* (1989)
Faces (1990) *WordTris* (1991)

Publisher: Spectrum Holobyte **Ages:** 8 and up for Tetris; 10 and up for others

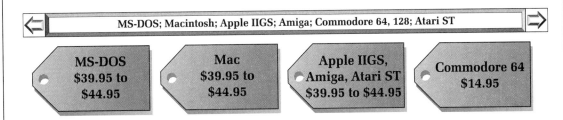

MS-DOS; Macintosh; Apple IIGS; Amiga; Commodore 64, 128; Atari ST

MS-DOS
$39.95 to
$44.95

Mac
$39.95 to
$44.95

Apple IIGS,
Amiga, Atari ST
$39.95 to $44.95

Commodore 64
$14.95

The 'Tris family of computer games represents a highly addictive collection of fast-action brainteasers. *Tetris* is the most popular cerebral puzzler of the series. Play takes place in a multilayered pit. Geometric shapes (each composed of four blocks in different configurations) appear at the top of the pit and begin their descent. Challengers must flip or rotate the falling geometric blocks to form solid rows. Completed layers (rows without holes) disappear from the screen, leaving more room to maneuver. When a column of blocks reaches the top of the pit, the game ends.

After players complete 10 solid rows, *Tetris* advances to a new level. The higher the level, the more difficult the game. Blocks fall faster and faster. Challengers must become increasingly more quick-witted to sort and position shapes correctly. An optional Preview mode enables players to see the "next" shape and plan for its placement.

WellTris adds a three-dimensional challenge to the spatial puzzle-solving task. Shapes descend from the top of a four-sided, multilayer well. Players

Tetris, from Spectrum Holobyte

flip, rotate, and reposition the falling blocks to fill horizontal or vertical eight-block layers at the bottom of the well. They use the corners of the well to split larger shapes into smaller ones. Completed rows and columns disappear, leaving more room to manipulate falling geometric shapes. The game ends when strategists can no longer bring pieces into the bottom of the well or when a stack of shapes reaches the top of a side wall.

In *Faces*, instead of falling blocks, game pieces have pictures of facial parts. Strategists reposition falling portrait segments to form complete faces, some of which belong to famous people, such as Sigmund Freud, Margaret Thatcher, Shakespeare, or Santa Claus. Whole faces disappear from the playing screen, but if a stack of mismatched facial parts reaches the top of a playing area, the game ends. As with other games in the series, the faster a piece is positioned, the more points are scored.

The newest program in the series, *WordTris*, requires players to use falling letters to create words on the screen. As the letters reach the bottom of the Tetris-like well, falling into whatever column the player specifies, they hit "water" and remain floating until another letter lands on top of them, pushing them down one row. Completed words (formed either

vertically or horizontally) disappear from the well, leaving more room for play. Longer or more complex words (that is, words with the letter *Q* or *Z*) earn the most points. As with the other 'Tris programs, blocks fall at increasingly faster rates at higher levels of play.

Comments

Kids enjoy the programs in this series because each activity features gamelike puzzle-solving challenges. Adults encourage children to play because the software helps strengthen depth perception and visual acuity while teaching youngsters the importance of tactical planning. To be successful, 'Tris enthusiasts must plan moves in advance. The faster a piece comes to rest, the higher the points.

Success at *Tetris*, *WellTris*, *Faces*, or *WordTris* also depends on quick reflexes and keyboard dexterity. If your child has difficulty with fast finger action or hates to compete against a clock, game play may be more frustrating than fun. However, there are ways of modifying the software to meet the styles of individual players. For example, although the programs advance players automatically, it is possible to determine the level at which to begin play each time and to turn on or off such options as the ability to preview the shape that will fall next.

WordTris is probably not the best program to start kids off with, because the required language arts skills combined with the strategy and reflexes involved in all the 'Tris games can be overwhelming at first. However, if your son or daughter has already gained confidence with one of the other programs in the series (*Tetris* is a good place to start), you might want to add this extra educational content. *WordTris* offers a kids' mode that slows down the timer considerably. Your 10-year-old is not likely to know a number of the words the program accepts (players do not have to indicate when they've made a word, because the program checks

each turn and removes any real words from the well), but perhaps he will do a little vocabulary expanding in the process.

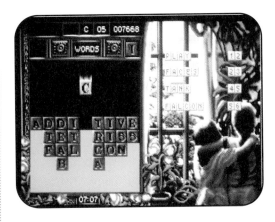

WordTris, from Spectrum Holobyte

Adventure Games

King's Quest (1984–1991)

Publisher: Sierra On-Line   **Ages:** 10 and up

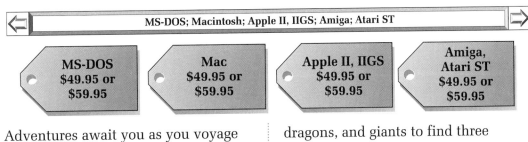

MS-DOS; Macintosh; Apple II, IIGS; Amiga; Atari ST

| MS-DOS $49.95 or $59.95 | Mac $49.95 or $59.95 | Apple II, IIGS $49.95 or $59.95 | Amiga, Atari ST $49.95 or $59.95 |

Adventures await you as you voyage into the Kingdom of Daventry. In *King's Quest I*, players take on the role of Sir Graham, who must brave ogres,

dragons, and giants to find three magical treasures and return them to the Kingdom. In later adventures, Graham (now King) and a variety of other characters (including Graham's daughter, the Princess Rosella, and his friend, Cedrick the owl) journey to distant parts of the world, searching for magical fruits, missing castles, and true love.

In each of the *King's Quest* adventures, you decide where the characters are to move and what they will do in every scene. You talk to other characters in the story to discover clues and hints about the location of important items. Occasionally, you must act quickly to escape from a threatening creature.

The program provides multiple choices for each action. If one action does not work, simply select another to see different results. When not making choices, you move your character from place to place on the screen, constantly discovering new things to explore and creatures to talk with.

Completing one of the *King's Quest* adventures can take hours. Fortunately, you can save the game at a number of points and return to that same point later. (Sometimes, if you don't make the right decision, your character dies, but you can restart the game at the last point you saved it.)

Comments

The plot of each of the *King's Quest* programs is complex and the characters well developed. The adventures offer plenty of suspense and perils to overcome without focusing on violence. (It's possible to die or to suffer the consequences of various decisions, but there is little emphasis on fights and battles.)

Educators and parents who were around in the early days of adventure games might lament the fact that today's programs no longer involve the reading and writing required in the past. Instead, in the latest *King's Quest* titles (as with many other popular adventure games today) choices are made using a pointer, and most program information is conveyed with graphics and sound rather than with text. While your child is not practicing reading skills, she is, however, being challenged to think because a lot of problem solving is involved in each new situation.

As your kids play these games, they will come to know and love the characters of Daventry. Fortunately, each story is independent of the others, making it possible to start with any title in the series. If your daughter prefers a female lead character, she can start off with *King's Quest IV: The Perils of Rosella*. If you have an MS-DOS computer with VGA graphics, you'll definitely want to select only those titles with Sierra's new VGA graphics. (*King's Quest I* and *V* were already available in this format when we reviewed them, and the other titles in the series were all being upgraded.) The color screens in VGA are works of art. Owners of MS-DOS machines will also be better off with a sound card that allows them to hear the elaborate music and sound effects produced by the programs.

The entire family will be drawn to the *King's Quest* series. Children under 10 are not likely to have the perseverance to complete any of the quests on their own. But because almost anyone can control the game,

both parents and children can team up to have some great adventures together.

King's Quest V, from Sierra On-Line

Loom (1990)

Publisher: LucasFilm Games   **Ages:** 12 and up

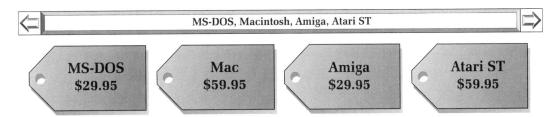

MS-DOS, Macintosh, Amiga, Atari ST

MS-DOS $29.95	Mac $59.95	Amiga $29.95	Atari ST $59.95

Loom, LucasFilm Games' first fantasy adventure and our favorite program in their line, places you in the role of Bobbin, the weaver boy, who must rescue the Weaver's Guild by finding and defeating a strange power. Bobbin is the only remaining member of the

Guild in human form and must learn progressively more complicated tunes (up to eight notes) to move to the next level. In the advanced mode, you only hear the notes. In the beginner's mode, you see the notes on a musical staff as well as hear them.

All the LucasFilm games are very movielike. (Other popular titles from Lucas include *Monkey Island* and *Raiders of the Lost Ark*). At some points in these games, you sit back and watch for two or three minutes as the story unfolds. (If you have already viewed the sequence, you can press the Escape key to jump directly to the next scene.) Decisions are made using multiple-choice menus. If a choice does not work, you can back up and try again.

Because *Loom* is based on music, the package includes a 30-minute audio cassette to provide a dramatic beginning to the story.

Comments

Although there are several scenes in this program that could easily scare younger children, the game is not violent. Bobbin does not fight other characters but uses his magical notes to deal with them.

For kids who are new to adventure games, *Loom* provides a gentle introduction. It is not as hard to complete as many other programs, and because of its unusual emphasis on music, it appeals to many users who aren't normally drawn to action and adventure games. (In order to fully appreciate the music, owners of MS-DOS computers will want to have a sound board.)

Like *Kings Quest, Loom* is an adventure that will engage the whole family. The game controls are easily learned while the challenges are difficult enough to keep everyone interested. Even kids under the recommended age level (especially kids over 9 or 10) can participate comfortably as the family plays this game.

CD-ROM

A relatively new technology, CD-ROM is used widely by businesses, libraries, and other facilities that need regular access to huge quantities of data. Even though CD-ROM drives have only recently begun making their way into the home, there are several family-oriented titles on the market, and the list of available programs is growing every day.

If you've just invested in a CD-ROM drive for your computer or are considering one and wondering what's available for children and young teenagers, we have a few titles to recommend. Some of these programs, oriented to younger children, allow users to explore strange electronic fantasy worlds, listen to their favorite storybooks being read aloud, or solve puzzles that reinforce a variety of basic skills. Taking advantage of the CD-ROM's storage capacity, these titles come alive with high-resolution images and realistic sound.

The second group of CD-ROM titles will be of interest to parents of kids over 9 or 10 years of age. These are electronic reference tools that make accessing information a matter of a few simple keystrokes. With a CD-ROM encyclopedia, youngsters usually don't mind following a variety of research leads, because they don't have to return to the bookshelf to check on cross-references. Most CD-ROM encyclopedias also feature several electronic options that enable youngsters to mark important passages with "bookmarks," look up difficult words in an on-line dictionary, save articles to disk for use with a word processor, or print relevant data. It's a researcher's dream come true!

As you'll see, none of the CD-ROM titles are cheap. In part that's because of the market—with few CD-ROM drives in homes, early adopters are called upon to pay a larger share of the publishers' development costs. However, before you balk at the prices, keep in mind that a CD-ROM is capable of holding many times more information than a standard floppy disk. It may seem outrageous to spend hundreds of dollars on a single disc that you can hold in one hand, but when you consider that the disc might contain as much information as a multivolume encyclopedia—in a form that's much easier to use—the price may not seem so high after all.

As with the reviews in previous chapters, we have indicated the basic platform on which each title will run. Obviously, your computer must also have a CD-ROM drive in order to run these programs. In a few cases, you will see a reference to an MPC computer. By this, we are referring to titles developed for "Multimedia PCs"—IBM PCs and compatibles that run *Windows* and conform to a new standard described in Chapter 12, "Peripherals and Other Options."

 For other programs on CD-ROM, see also King's Quest *(Chapter 25) and* Living Books *and* Macmillan Multimedia Dictionary for Children *(Chapter 27).*

Exploration and Play

Discis Books (1990)

Publisher: Discis Knowledge Research   **Ages:** 4 and up

Macintosh

**Mac
$74.95 to
$89.95**

How about curling up in front of the computer and reading along with a good book? These electronic texts

introduce young children to the magic of interactive storytelling. The series consists of 10 popular titles by well-known children's authors, including Robert Munsch (*Thomas' Snowsuit, Mud Puddle*), Beatrix Potter (*The Tale of Peter Rabbit, The Tale of Benjamin Bunny*), Sean O. Huigin (*Scary Poems for Rotten Kids*), and Audrey Nelson (*A Long Hard Day on the Ranch*).

Kids listen to the computer read the story aloud while they follow along with the text on the screen. Each Discis Book features complete story text along with original illustrations. Sound effects and music enhance the dramatized delivery. When youngsters click on a word in the story, they hear its pronunciation. For some of the words, they can also request a dictionary definition. When a storybook picture is selected, a printed label appears and is pronounced aloud.

A "customize" menu allows parents to personalize the book for their kids, determining how the story should be read and which features should be turned on or off. The program will also translate selected words and pictures into Spanish.

Comments

With only one title per disc, Discis Books are quite expensive for what you get. You'll have to decide for yourself how much more useful they are to you than a less-expensive printed book. Some parents may be happier to curl up on the couch and read to their kids. Some may also be annoyed, as we were, at the program's dictionary. The definitions, taken from a source clearly written for an older audience, tend to be quite incomprehensible to any child young enough to need the help.

On the other hand, for many kids these CD-ROM books do a lot to make reading fun. The children don't listen passively to the story being read aloud; they interact with the words and pictures, directing the program to deliver translations and pronunciations. Reading fluency is reinforced by the way in which the program highlights phrases as they are read aloud. "Reading" a Discis book need not preclude the time you spend exploring literature with your youngster; instead, you and your child can watch together as your favorite storybook characters come alive on a computer screen.

The Manhole (1989)
Cosmic Osmo (1990)

Publisher: Activision   **Ages:** 4 and up

Macintosh; Manhole also available in MS-DOS format

MS-DOS
$79.95
(Manhole)

Mac
$59.95
(Manhole)

Mac
$69.95
(Cosmic Osmo)

The Manhole is reminiscent of the adventures experienced by Alice in *Through the Looking Glass,* or Jack in his travels up the beanstalk. It was one of the first programs on the market to provide an open-ended and fun-filled environment in which players move from scene to scene by clicking on objects of interest. There are two worlds for your children to explore: a mysterious castle perched high in the sky and a sunken ship nestled deep on an ocean floor.

As they travel, kids meet a variety of fanciful characters, including a talking flamingo, a walrus who likes to nap, dancing seahorses, a tea-sipping rabbit, and a French-speaking turtle. Each setting is as unusual as it is inviting, and there are enough unpredictable events packed into the story to keep viewers of all ages glued to the computer screen for many hours.

Cosmic Osmo sends children on another interactive adventure, this time into hyperspace aboard the Osmobile, a "magical mystery" electronic spaceship. Players visit seven different planets, including a Vegetable Moon and a Holy Mackerel. Each planet in the Osmo universe offers many surprises. Travelers meet several whimsical characters, who include an opera-singing ketchup bottle, a disenchanted digger ant, Professor Osmostein, and the great Osmo himself. They find phone numbers to dial, a museum to visit, puzzles to solve, electronic toys to construct, elevators to ride, and much more.

Animated graphics, sound effects, and toe-tapping musical scores provided by both of these programs encourage youngsters to delve deeper and deeper into the mysteries that lie behind closed doors, inside desk drawers, or down uncharted tunnels.

Comments

These CDs won't teach your kids basic reading or writing skills, but they're a terrific way to introduce them to computers and encourage their imaginations to run wild. Both titles will keep young people delightfully entertained for hours, stimulating curiosity and investigation while introducing newcomers to using a mouse. There are no clocks to beat, battles to win, or competitive pressures to overcome.

The one thing to be aware of if you're considering buying one of these titles is that they may have some outdated system requirements. When this book was being written, the Mac CD-ROM programs had not yet been upgraded to work with the most current versions of *HyperCard* and the Macintosh System software. Check the requirements on the package carefully to make sure that the title you're considering will run on your system.

If you do have the hardware and software that's needed, go ahead and give *The Manhole* or *Cosmic Osmo* a try. Preschoolers and adults alike will delight in exploring these two new worlds. They're fun places to visit and a great way to spend a rainy afternoon!

Note: There also are Macintosh floppy disk versions of these programs, although we haven't seen them in many stores recently.

Mixed-Up Mother Goose, CD-ROM version (1991)

Publisher: Sierra On-Line   **Ages:** 4 and up

MS-DOS, MPC

MS-DOS
$59.95

MPC
$59.95

Sierra's *Mixed-Up Mother Goose*, described in detail in Chapter 20, "Software for Preschoolers," is even more captivating when translated to CD-ROM. The basic plot remains the same, but the graphics have been redone in stunning VGA resolution. And in this version of the program, the characters that inhabit Mother Goose Land talk and sing.

Two CDs ship in the package. One contains only the English-language version, which outputs the audio to headphones or amplified speakers. The other contains a multilingual version that lets children choose whether characters sing and speak in English, Spanish, French, German, or Japanese. For this version, your computer must be equipped with a sound card capable of playing digitized sounds.

Comments

Mixed-Up Mother Goose is delightful in both its floppy and CD-ROM versions. If you have a CD-ROM drive, the enhanced graphics and sound may make the extra cost of this version worth it to your child. One thing to be aware of, however, if you're interested in helping your child learn to read at

Mixed-Up Mother Goose, CD-ROM, from Sierra On-Line

the computer: in "improving" this program, its developers decided to eliminate all the written text used in the floppy version rather than simply supplement it with spoken voice. It's too bad, because in the process they passed up a great chance to reinforce beginning reading skills.

There is no difference in content between the MS-DOS and MPC versions of this program, but the MPC version does operate faster and take advantage of the *Windows* interface.

Reference Tools

Compton's MultiMedia Encyclopedia (1991)
Compton's Family Encyclopedia (1991)

Publisher: Britannica Software   **Ages:** 6 and up

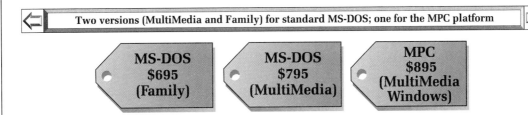

Two versions (MultiMedia and Family) for standard MS-DOS; one for the MPC platform

MS-DOS $695 (Family)   **MS-DOS $795 (MultiMedia)**   **MPC $895 (MultiMedia Windows)**

Each of Britannica's CD-ROM encyclopedias features all 26 volumes of the 1991 print edition of *Compton's Encyclopedia,* plus a lot more. In addition to articles, there are maps, graphs, drawings, captioned photographs, recorded sounds, and speech. The version of this encyclopedia that we actually reviewed is known as *Compton's*

MultiMedia Encyclopedia and is marketed primarily to schools and libraries. Two other versions were being completed as we went to press.

With the family version of the encyclopedia, the price is kept down by offering fewer multimedia features: there are none of the animated effects provided by the standard MultiMedia version, and the new version offers 30 minutes of music and sound, as opposed to 60, and 10,000 images instead of 15,000. On the other end of the spectrum, the *Windows* version adds value to the product, although not by increasing its content. Instead, the *Windows* interface makes the encyclopedia even easier to use, and such technical features as the ability to hear audio effects while reading the text have been improved.

With these programs, students access information by directing the computer to search for ideas, major topics, article titles, pictures, or picture captions. Alternatively, they use the electronic atlas to locate places on a world map, explore a time line of United States history (1490–1990), or concentrate on science themes by proceeding directly to 20 of the most interesting science articles in the encyclopedia.

Unlike conventional print encyclopedias, the CD version of *Compton's Encyclopedia* provides special tools to facilitate on-line research. A "Bookmark" option lets users mark a section of an article for later reference. A Glossary contains definitions for underlined article words. The encyclopedia's on-line version of *Merriam-Webster's Intermediate Dictionary* lets individuals look up the meaning of any difficult word.

When researchers choose the "Find a Word" option, they can quickly search an article for all instances of a particular word. Copy and save options allow students to store portions of an article (up to a maximum of 108 lines of text) in a Notebook file for future reference. A print function makes it possible to generate hard copy of up to five screens of text.

Comments

A friendly icon-based interface makes this encyclopedia quite easy to use. For example, when youngsters click on a camera icon, they see pictures. If they select the headphones icon, they listen to digitized recordings of speech, music, or other sounds. Students who have difficulty selecting a research topic can call upon the encyclopedia's Research Assistant to obtain a list of suggested themes and

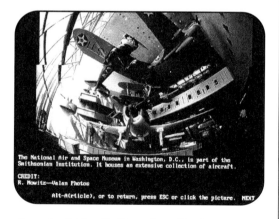

The National Air and Space Museum in Washington, D.C., is part of the Smithsonian Institution. It houses an extensive collection of aircraft.
CREDIT:
R. Mowitz—Valan Photos
Alt-A(rticle), or to return, press ESC or click the picture. NEXT

Compton's Family Encyclopedia, from Britannica Software

topics, complete with helpful questions and instructions for quick information retrieval. Because of the sheer number of options, however, some people will find the program overwhelming at first. Before you leave your child to work with this reference tool, it's a good idea to take a complete tour of the encyclopedia together, making sure he understands the many icons and the levels from which they can be reached.

We think that you should be aware of the three options open to you when considering this electronic encyclopedia. Although you're likely to find only the family version of the encyclopedia in the retail stores, if you like what you see but want even more in the way of multimedia

capabilities, contact Britannica about ordering one of the other versions. All of the versions require a hefty investment, but there's a good chance that you'll feel it's money well spent.

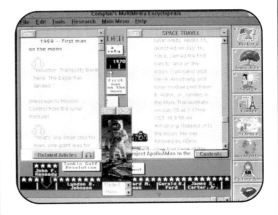

Compton's MultiMedia Encyclopedia, from Britannica Software

Guinness Disc of Records (1991)

Publisher: UniDisc/Britannica Software (order from Britannica)

Ages: 14 and up

MS-DOS, MPC (Macintosh in development)

MS-DOS	Mac	MPC
$99.95	$99.95	$149.95

The CD-ROM version of the official *Guinness Book of Records* compiles information on more than 7,000 human achievements. It details superlative accomplishments in many areas, including science, technology, sports, business, transportation, buildings, the arts, and entertainment. Three hundred color photographs, taken directly from the print edition, add an element of realism to the presentation.

The disc sports a point-and-click interface with simple menus that make record retrieval a breeze. As you search for the biggest, longest, fastest, shortest, most valuable record-holders, etc., you can look them up by topic, idea, entry title, and picture. A "Picture Tour" option allows users with VGA monitors and graphics cards to view a slide show of the photograph library, complete with captions, or to proceed from any picture to its related record.

On-line help details operation specifics. The disc incorporates an electronic version of *Merriam-Webster's Intermediate Dictionary* for definitions of any word in the text. Viewers even have the option of printing the contents of text windows if the computer is connected to a printer that supports the IBM character set.

Guinness Disc of Records, from UniDisc/Britannica Software

266

The Guinness MultiMedia Disc of Records, a new version for owners of MPC or other Windows-based computers, offers the same basic features, plus recorded sound to accompany 70 of the entries.

Comments

No, this is not a "serious" reference tool. But that's where its appeal lies. Unlike conventional encyclopedias or technical databases, Guinness Disc of Records is extremely entertaining.

Kids feel motivated to search for information on the strangest as well as the greatest human achievements. The information may or may not be relevant to anything your child is doing in school, but in the process of browsing the database for authenticated facts or bizarre testimonials, youngsters develop and refine their analytical skills. This is the sort of program that is fun for the whole family.

Information Finder (1991)

Publisher: World Book Educational Products   **Ages:** 10 and up

MS-DOS

MS-DOS
$599

Information Finder is a CD-ROM with articles and "Quick Fact" tables taken from the 22-volume World Book Encyclopedia. Like the Grolier and Compton's electronic encyclopedias (also featured in this chapter), Information Finder incorporates a variety of research tools that simplify electronic investigation. Users look up information by topic or key word.

They obtain definitions for difficult words by accessing an on-line dictionary. Hot-link cross-references provide instant access to related articles.

An on-disc tutorial presents step-by-step operating instructions. "Context sensitive" on-line help (tailored to where you are in the program) explains all software functions. Program options may be invoked by typing in keyboard command shortcuts or selecting functions from drop-down menus.

Articles appear on-screen with text in one window and an outline summary in another. Researchers read an article by using keyboard arrow keys or mouse-controlled screen scroll arrows to browse. Alternatively, they can move quickly through an article by selecting major headings from its outline window.

Information Finder's Notepad offers a convenient way to record personal notes and reminders or transfer information from CD-ROM to disk. A "Bookmark" option lets researchers place up to 25 tags for later reference. Articles and tables may be output to a printer or saved to disk for use with a word processor.

Comment

World Book's *Information Finder* is a serious electronic reference tool. Without the multimedia elements (pictures, maps, sounds, drawings, or graphic illustrations) provided by

other CD-ROM encyclopedias, it's not likely to be as appealing to your child as the other tools listed in this chapter. However, we know of some school librarians who have chosen *Information Finder* over a more entertaining alternative because they think that the print encyclopedia on which it's based is better written than most. (However, it does not include bibliographies—a shortcoming in our opinion.) With more than 17,000 articles, 60,000 cross-references, 1,700 tables, powerful search capabilities, and a slightly lower price tag than *Compton's,* the program certainly is worth considering.

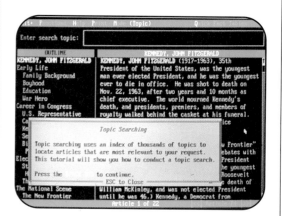

Information Finder, from World Book Educational Products

Mammals: A Multimedia Encyclopedia (1990)

Publisher: National Geographic Society   **Ages:** 10 and up

MS-DOS

**MS-DOS
$149.95**

Mammals: A Multimedia Encyclopedia features an expanded and updated version of National Geographic's popular two-volume print edition of the *Book of Mammals*. The disc contains articles, fact screens, and vital statistics on 201 animals. Researchers can view 700 full-screen color photographs and drawings (complete with captions), 150 range (habitat) maps, and 45 motion-video clips from National Geographic television documentaries. In addition, the disc offers digitized sound clips of 155 animal vocalizations. These multimedia elements bring animals to life on the computer screen.

A graphical user interface with click-on buttons makes it easy for youngsters to conduct scientific research. An on-line tutorial explains how to navigate the database, view pictures and movie clips, listen to animal sounds, print article text, and much more. Hot-link cross-references to related topics encourage students to expand investigations. A glossary provides definitions for difficult terms.

Researchers look up information about specific animals by searching an alphabetical listing called "Mammals A to Z." A section called "About Mammals" features 10 general essays, covering topics such as habitat, caring for young, survival, and foods mammals eat. A chapter called "Orders of Mammals" classifies the animals into 20 different orders and shows how mammals within each group share common characteristics.

Once children feel comfortable with the information presented on disc, they can test their knowledge by playing an amusing game. The activity challenges them to identify a mystery animal from a series of clues, locate the animal on a map, and then photograph it. There are 36 missions at three levels of difficulty.

Contestants can access the mammals encyclopedia for help with clues during play.

Comments

Unlike printed textbooks, this multimedia encyclopedia offers a range of sensory experiences. The interactive nature of the program allows youngsters to chart their own research paths and become active learners. Kids not only read articles, they see pictures, watch movies, and listen to animal sounds.

If you compare the encyclopedia's "movie" clips to real video, you may find yourself wondering why they look a bit funny. Because of the limitations of CD-ROM and how difficult it is to use this medium for motion video, the video clips that were included were not only limited in number but displayed at a fairly low resolution with fewer frames per second than a normal movie. Nevertheless, they're appealing if only for their novelty. The digitized sound effects are equally likely to keep your kids entranced.

This reference tool is one of the easiest to use. And if your kids need help getting oriented, it has a great tutorial. Will this program keep your kids occupied for long enough to justify the investment? It depends on how interested they (and you) are in animals. If you want children to learn all about mammals, from aardvarks to zorillas, this is the perfect place to start.

Mammals: A Multimedia Encyclopedia, from National Geographic Society

The New Grolier Encyclopedia (1991 edition)

Publisher: Grolier Electronic Publishing   **Ages:** 10 and up

 MS-DOS, Macintosh

MS-DOS
$395

Mac
$395

In 1986, Grolier was the first company to publish an electronic encyclopedia. In its 1991 version, *The New Grolier Encyclopedia* features 33,000 articles (all 21 volumes of the *Academic American Encyclopedia*), hundreds of digitized CD-quality sounds (excerpts from speeches, musical compositions, and animal vocalizations), more than 2,000 pictures, and 250 political maps. It's a veritable wealth of reference information on a single disc.

Simple search and retrieve procedures let users call up information with minimal effort. Kids can search for articles by Title, Word, Picture, or Map. Alternatively, they can narrow a search using combinations of words, wild cards, truncation (partial words), or retrieval restrictions. Articles (or selected portions of text) can be copied from disc, saved to a floppy or hard disk, and printed. A "Bookmark" option makes it possible to reference a specific section of an article and return to it at any time.

Comments

This is the least expensive encyclopedia on CD-ROM and the

The New Grolier Encyclopedia, from Grolier Electronic Publishing

only CD-ROM encyclopedia with versions for both Macintosh and MS-DOS computers. A friendly user interface (with context-sensitive help) simplifies research. Articles usually include hot-link cross-references to related on-line articles and bibliographies listing suggested readings from conventional print sources. This tool may not offer as rich a set of options as the *Compton's* disc, but as a result it's a bit simpler to use—and definitely more affordable.

Sneak Peeks: A Look at Some Brand-New Programs

With exciting new programs hitting the market every month, it's inevitable that some great titles will appear shortly after this book does. So that we could provide you with the most timely information possible, we were able to get several just-released programs into the hands of kids and parents in time to review them in other chapters of this book. In addition, however, there were a few programs that looked exciting to us but weren't in a final-enough form to test by the time we went to press. This chapter is devoted to such software.

We've seen demonstrations of the following programs at some point in the development process, and while we can't vouch for the final quality of any of the titles, they all look like good bets to us.

Edmark's Early Childhood Series

Publisher: Edmark

These programs were in a fairly early stage of development when we saw them, but they look as though they're going to appeal to fans of *The Playroom* or any other early childhood program that takes a playful, exploratory approach. The first two titles in the series, which will be available in both Macintosh and MS-DOS formats, focus on math and early reading skills.

Both programs use colorful graphics, digitized speech, music, animation, and friendly animal characters to capture the attention of preschoolers. Each offers six different activities, accessed by clicking or touching on a portion of an opening scene that serves as the menu. (Since Edmark manufactures its own touch window, the software is designed to work well with the Touch Window, but it also can be used with a mouse.)

In *Millicent's Math House,* several activities allow children to play with numbers and counting. The kids press numbers on a cash register and watch as the appropriate number of critters pop out; design cookies by controlling the number of jelly beans placed on each cookie; and create funny bugs by selecting the number of eyes, ears, feet, and other body parts the bug should have. Players can also visit the shoe store where they experiment with the concept of big, medium, and little by fitting three colorful characters for shoes. Or they can build

pictures using geometric shapes and complete patterns involving pictures, shapes, and sound effects. A number of the activities have a challenge mode (where kids are asked to supply a correct answer) as well as encouraging exploration and observation.

Bartholomew's Book House takes a similar approach but focuses on the letters of the alphabet, rhyming sentences, simple prepositions (in, on, through, etc.), story creation, the design of simple greeting cards, and more. The activities in this program use a combination of words and graphics to reinforce word recognition without requiring kids to be able to read in order to use the software.

If our first impressions are correct, it looks as though Edmark's first venture into the early childhood and home markets will be worth watching for.

KidWorks

Publisher: Davidson & Associates

This word processor and story illustrator for young kids was not quite finished at the time we went to press, but it promises to fill a real need in the market. *KidWorks* uses synthesized speech (words "sounded

out" by the computer) and extra-large text to create an introductory word processor that reads back what kids have written. A variety of brightly colored icons can be used in place of individual words within the story.

(Kids choose from menus of nouns, verbs, and adjectives, and once the icon has been placed in the story, the computer reads it back as a word.)

KidWorks also offers an impressive array of graphics tools that allow kids to draw their own story illustrations or create their own icons to use within the text. When they are ready, the young authors can direct the computer to play back their stories, complete with sound effects, illustrations, and speech.

We haven't seen kids using this program yet, but we think that the ease of use, varied drawing options, and ability to hear their own words read back to them will appeal to most young children. Parents may be bothered by the robotic sound of the synthesized speech (the only type of speech feasible for talking word processors), but we're not sure how much kids will mind. With similar speech-based programs in the past, we've found that most young people adjust quickly, often enjoying the funny way the computer speaks or at least tolerating it. However, now that kids are becoming used to highly realistic digitized speech (which is showing up in a number of programs these days), we're not sure whether their expectations will have changed. Overall, however, we expect reactions from both kids and parents to this tool to be very positive.

Living Books

Publisher: Broderbund Software

Broderbund is making a serious investment in CD-ROM development with this new line of interactive storybooks. Using existing titles by well-known authors of children's books, *Living Books* turns the stories into exploratory on-screen adventures. The first three titles are picture books oriented to pre- or beginning readers.

In Mercer Mayer's *Just Grandma and Me* (the book we saw in devel-opment), Little Critter and his Grandma take a trip to the beach. Children can choose to have the entire story read to them by the computer, using digitized speech, on-screen text, and graphics from the original story. Or they can switch into interactive mode and explore. As each new page appears on the screen, the text is read aloud and then the computer waits. Almost everything on the screen comes alive when selected. Click on Grandma or Little Critter, for example, and they will speak aloud (accompanied by voice balloons with written text). Click on the bird and it flies away; on the cow and it moos; on the fish and it blows kisses. Even the inanimate objects entertain you when asked.

Animated effects (the bus rolling up to the beach and depositing the two characters, hats blowing in the breeze) and sound effects (the crunch of sand underfoot, the rush of waves) add to the overall effect. Kids can page forward or backward in the living book, although in an attempt to remain true to the original story, the software is not set up to encourage jumping around.

The programs are ideal for prereaders although they also reinforce early reading skills. Children can click on any word from the story and hear it read aloud or select a special icon to hear entire sentences reread. Later titles for a slightly older audience may do even more to encourage reading, allowing kids to rearrange words in a poem, for example, and listen to the results.

In addition to *Just Grandma and Me*, Marc Brown's *Arthur's Teacher Troubles* and Aesop's fable *The Tortoise and the Hare* will be among the first titles in the Living Books series. If all goes well, many others will follow. The programs will require a CD-ROM drive and will come out in both Macintosh and MPC versions. (See Chapter 12, "Peripherals and Other Options," for an explanation of the Multimedia PC (MPC) standard.)

Multimedia Edition of the Macmillan Dictionary for Children

Publisher: Maxwell Electronic Publishing

This multimedia dictionary for kids, due to be released in late 1991, is another CD-ROM title of interest to parents considering a Multimedia PC for the family. In bringing this well-established resource to the computer, the program's developers have stuck closely to the text and graphics from the print edition while adding value in a variety of ways.

Kids can search for a word by clicking on its first letter and the appropriate guide word and then scrolling to the right spot on the page. If they know the exact word they want, they can enter it and jump there instantly. Click on the pronunciation guide given after a word's definition and the computer will read the word aloud. Several of the entries are accompanied by buttons that call up word histories and other language notes (taken from the print dictionary) or sound effects relevant to the entry word. There's also a friendly character named Zak, who appears occasionally to act out some of the words (smiling at words that are entertaining, jumping up and down in joy to illustrate the word "allowance," and so on).

In addition, the program offers three games: a spelling bee, a version of hangman, and an anagram game. Children can choose whether the computer should select words randomly from the dictionary or take them from a personalized word list. (Such a list is created ahead of time by saving words found in the dictionary into an electronic notebook.)

With this multimedia reference tool, we suspect that kids who never before showed much interest in the family dictionary will be clamoring for a chance to sit down at the computer and look up words.

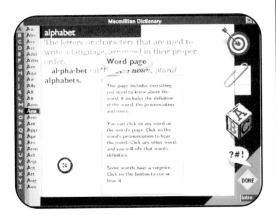

Multimedia Macmillan Dictionary for Children, from Maxwell Electronic Publishing

Mutanoid Math Challenge

Publisher: Legacy Software, distributed by Grace Software Distribution

Mutanoid Math Challenge was in the final stages of development (for MS-DOS computers) at the time we went to press. Aimed at kids between the ages of 7 and 14, it combines a Scrabble-like math game with arcade action and a huge cast of wacky characters. When the program opens, you learn that 15 Mutanoids, inhabiting old appliances dumped into space by thoughtless Earthlings, are about to drop "glop" on the Earth unless you can beat them at a math contest.

Kids play entire tournaments, selecting a different Mutanoid opponent for each game. Success is based partially on luck; the boxes that are added to the screen each turn (some filled with numbers and operands, others left blank) are randomly generated. In addition, however, players earn points by calculating accurately; by manip-ulating "gelatoids" that fly across the screen at the beginning of each turn, causing them to "splat" onto a box and triple its value; and by using strategy to include harder operands (an x sign earns more than a + or − but less than a /) and take advantage of the triple points.

Whether your kid loves this program or finds it frustrating will be determined in part by his or her personal style and in part by some decisions still to be made by the developer. At the time we tested the software, it was very hard to beat the Mutanoids. (Even good math students who paid attention to strategy found themselves losing more often than winning.) We were told that the difficulty level was being adjusted; even with such a change, however, this game will probably work best for kids who already enjoy both math and reading and are not easily overwhelmed.

In addition to the quick reflexes and math problem-solving involved, the program's characters "chatter" away (in text on the screen) using language filled with puns. Kids who like to read may be amused; others may find the comments distracting, especially since they rarely help with the game. The good news: those who take the time to explore the program's many options will discover that they have great control over the game. It's possible to turn off much of the conversation, request a variety of types of help, adjust or turn off the timer, and play at three levels of difficulty. Every time they do win a game, kids will love returning to the Cantina, where they can read about themselves in the *Cubix Chronicle* and see their trophies displayed in the trophy case.

Appendix

This listing provides names and addresses of publishers and distributors mentioned in this book.

Activision/MEDIAGENIC
P.O. Box 3048
Menlo Park, CA 94025
(415) 617-8161

Britannica Software
345 Fourth St.
San Francisco, CA 94107
(800) 572-2272 (for
software)
(800) 4CD-NEWS (for
CD-ROM titles)

Broderbund Software
500 Redwood Blvd.
Novato, CA 94948-6121
(800) 521-6263

Claris Corporation
5201 Patrick Henry Dr.
Santa Clara, CA 95052
(800) 538-9696

Davidson & Associates,
Inc.
P.O. Box 2961
Torrance, CA 90509
(800) 545-7677

Discis Knowledge
Research, Inc.
45 Sheppard Ave. East
Suite 410
Toronto, Ontario,
Canada M2N 5W9
(800) 567-4321

Electronic Arts
1820 Gateway Dr.
San Mateo, CA 94404
(800) 245-4525

Great Wave Software
5353 Scotts Valley Dr.
Scotts Valley, CA 95066
(408) 438-1990

Grolier Electronic
Publishing
Sherman Turnpike
Danbury, CT 06816
(800) 356-5590

Inline Design
5 West Mountain Rd.
Sharon, CT 06069
(203) 364-0063

Interplay Productions
3710 S. Susan
Suite 100
Santa Ana, CA 92704
(800) 969-4263

Lawrence Productions
1800 S. 35th St.
Galesburg, MI 49053
(800) 421-4157

The Learning Company
6493 Kaiser Dr.
Fremont, CA 94555
(800) 852-2255

Legacy Software
8817 Reseda Blvd.
Suite B
Northridge, CA 91324
(800) 532-7692

LucasFilm Games
P.O. Box 10307
San Rafael, CA 94912
(800) STARWARS

Maxis
Two Theatre Square
Suite 230
Orinda, CA 94563-3041
(800) 33MAXIS

Maxwell Electronic
Publishing
124 Mt. Auburn St.
Cambridge, MA 02138
(617) 661-2955

MECC
6160 Summit Dr. North
Minneapolis, MN
55430-4003
(800) 685-6322

Merit Software
13635 Gamma Rd.
Dallas, TX 75244
(800) 238-4277

Microsoft Corporation
One Microsoft Way
Redmond, WA
98052-6399
(800) 426-9400

National Geographic
Society
17th & M Streets, NW
Washington, D.C. 20036
(800) 368-2728

PC Globe, Inc.
4700 S. McClintock Dr.
Tempe, AZ 85282
(800) 255-2789

Scholastic Software
2931 East McCarty St.
P.O. Box 7502
Jefferson City, MO
65102
(800) 541-5513

Sierra On-Line, Inc.
P.O. Box 485
Coarsegold, CA 93614
(800) 326-6654

Software Toolworks
71 Leveroni Ct.
Novato, CA 94949
(800) 231-3088

Spectrum Holobyte
2061 Challenger Dr.
Alameda, CA 94501
(415) 522-3584

Spinnaker Software
201 Broadway
Cambridge, MA 02139
(800) 826-0706

Tom Snyder
Productions
90 Sherman St.
Cambridge, MA 02140
(800) 342-0236

Virgin Games
5070 Santa Fe St.
San Diego, CA 92109
(800) 874-4607

Walt Disney Computer
Software, Inc.
500 S. Buena Vista St.
Burbank, CA 91521
(800) 688-1520

World Book, Inc.
Merchandise Mart Plaza
Chicago, Il 60654
(800) 621-8202

Index

Trademark Acknowledgments

All terms mentioned in this book that are known to be trademarks or service marks are listed below. In addition, terms suspected of being trademarks or service marks have been appropriately capitalized. Sams cannot attest to the accuracy of this information. Use of a term in this book should not be regarded as affecting the validity of any trademark or service mark.

Shanghai II: Dragon's Eye is a registered trademark of Activision.

Apple IIGS, Macintosh, Mac, and Classic are registered trademarks and SuperDrive is a trademark of Apple Computer.

AppleWorks, HyperCard, and MacPaint are registered trademarks of Apple Computer, licensed to Claris Corporation.

Scrabble is a registered trademark of Milton Bradley.

Print Shop, The New Print Shop, BannerMania, Where in the USA Is Carmen Sandiego?, and Where in the World Is Carmen Sandiego? are registered trademarks of Broderbund Software. Kid Pix, The Playroom, The Treehouse, Where in America's Past Is Carmen Sandiego?, Where in Europe Is Carmen Sandiego?, and Where in Time Is Carmen Sandiego? are trademarks of Broderbund Software.

Amiga is a registered trademark of Commodore.

CompuServe is a registered trademark of CompuServe Incorporated and H&R Block.

The Manhole and Cosmic Osmo are trademarks of Cyan.

Headline Harry and Headline Harry and the Great Paper Race, KidWorks, Math Blaster, and Spell It are registered trademarks of Davidson & Associates.

Cartooners is a trademark and DeluxePaint is a registered trademark of Electronic Arts.

MacRecorder is a registered trademark of Farallon.

Dinosaur Discovery Kit and Puzzle Story Book are registered trademarks and Eco-Saurus is a trademark of First Byte.

KidsMath and ReadingMaze are trademarks and NumberMaze and KidsTime are registered trademarks of Great Wave Software.

New Grolier Encyclopedia is a trademark of Grolier Electronic Publishing.

Tesserae is a trademark of Inline Design.

IBM, Linkway, Personal Computer AT, PS/1, Screen Reader, Speech Viewer, and Storyboard are trademarks of International Business Machines.

Castles is a trademark of Interplay.

Katie's Farm, McGee, McGee at the Fun Fair, and Nigel's World are trademarks of Lawrence Productions.

Reader Rabbit is a registered trademark and The Children's Writing and Publishing Center, Operation Neptune, Super Solvers Challenge of Ancient Empires, Super Solvers Midnight Rescue, Super Solvers Outnumbered!, Super Solvers Spellbound, Super Solvers Treasure Mountain, and The Writing Center are trademarks of The Learning Company.

Mutanoid Math Challenge is a a registered trademark of Legacy Software.

Loom and PipeDream are trademarks of LucasFilm Games.

SimCity is a registered trademark of Maxis.

Number Munchers, Oregon Trail, and Super Munchers are registered trademarks of MECC.

All Dogs Go to Heaven, At the Zoo, Inspector Gadget Safety Patrol, Mutant Ninja Turtles, and Super Mario Brothers: When I Grow Up are registered trademarks of Merit Software.

MS-DOS, Microsoft Mouse, and Microsoft Works are registered trademarks and Microsoft Windows is a trademark of Microsoft Corporation.

Nintendo and Tetris are registered trademarks of Nintendo of America.

Boggle is a registered trademark of Parker Brothers.

Bushbuck Charms, Viking Ships and Dodo Eggs is a trademark of PC Globe.

Prodigy is a registered trademark of Prodigy Systems.

Math Shop and SuperPrint are registered trademarks of Scholastic Software.

Spot is a registered trademark of Seven-Up Co.

King's Quest is a registered trademark and Mixed-Up Mother Goose is a trademark of Sierra On-Line, Inc.

WellTris and WordTris are trademarks of Spectrum Holobyte.

PFS: is a registered trademark and First Publisher is a trademark of Spinnaker Software.

Publish It! is a registered trademark of Timeworks.

Inner Body Works, International Inspirer, and National Inspirer are trademarks and Flodd, the Bad Guy, Reading Magic, and Reading Magic Library are registered trademarks of Tom Snyder Productions.

Information Finder is a trademark of World Book Publishing.

Sams Guarantees Your Success In 10 Minutes!

The *10 Minute Guides* provide a new approach to learning computer programs. Each book teaches you the most often used features of a particular program in 15 to 20 short lessons—all of which can be completed in 10 minutes or less. What's more, the *10 Minute Guides* are simple to use. You won't find any "computerese" or technical jargon—just plain English explanations. With straightforward instructions, easy-to-follow steps, and special margin icons to call attention to important tips and definitions, the *10 Minute Guides* make learning a new software program easy and fun!

10 Minute Guide to WordPerfect 5.1
Katherine Murray & Doug Sabotin
$9.95 USA, 160 pages, 5¹/₂ x 8¹/₂
0-672-22808-4

10 Minute Guide to MS-DOS 5
Jack Nimersheim
$9.95 USA, 160 pages, 5¹/₂ x 8¹/₂
0-672-22807-6

10 Minute Guide to Windows 3
Katherine Murray & Doug Sabotin
$9.95 USA, 160 pages, 5¹/₂ x 8¹/₂
0-672-22812-2

10 Minute Guide to PC Tools Deluxe 7.0
Joe Kraynak
$9.95 USA, 160 pages, 5¹/₂ x 8¹/₂
0-672-30021-4

10 Minute Guide to Lotus 1-2-3
Katherine Murray & Doug Sabotin
$9.95 USA, 160 pages, 5¹/₂ x 8¹/₂
0-672-22809-2

10 Minute Guide to Q&A 4, Revised Edition
Arlene Azzarello
$9.95 USA, 160 pages, 5¹/₂ x 8¹/₂
0-672-30035-4

10 Minute Guide to Harvard Graphics 2.3
Lisa Bucki
$9.95 USA, 160 pages, 5¹/₂ x 8¹/₂
0-672-22837-8

A Division of Prentice Hall Computer Publishing

See your local retailer or call: 1-800-428-5331

Sams Keeps You Up-to-Date In Graphics

Turn to Sams for Complete Hardware and Networking Information

The Business Guide to Local Area Networks
William Stallings
$24.95 USA, 400 pages, $7^3/_8$ x$9^1/_4$
0-672-22728-2

LAN Desktop Guide to Printing with NetWare
Donna J. King
$27.95 USA, 350 pages, $7^3/_8$ x$9^1/_4$
0-672-30084-2

See your local retailer or call
1-800-428-5331

SAMS

A Division of Prentice Hall Computer Publishing

(Fill in the information that is applicable)

1. Computer Name and Model (e.g., Macintosh Classic or Tandy 2500 SL):

   _____

2. Operating System Software Version (e.g., Macintosh System 6.0.7;
   MS-DOS 3.3):

   _____

   Other Relevant Software (e.g., HyperCard 2.0 or Windows 3.0):

   _____

3. Microprocessor (e.g., 80286 or 68020):_____

4. Microprocessor Speed in Megahertz (e.g., 4.77 MHz, 20 MHz):_____

5. System Memory (RAM) (e.g., 640K, 1M, 5M):_____

6. Hard-Disk-Drive Capacity (e.g., 40M, 80M):_____

7. Floppy Disk Drives, Size and Capacity:_____

   ### MS-DOS

   5.25", low-density (320K/360K) _____ 5.25", high-density (1.2M)_____

   3.5", low-density (720K)_____ 3.5", high-density (1.44M) _____

   other_____

   ### Macintosh

   3.5", single-sided (400K)_____ 3.5", double-sided (800K)_____

   3.5", high-density (1.4M) _____ other_____

8. Video Display Card (e.g., EGA, VGA, Super VGA, Apple 8-bit):_____

9. Monitor Name, Model and Type (e.g., Tandy VGM-300, VGA monitor):

   _____

10. Printer Name, Model and Type (e.g., Hewlett-Packard DeskJet, inkjet
    printer):_____

11. Sound Cards for output/input (e.g., AdLib, Sound Blaster, MacRecorder, etc.):

    _____

12. Other Options (e.g., Microsoft Mouse, serial interface or Hitachi CD-ROM
    drive):_____

    _____